LIFE OF CHE

AN IMPRESSIONISTIC BIOGRAPHY

Translator: Erica Mena
Editor: Kristy Valenti
Supervising Editor: Gary Groth
Designer: Justin Allan-Spencer
Production: Christina Hwang & Paul Baresh

Editorial Assistance: Aidan Lee
Associate Publisher: Eric Reynolds
Publicity: Jacq Cohen
Publisher: Gary Groth

 Fantagraphics Books, Inc. 7563 Lake City Way NE, Seattle, WA 98115 (800) 657-1100 www.fantagraphics.com.

Follow us on Twitter and Instagram @fantagraphics and on Facebook at Facebook.com/Fantagraphics.

ISBN: 978-1-68396-522-0
LOC Number: 2021944206
First Edition: 2022
Printed in Republic of Korea

PUBLICATION HISTORY

In the late 1960s, independent and influential Argentine publisher Jorge Álvarez began an "Illustrated Lives" series, which subversively mixed traditional subjects with countercultural ones. Ernesto "Che" Guevara died in October 1967. Ripped from headlines and diaries, *Vida del Che* (Life of Che) was scheduled for an October 1968 release, but did not appear until 1969. Publishing a graphic biography about the revolutionary was dangerous under a military government, so Álvarez released *Life of Che* under a fictional imprint, Ediko, and offered to remove the creators' names from the covers. (As an act of political defiance, Oesterheld insisted that his name remain.) It would prove a tipping point. In 1973, governmental agents raided the publishing house, and the original art, printed copies, and the means to reprint the book were destroyed. The work was restored in Spain in 1987, from a printed copy.

WRITTEN BY
OESTERHELD

DRAWN BY
BRECCIA & BRECCIA

LIFE OF CHE

AN IMPRESSIONISTIC BIOGRAPHY

TRANSLATED BY
MENA

FANTAGRAPHICS BOOKS   SEATTLE, WASHINGTON

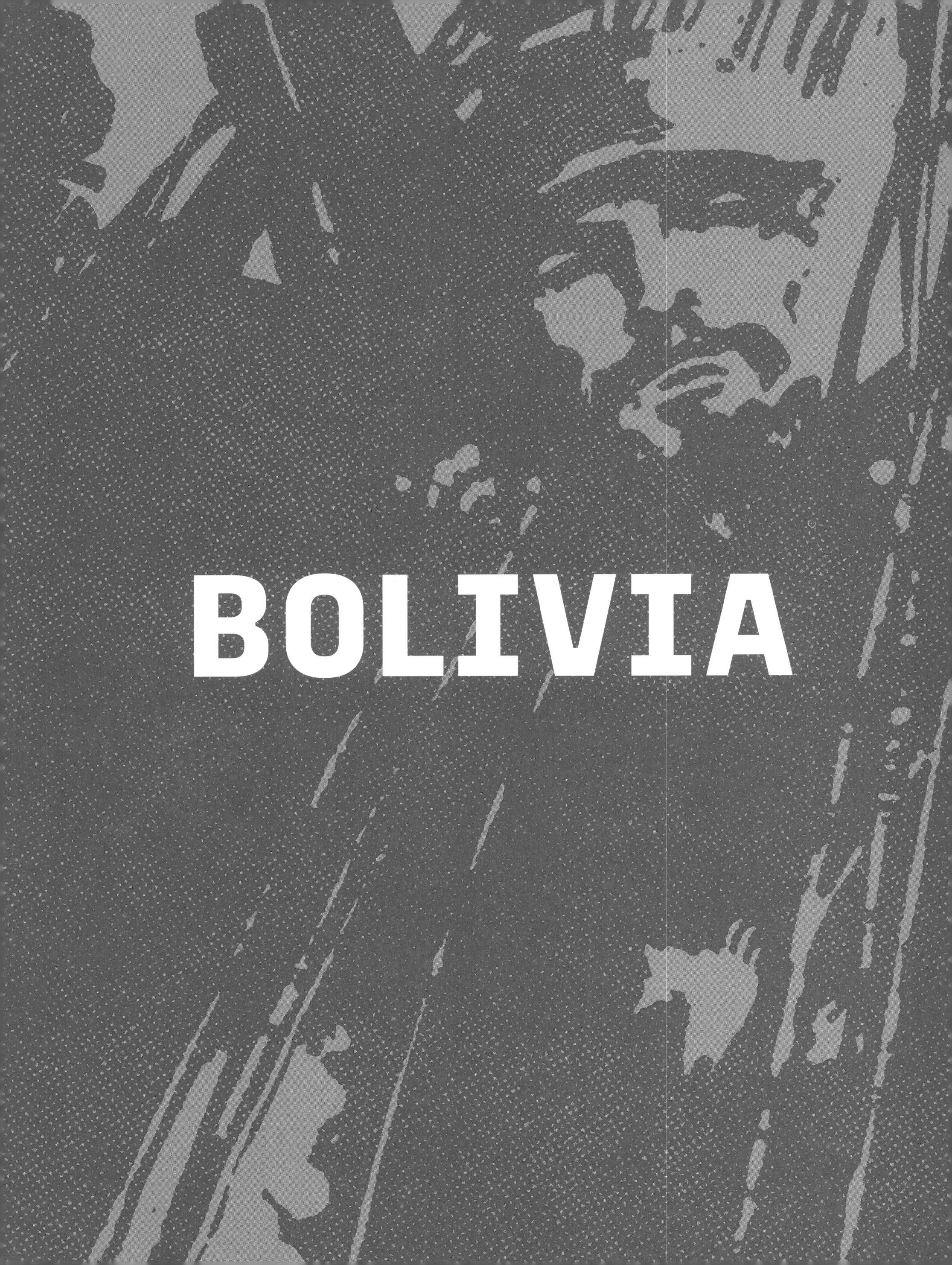

BOLIVIA

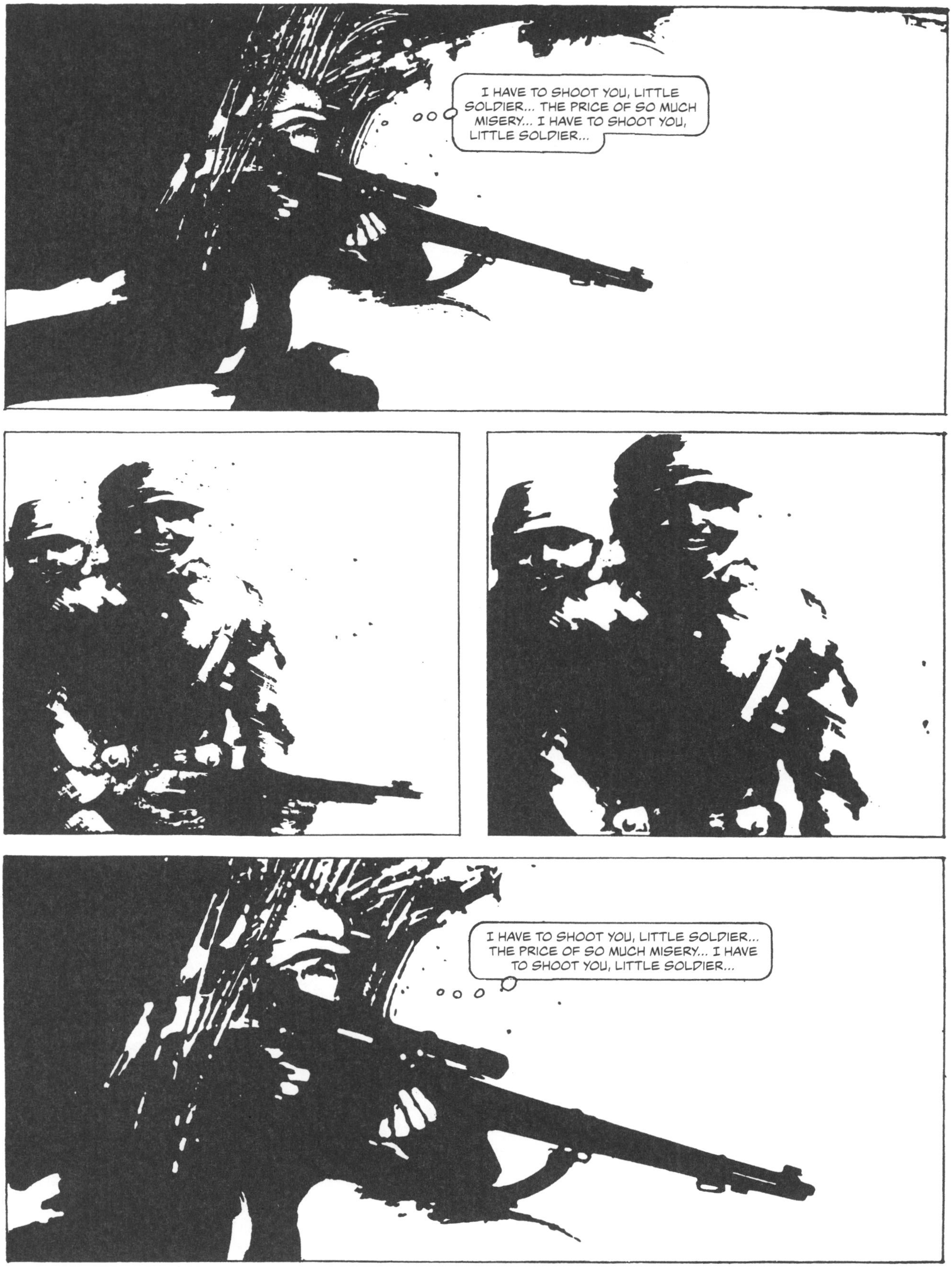
I HAVE TO SHOOT YOU, LITTLE SOLDIER... THE PRICE OF SO MUCH MISERY... I HAVE TO SHOOT YOU, LITTLE SOLDIER...
I HAVE TO SHOOT YOU, LITTLE SOLDIER... THE PRICE OF SO MUCH MISERY... I HAVE TO SHOOT YOU, LITTLE SOLDIER...

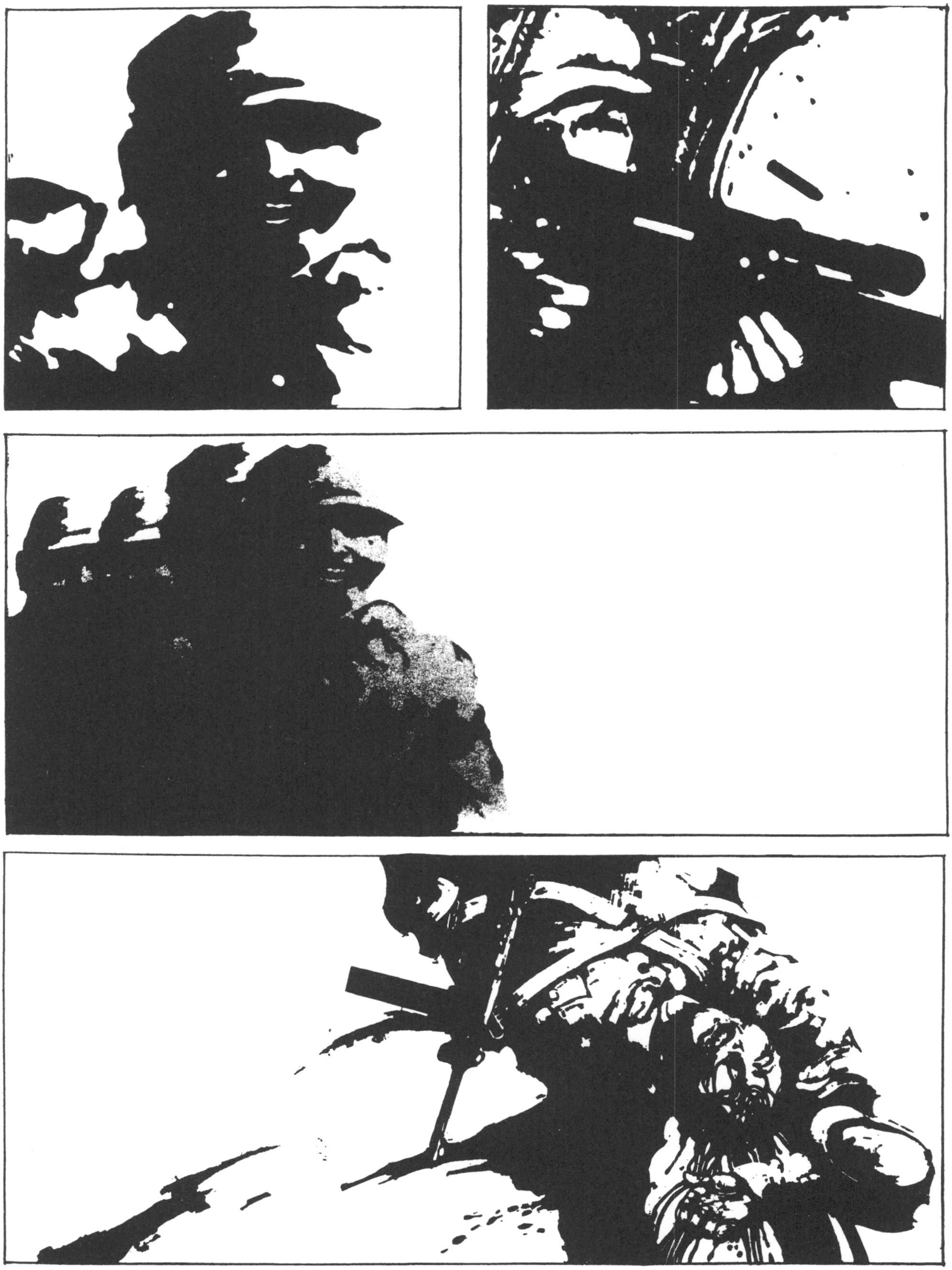

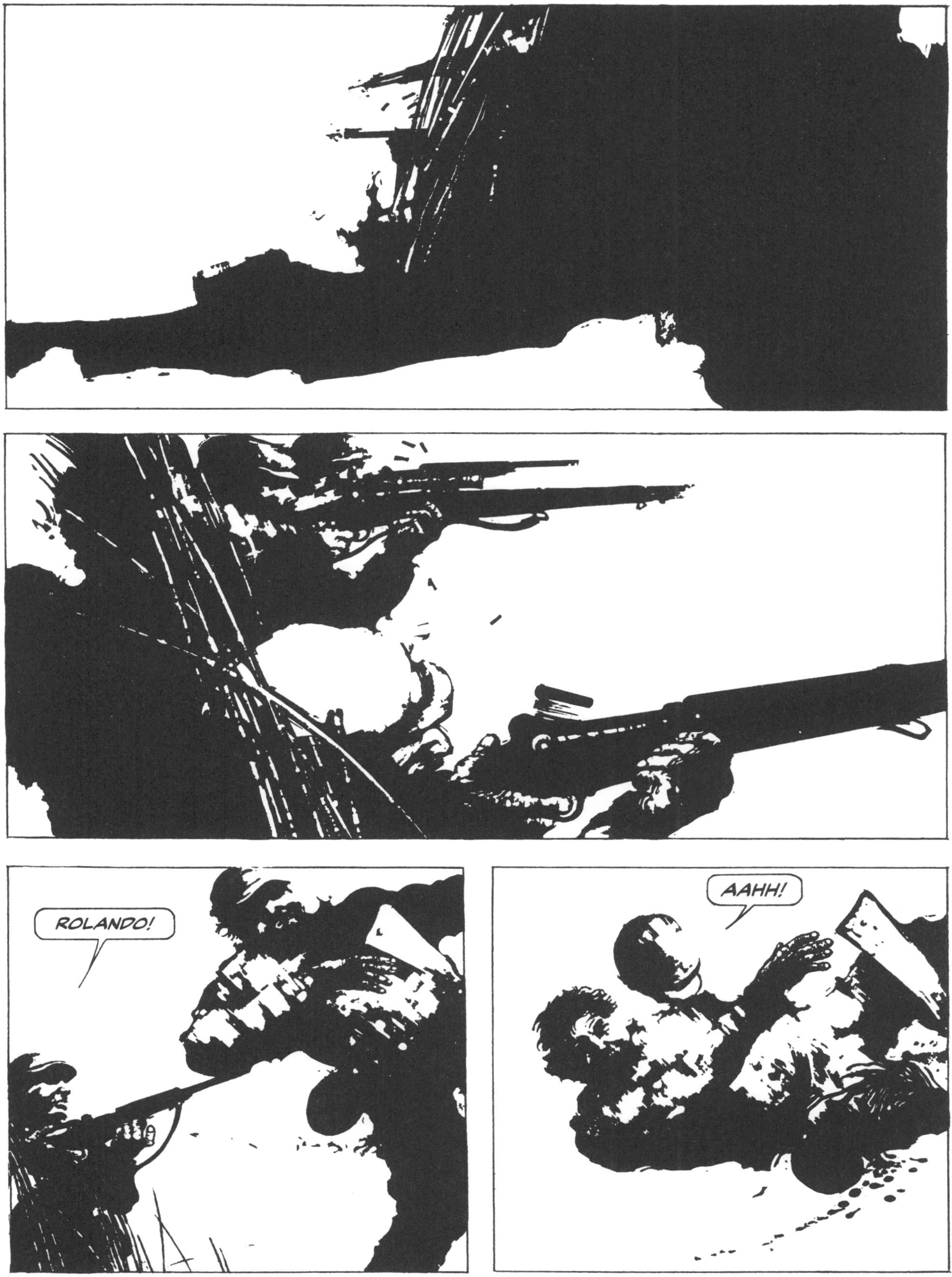
ROLANDO!
AAHH!

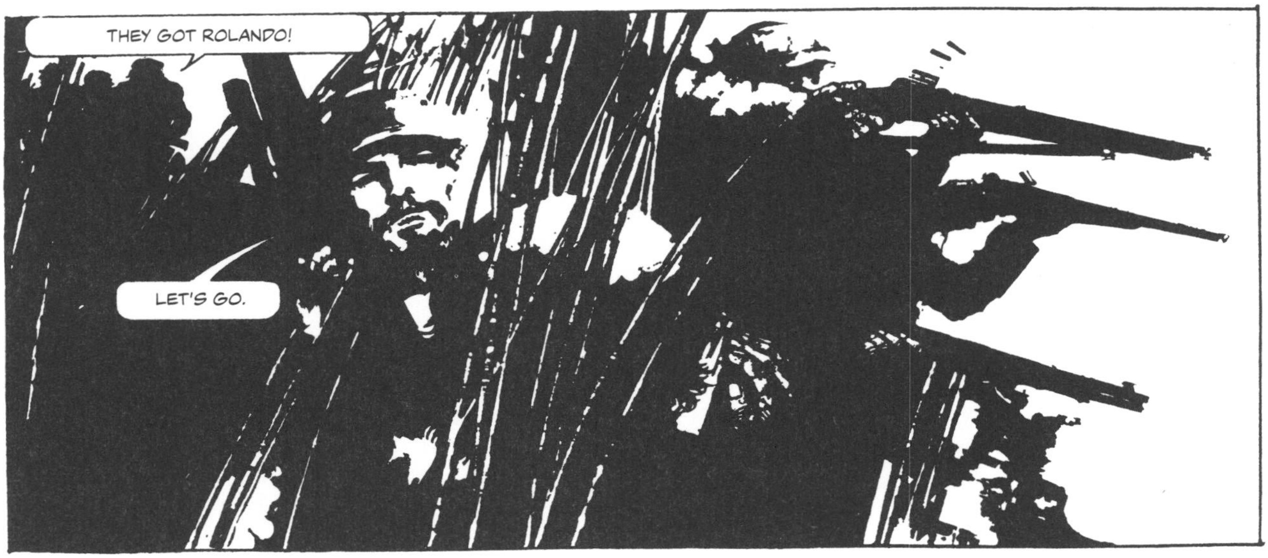
THEY GOT ROLANDO!
LET'S GO.

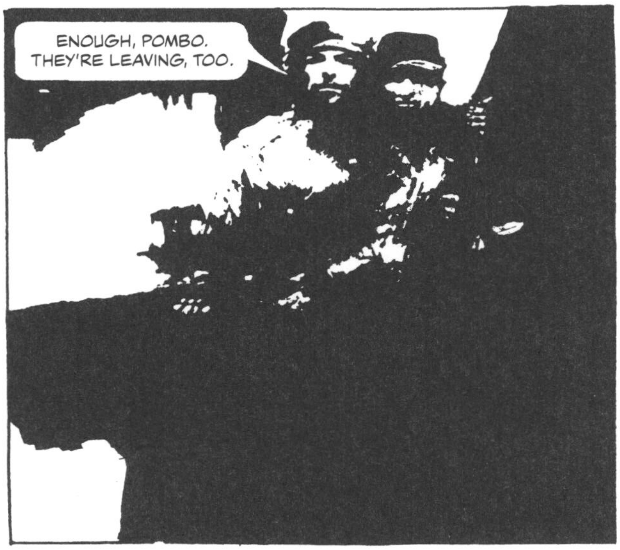
ENOUGH, POMBO. THEY'RE LEAVING, TOO.

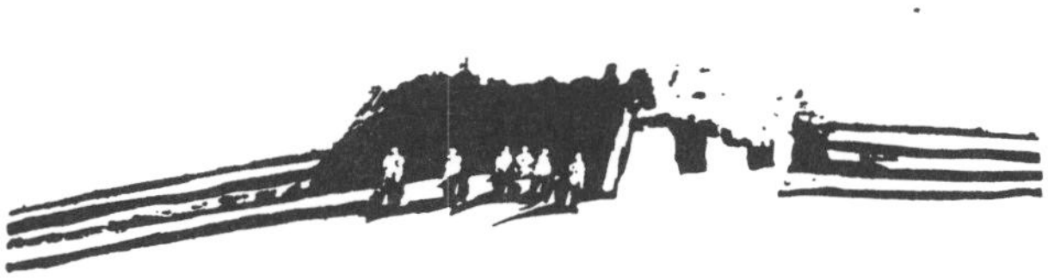

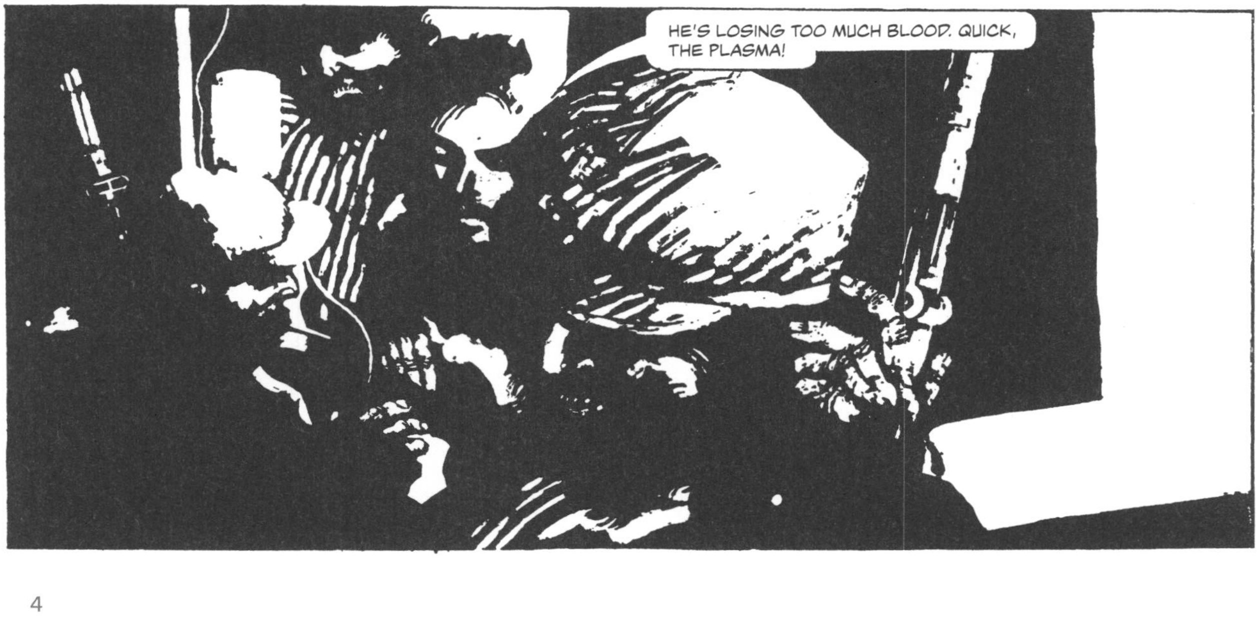
HE'S LOSING TOO MUCH BLOOD. QUICK, THE PLASMA!

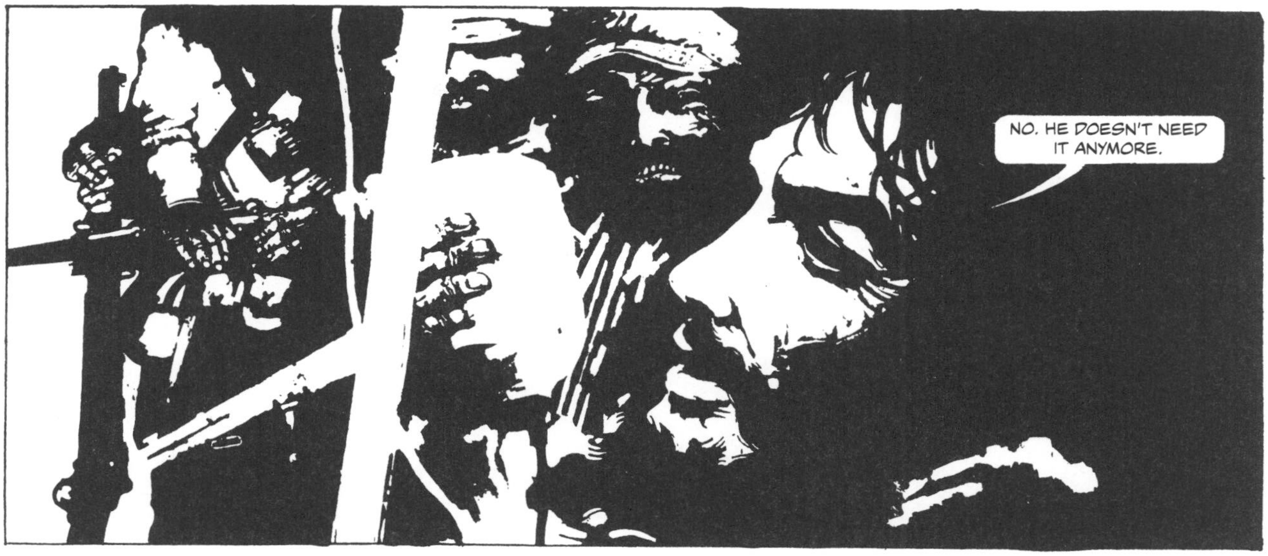
NO. HE DOESN'T NEED IT ANYMORE.

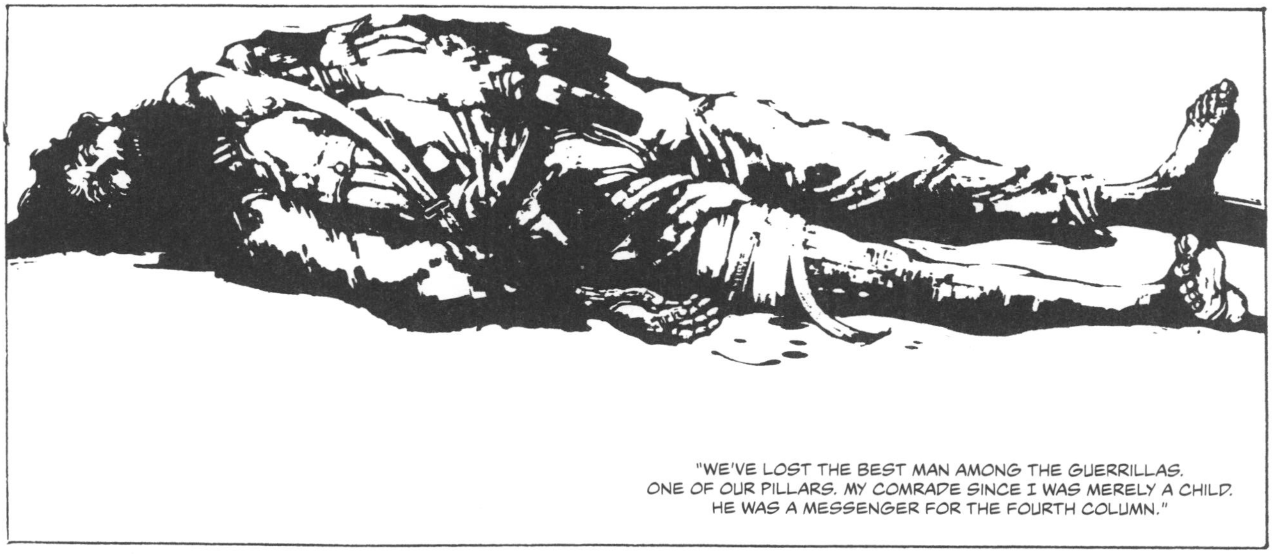
"WE'VE LOST THE BEST MAN AMONG THE GUERRILLAS. ONE OF OUR PILLARS. MY COMRADE SINCE I WAS MERELY A CHILD. HE WAS A MESSENGER FOR THE FOURTH COLUMN."

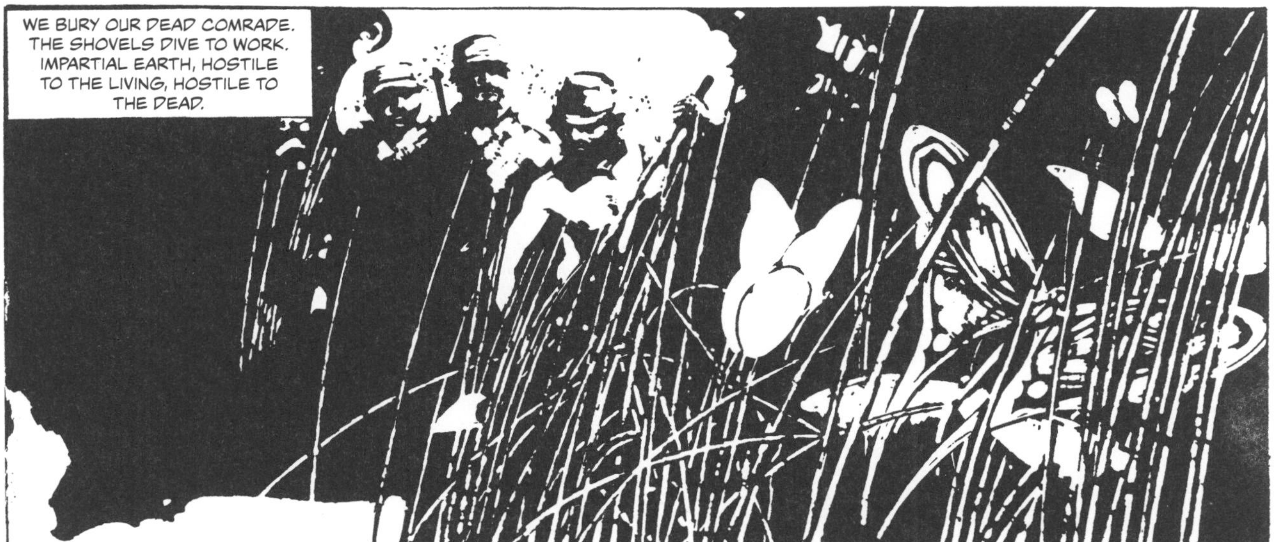
WE BURY OUR DEAD COMRADE. THE SHOVELS DIVE TO WORK. IMPARTIAL EARTH, HOSTILE TO THE LIVING, HOSTILE TO THE DEAD.

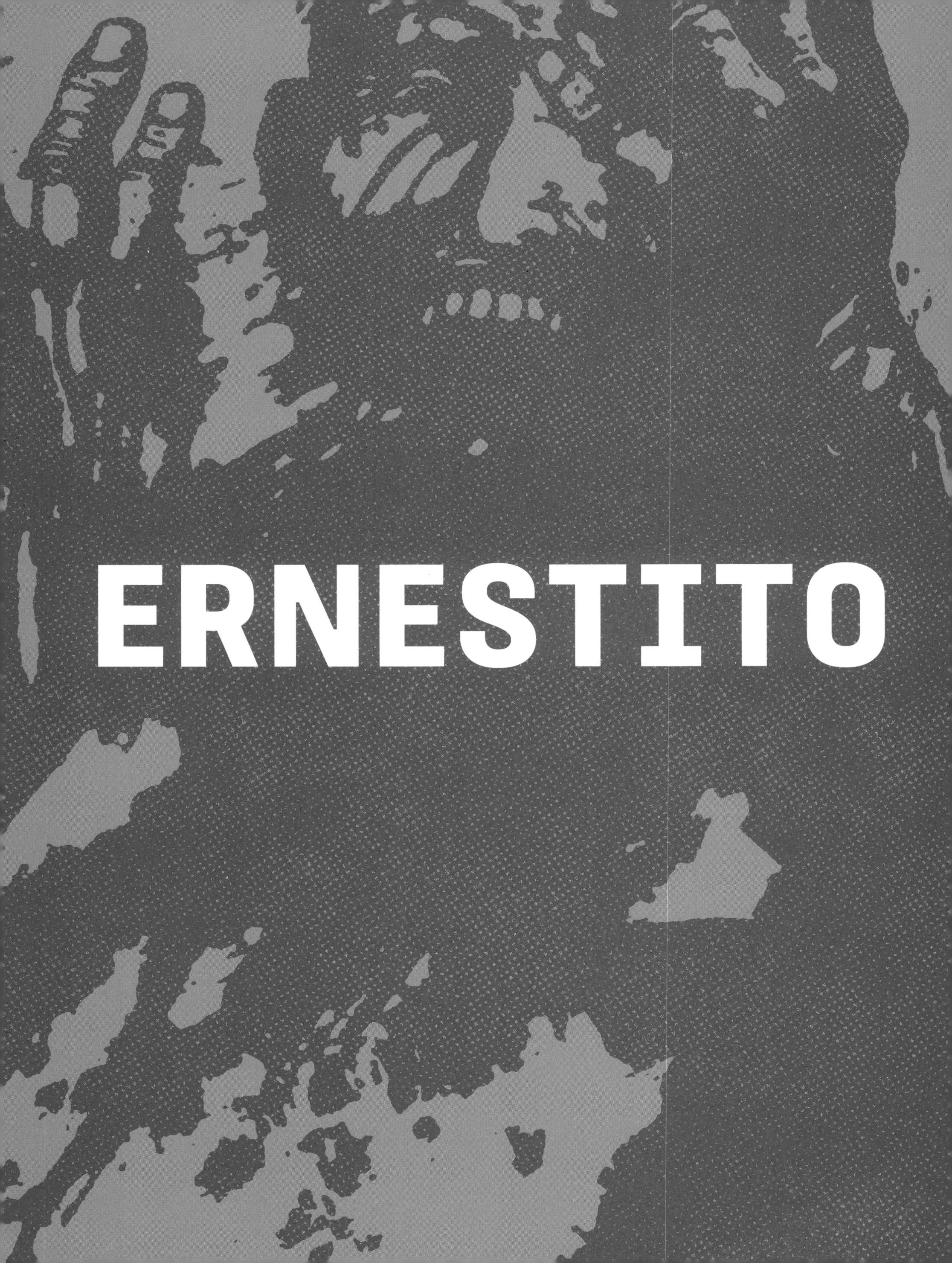
ERNESTITO

*

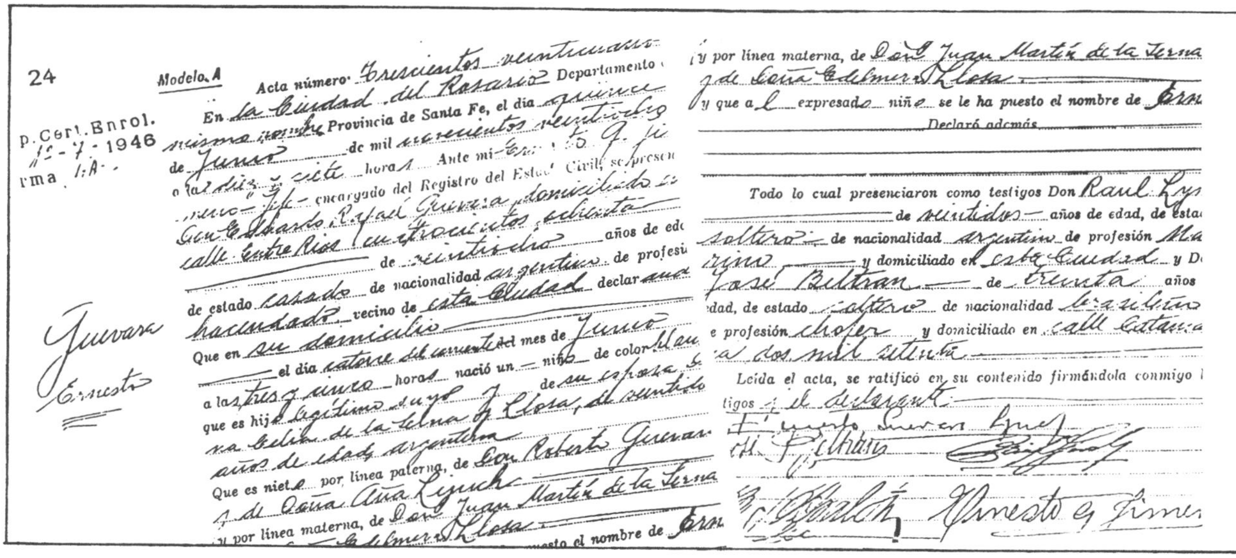

24

Modelo A

p. Cert. Enrol. 15-7-1946 ... rma 1:A.

Acta número trescientos veinticuatro Departamento ...

En la Ciudad del Rosario mismo nombre Provincia de Santa Fe, el día quince de Junio de mil novecientos veintiocho a las diez y siete horas. Ante mí ... encargado del Registro del Estado Civil, se presentó Don Ernesto Rafael Guevara, domiciliado en calle Entre Ríos ... de veintiocho años de edad, de nacionalidad argentino, de profesión hacendado, de estado casado, vecino de esta Ciudad, declaró que en su domicilio el día catorce del corriente mes de Junio a las tres y cinco horas nació un niño de color blanco que es hijo legítimo suyo y de su esposa Doña Celia de la Serna y Llosa, de veintiún años de edad, argentina.

Que es nieto por línea paterna, de Don Roberto Guevara y de Doña Ana Lynch

y por línea materna, de Don Juan Martín de la Serna y de Doña Edelmira Llosa

y que al expresado niño se le ha puesto el nombre de Ernesto

Declaró además ...

Todo lo cual presenciaron como testigos Don Raúl Lynch de veintidós años de edad, de estado soltero de nacionalidad argentino de profesión marino y domiciliado en esta Ciudad y Don José Beltrán de treinta años de edad, de estado soltero de nacionalidad brasileño de profesión chofer y domiciliado en calle Catamarca dos mil setenta.

Leída el acta, se ratificó en su contenido firmándola conmigo los testigos y el declarante.

Guevara

Ernesto

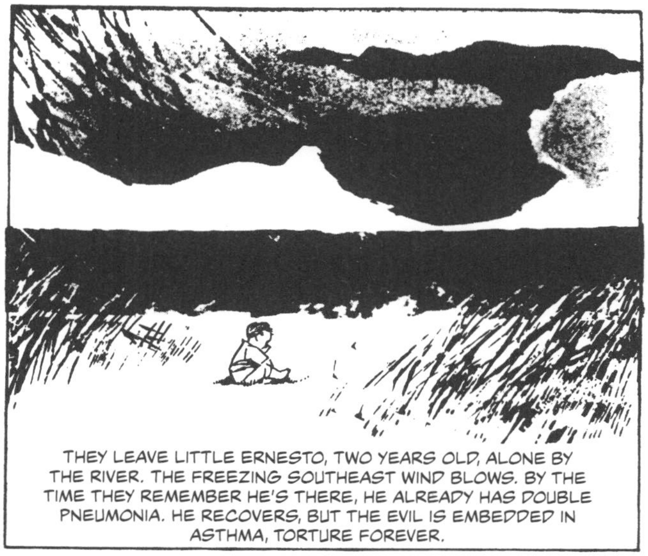

THEY LEAVE LITTLE ERNESTO, TWO YEARS OLD, ALONE BY THE RIVER. THE FREEZING SOUTHEAST WIND BLOWS. BY THE TIME THEY REMEMBER HE'S THERE, HE ALREADY HAS DOUBLE PNEUMONIA. HE RECOVERS, BUT THE EVIL IS EMBEDDED IN ASTHMA, TORTURE FOREVER.

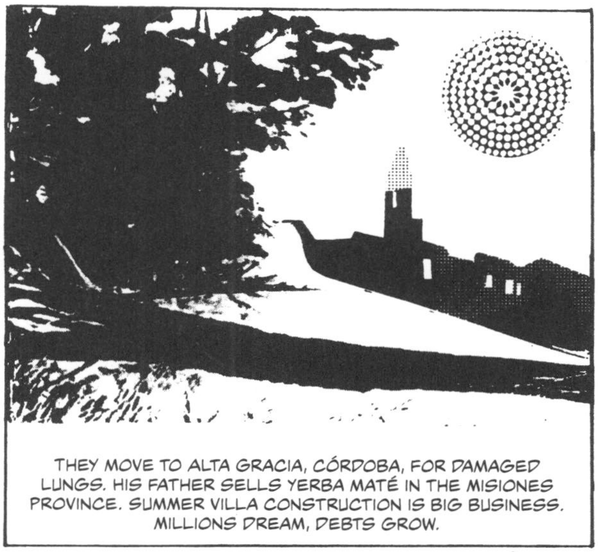

THEY MOVE TO ALTA GRACIA, CÓRDOBA, FOR DAMAGED LUNGS. HIS FATHER SELLS YERBA MATÉ IN THE MISIONES PROVINCE. SUMMER VILLA CONSTRUCTION IS BIG BUSINESS. MILLIONS DREAM, DEBTS GROW.

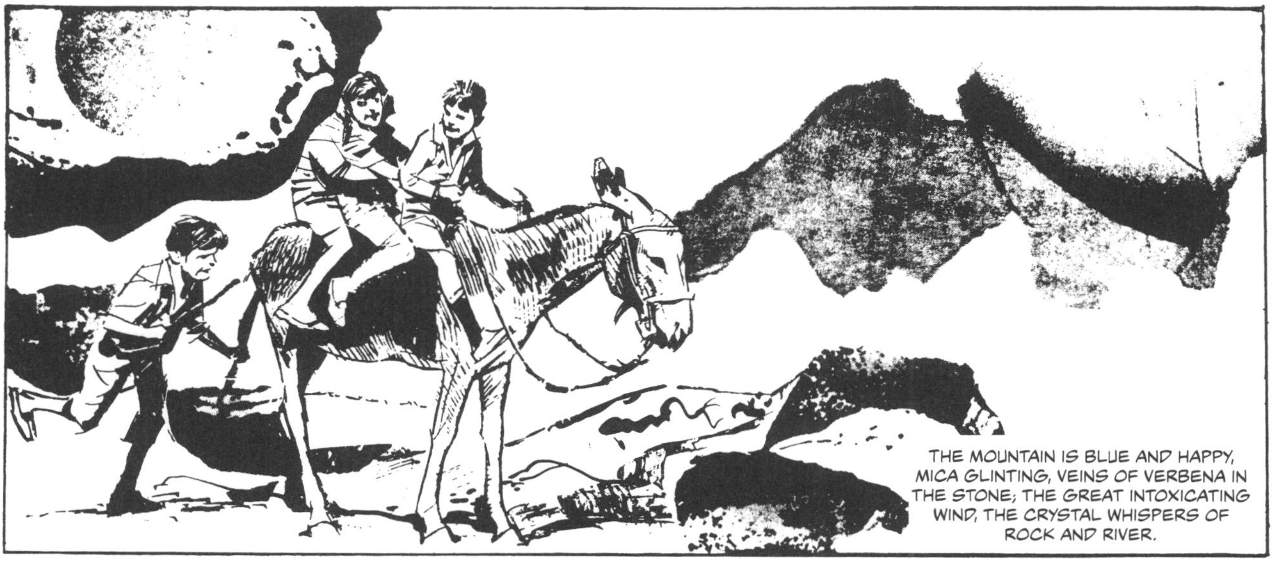

THE MOUNTAIN IS BLUE AND HAPPY, MICA GLINTING, VEINS OF VERBENA IN THE STONE; THE GREAT INTOXICATING WIND, THE CRYSTAL WHISPERS OF ROCK AND RIVER.

* CHE'S BIRTH CERTIFICATE. TRANSLATION ON PAGE 91.

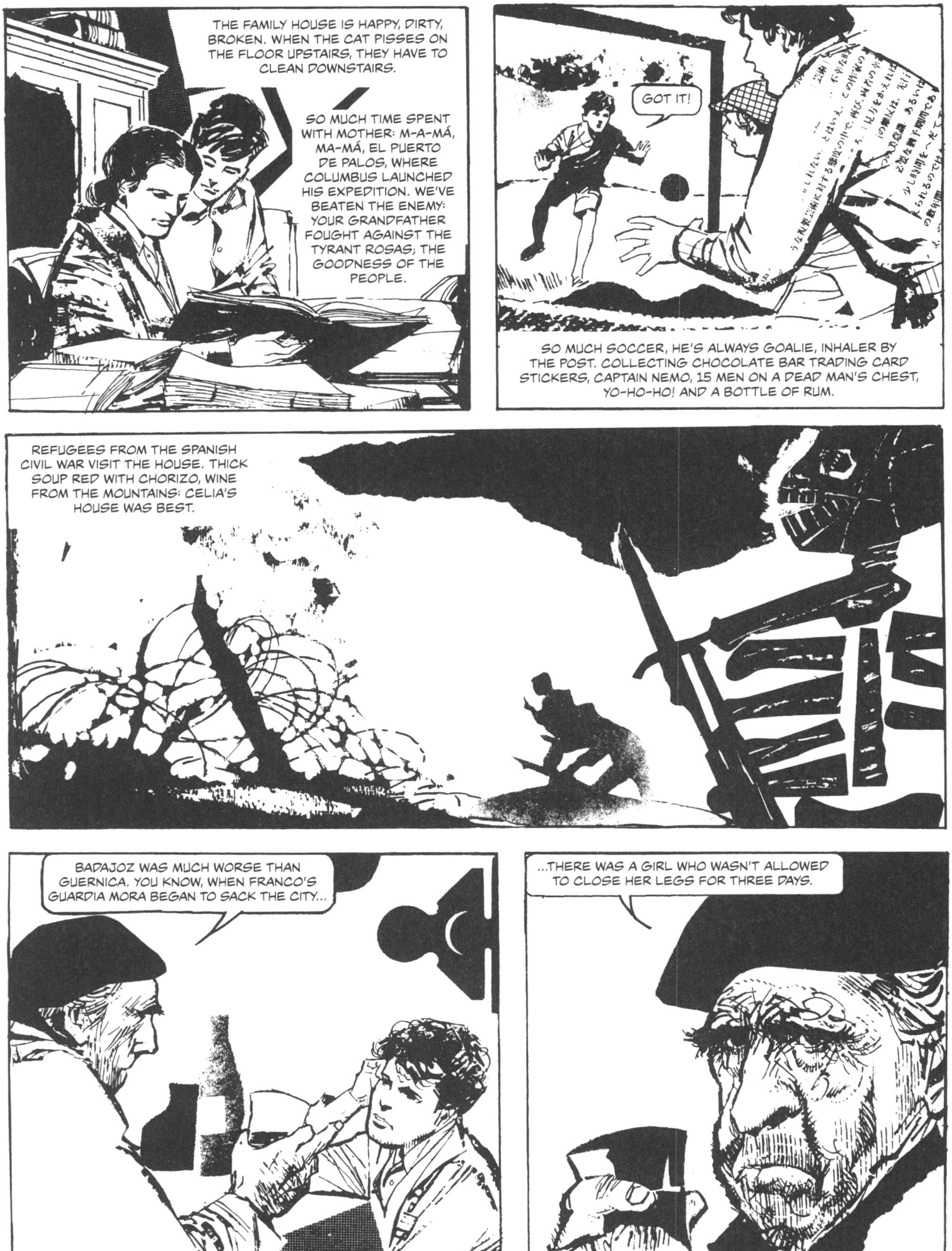
THE FAMILY HOUSE IS HAPPY, DIRTY, BROKEN. WHEN THE CAT PISSES ON THE FLOOR UPSTAIRS, THEY HAVE TO CLEAN DOWNSTAIRS.
SO MUCH TIME SPENT WITH MOTHER: M-A-MÁ, MA-MÁ, EL PUERTO DE PALOS, WHERE COLUMBUS LAUNCHED HIS EXPEDITION. WE'VE BEATEN THE ENEMY: YOUR GRANDFATHER FOUGHT AGAINST THE TYRANT ROSAS; THE GOODNESS OF THE PEOPLE.
GOT IT!
SO MUCH SOCCER, HE'S ALWAYS GOALIE, INHALER BY THE POST. COLLECTING CHOCOLATE BAR TRADING CARD STICKERS, CAPTAIN NEMO, 15 MEN ON A DEAD MAN'S CHEST, YO-HO-HO! AND A BOTTLE OF RUM.
REFUGEES FROM THE SPANISH CIVIL WAR VISIT THE HOUSE. THICK SOUP RED WITH CHORIZO, WINE FROM THE MOUNTAINS: CELIA'S HOUSE WAS BEST.
BADAJOZ WAS MUCH WORSE THAN GUERNICA. YOU KNOW, WHEN FRANCO'S GUARDIA MORA BEGAN TO SACK THE CITY...
...THERE WAS A GIRL WHO WASN'T ALLOWED TO CLOSE HER LEGS FOR THREE DAYS.

THE SECOND WORLD WAR.
MOTHER WEEPING FOR ANOTHER COUNTRY.

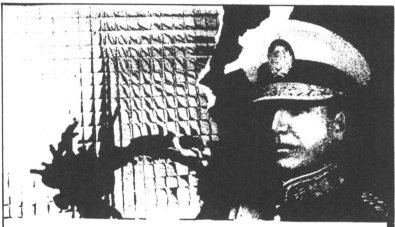

WORSE THAN HITLER OR MUSSOLINI, THE SMELL OF HORSE SHIT IN THE TEATRO COLÓN OPERA HOUSE. SHE'S A RUIN, WORMS IN THE EARTH, HAVE YOU HEARD THE LATEST ABOUT PRESIDENT FARRELL? THEY HAVE TO PULL HIS TEETH OUT THROUGH HIS ASS. VICE PRESIDENT PERÓN WON'T LET HIM OPEN HIS MOUTH.

PERÓN, QUIJANO! TWO HAMS, HAND-IN-HAND!

"LIGHTENING" PROTESTS, ANTI-PERÓNISM SIGNS BY NIGHT, BOMBS ALWAYS PLACED BY OTHERS. RUGBY AND COLLEGE, THEY LEFT HIM NO TIME, AND THEN--

--CHICHINA FERREYRA, TEA WITH THE MASSES IN THE CAFETERIA, A QUIET TREE-LINED STREET AT TWILIGHT, THE ALREADY-EXPERT KISS.

EIGHTH OF MAY

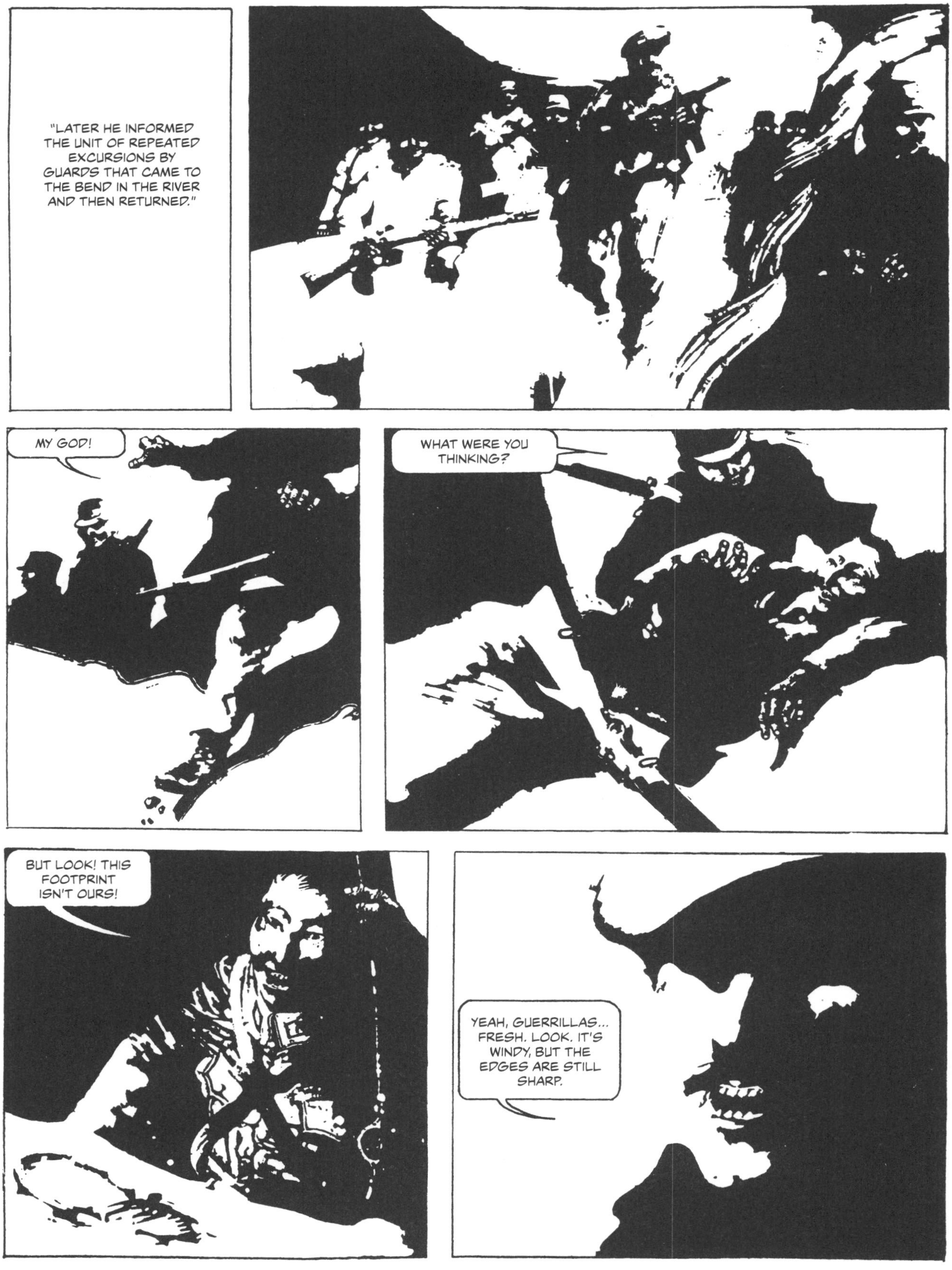

"LATER HE INFORMED THE UNIT OF REPEATED EXCURSIONS BY GUARDS THAT CAME TO THE BEND IN THE RIVER AND THEN RETURNED."
MY GOD!
WHAT WERE YOU THINKING?
BUT LOOK! THIS FOOTPRINT ISN'T OURS!
YEAH, GUERRILLAS... FRESH. LOOK. IT'S WINDY, BUT THE EDGES ARE STILL SHARP.

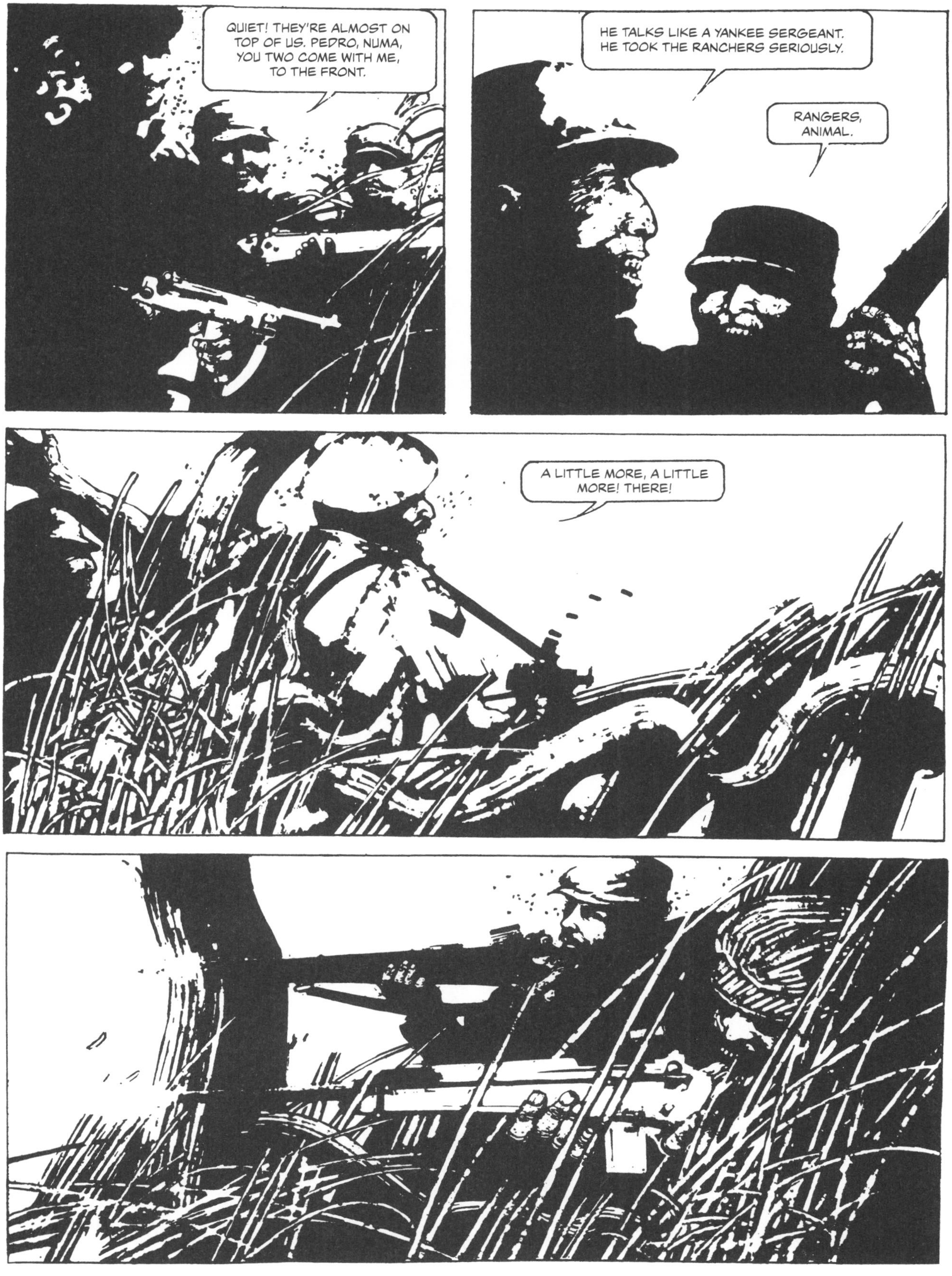
QUIET! THEY'RE ALMOST ON TOP OF US. PEDRO, NUMA, YOU TWO COME WITH ME, TO THE FRONT.
HE TALKS LIKE A YANKEE SERGEANT. HE TOOK THE RANCHERS SERIOUSLY.
RANGERS, ANIMAL.
A LITTLE MORE, A LITTLE MORE! THERE!

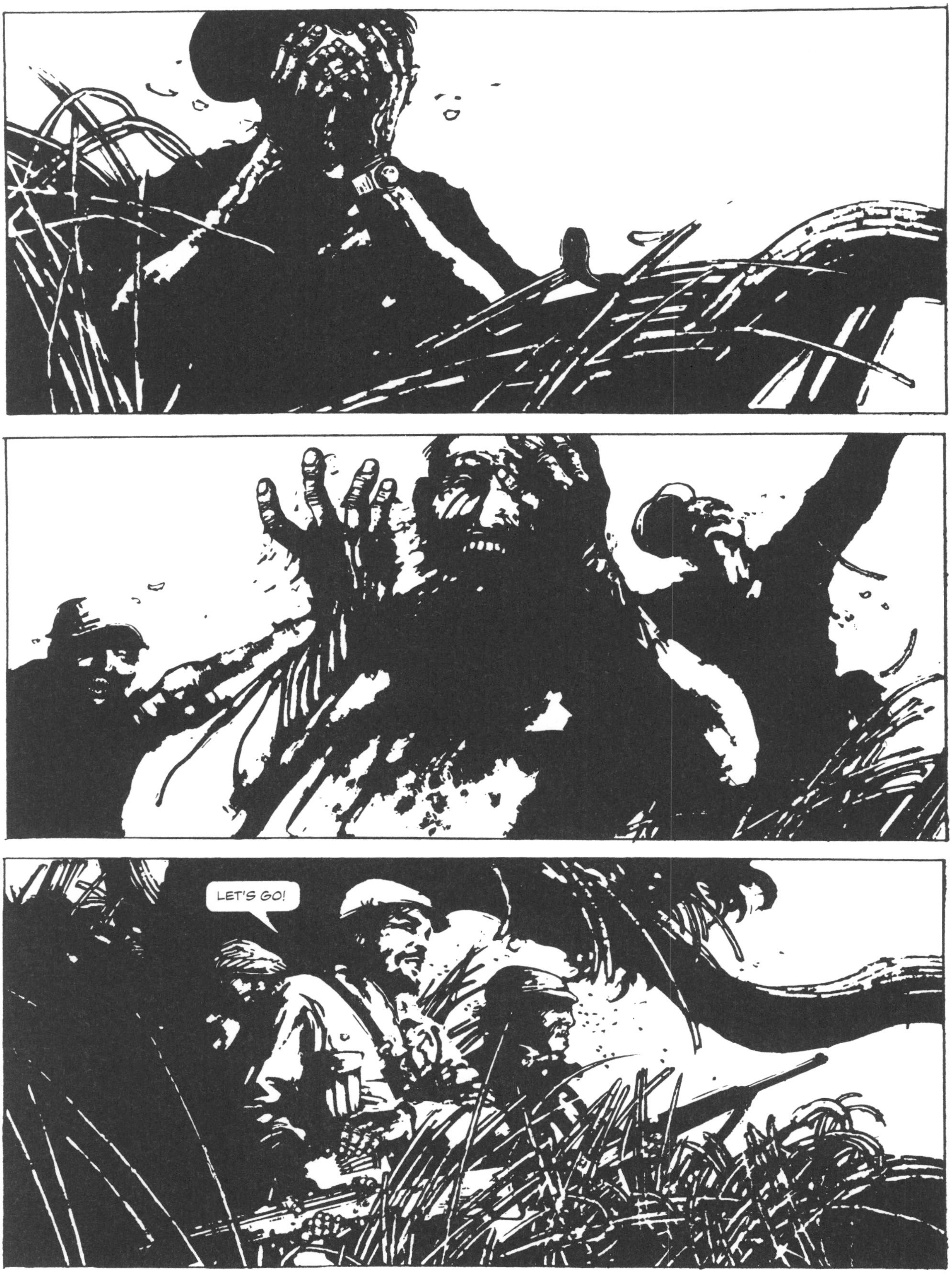
LET'S GO!

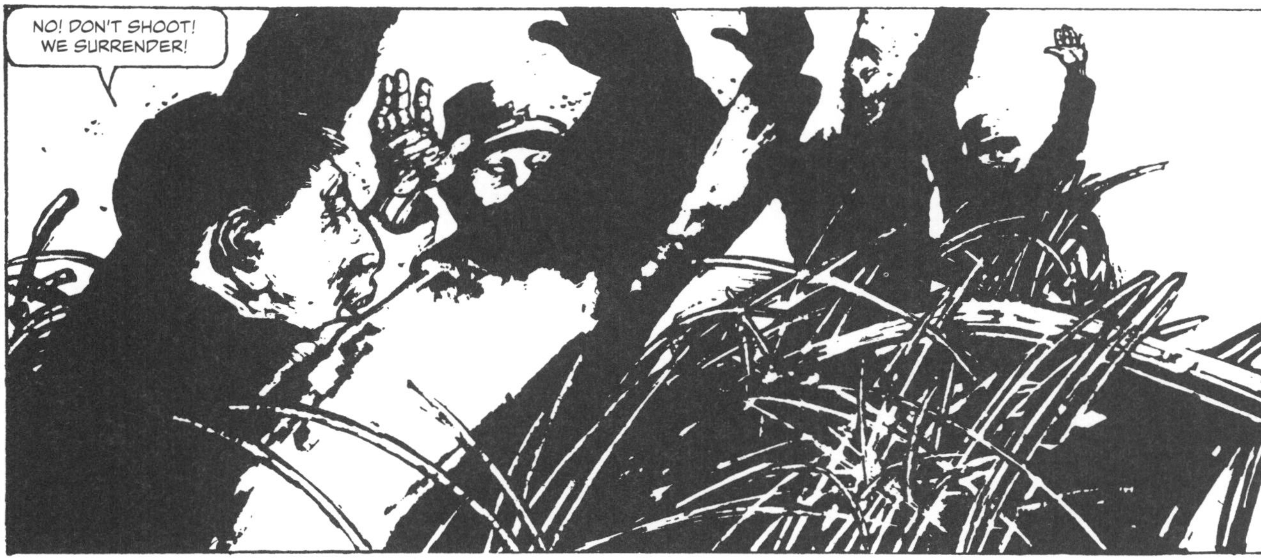
NO! DON'T SHOOT! WE SURRENDER!

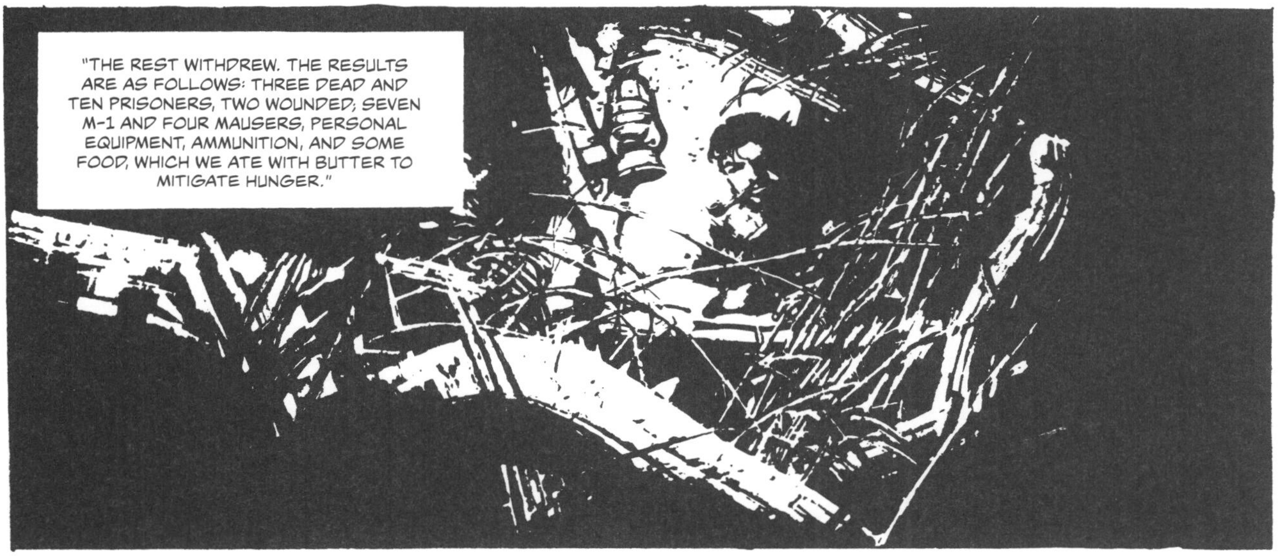
"THE REST WITHDREW. THE RESULTS ARE AS FOLLOWS: THREE DEAD AND TEN PRISONERS, TWO WOUNDED; SEVEN M-1 AND FOUR MAUSERS, PERSONAL EQUIPMENT, AMMUNITION, AND SOME FOOD, WHICH WE ATE WITH BUTTER TO MITIGATE HUNGER."

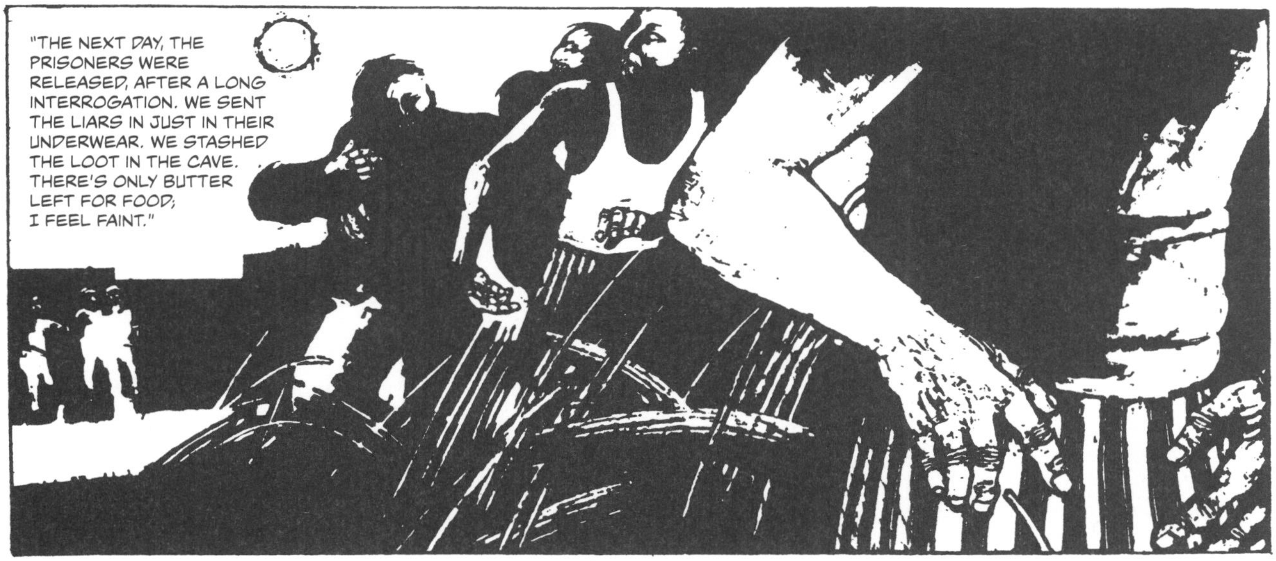
"THE NEXT DAY, THE PRISONERS WERE RELEASED, AFTER A LONG INTERROGATION. WE SENT THE LIARS IN JUST IN THEIR UNDERWEAR. WE STASHED THE LOOT IN THE CAVE. THERE'S ONLY BUTTER LEFT FOR FOOD; I FEEL FAINT."

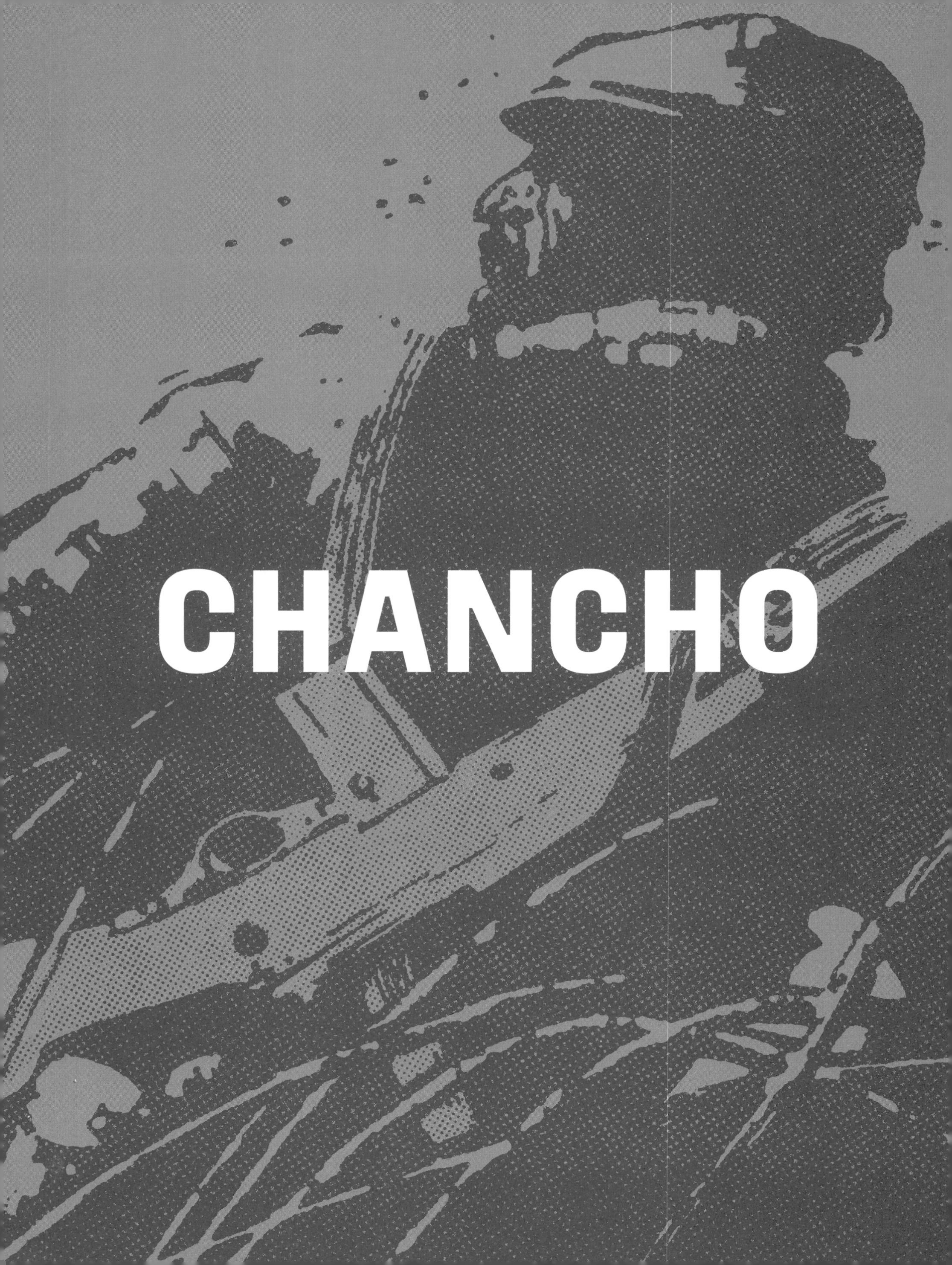
CHANCHO

YES, ERNESTO. THREE LEPERS. THE HEIGHT OF MISERY, OF HUNGER, OF LICE, IS LEPROSY... WHAT DO YOU THINK?

ALBERTO "MIAL" GRANADO. GOOD FRIEND (THOUGH FIVE YEARS OLDER). RECENTLY BECAME A DOCTOR, THE LEPER HOSPITAL. ERNESTO IS GOOD AT MATH, COULD BE AN ENGINEER OR AN ACCOUNTANT. BUT NO. HE, TOO, WOULD BE A DOCTOR.

BUENOS AIRES, THE SCHOOL OF MEDICINE. A MUNICIPAL EMPLOYEE: YOU SIGN AND LEAVE WHEN YOU WANT, RUGBY ON WEEKENDS, ATALAYA POLO CLUB, SCRUM-HALF, I CAN'T RUN MUCH. ASTHMA, YOU KNOW. AND THE SKINNY GUY? SEEMS OK... HEY, CHANCHO! YOU PLAYING TOMORROW?

PIRATES AND THE MOON GIVE WAY TO RASKOLNIKOV, TO ÉLISÉE RECLUS, TO NERUDA, ABOVE ALL NERUDA. HE READS EVERYTHING, DISCUSSES EVERYTHING: STEFAN ZWEIG, THE ANARCHISTS, LEÓN FELIPE'S *LA INSIGNIA*, NERUDA, ABOVE ALL NERUDA.

THE CHILDISH TRIP INTO THE MOUNTAINS IS NOW A GREATER ADVENTURE. A VACATION IS AN OIL TANKER. NEVER AGAIN, WE DIDN'T SEE EVEN HALF, FIFTEEN DAYS OUT, FOUR HOURS LOADING ON A FILTHY ISLAND, ANOTHER FOR PARTYING AND MARACAS, FIFTEEN DAYS BACK, NEVER AGAIN. ANOTHER VACATION ON A MOTORCYCLE WITH AN ENGINE MARKED "MICRON," ENDLESS ROADS, FOUR THOUSAND KILOMETERS, TWELVE PROVINCES...

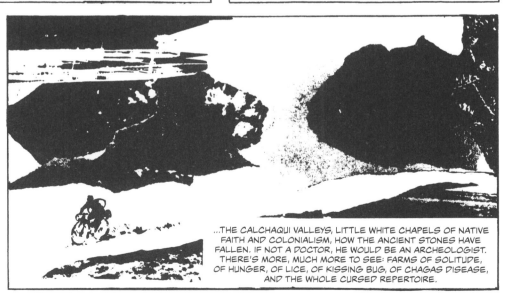

...THE CALCHAQUI VALLEYS, LITTLE WHITE CHAPELS OF NATIVE FAITH AND COLONIALISM, HOW THE ANCIENT STONES HAVE FALLEN. IF NOT A DOCTOR, HE WOULD BE AN ARCHEOLOGIST. THERE'S MORE, MUCH MORE TO SEE: FARMS OF SOLITUDE, OF HUNGER, OF LICE, OF KISSING BUG, OF CHAGAS DISEASE, AND THE WHOLE CURSED REPERTOIRE.

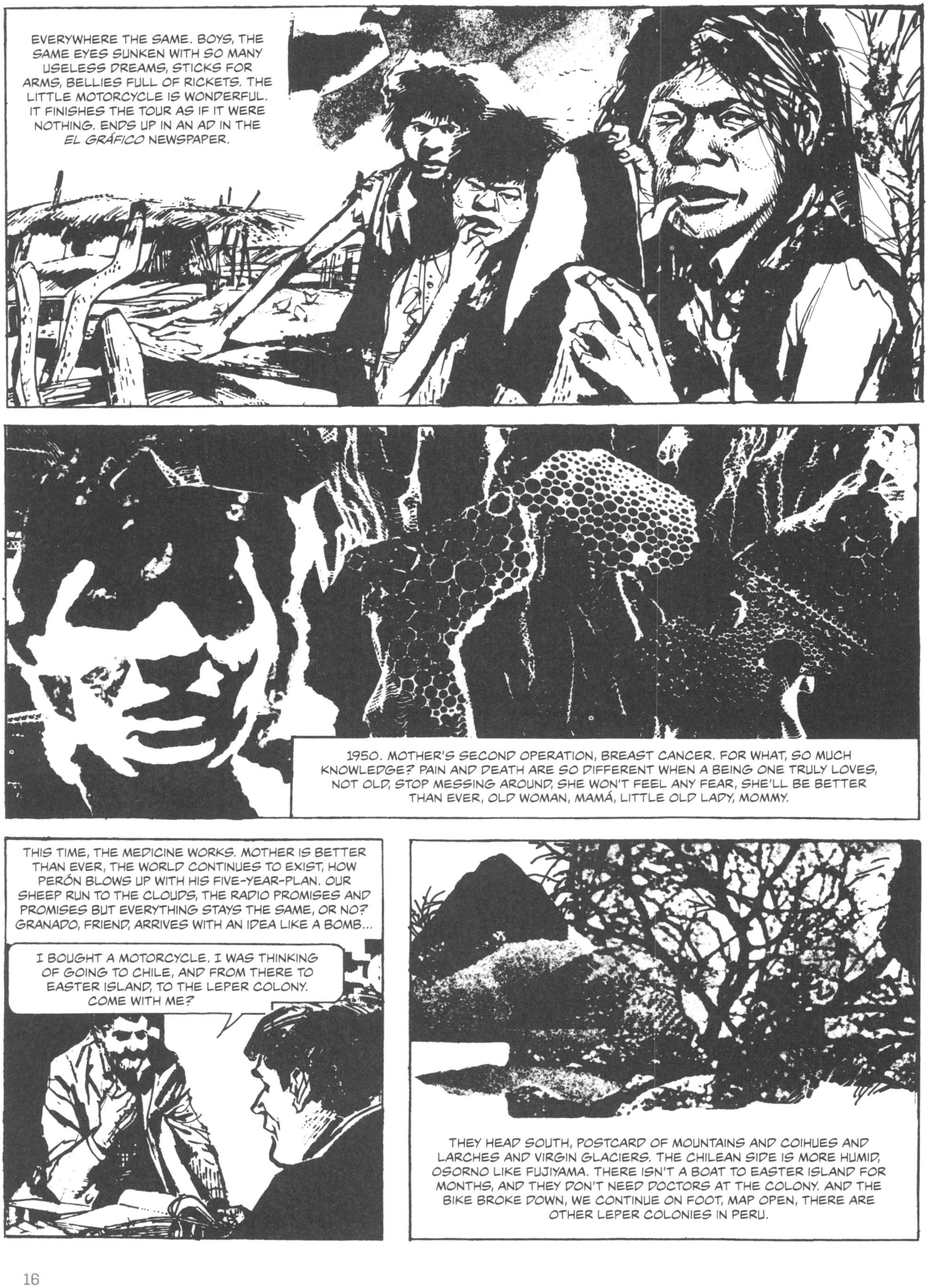
EVERYWHERE THE SAME. BOYS, THE SAME EYES SUNKEN WITH SO MANY USELESS DREAMS, STICKS FOR ARMS, BELLIES FULL OF RICKETS. THE LITTLE MOTORCYCLE IS WONDERFUL. IT FINISHES THE TOUR AS IF IT WERE NOTHING. ENDS UP IN AN AD IN THE *EL GRÁFICO* NEWSPAPER.
1950. MOTHER'S SECOND OPERATION, BREAST CANCER. FOR WHAT, SO MUCH KNOWLEDGE? PAIN AND DEATH ARE SO DIFFERENT WHEN A BEING ONE TRULY LOVES, NOT OLD, STOP MESSING AROUND, SHE WON'T FEEL ANY FEAR, SHE'LL BE BETTER THAN EVER, OLD WOMAN, MAMÁ, LITTLE OLD LADY, MOMMY.
THIS TIME, THE MEDICINE WORKS. MOTHER IS BETTER THAN EVER, THE WORLD CONTINUES TO EXIST, HOW PERÓN BLOWS UP WITH HIS FIVE-YEAR-PLAN. OUR SHEEP RUN TO THE CLOUDS, THE RADIO PROMISES AND PROMISES BUT EVERYTHING STAYS THE SAME, OR NO? GRANADO, FRIEND, ARRIVES WITH AN IDEA LIKE A BOMB...
I BOUGHT A MOTORCYCLE. I WAS THINKING OF GOING TO CHILE, AND FROM THERE TO EASTER ISLAND, TO THE LEPER COLONY. COME WITH ME?
THEY HEAD SOUTH, POSTCARD OF MOUNTAINS AND COIHUES AND LARCHES AND VIRGIN GLACIERS. THE CHILEAN SIDE IS MORE HUMID, OSORNO LIKE FUJIYAMA. THERE ISN'T A BOAT TO EASTER ISLAND FOR MONTHS, AND THEY DON'T NEED DOCTORS AT THE COLONY. AND THE BIKE BROKE DOWN, WE CONTINUE ON FOOT, MAP OPEN, THERE ARE OTHER LEPER COLONIES IN PERU.

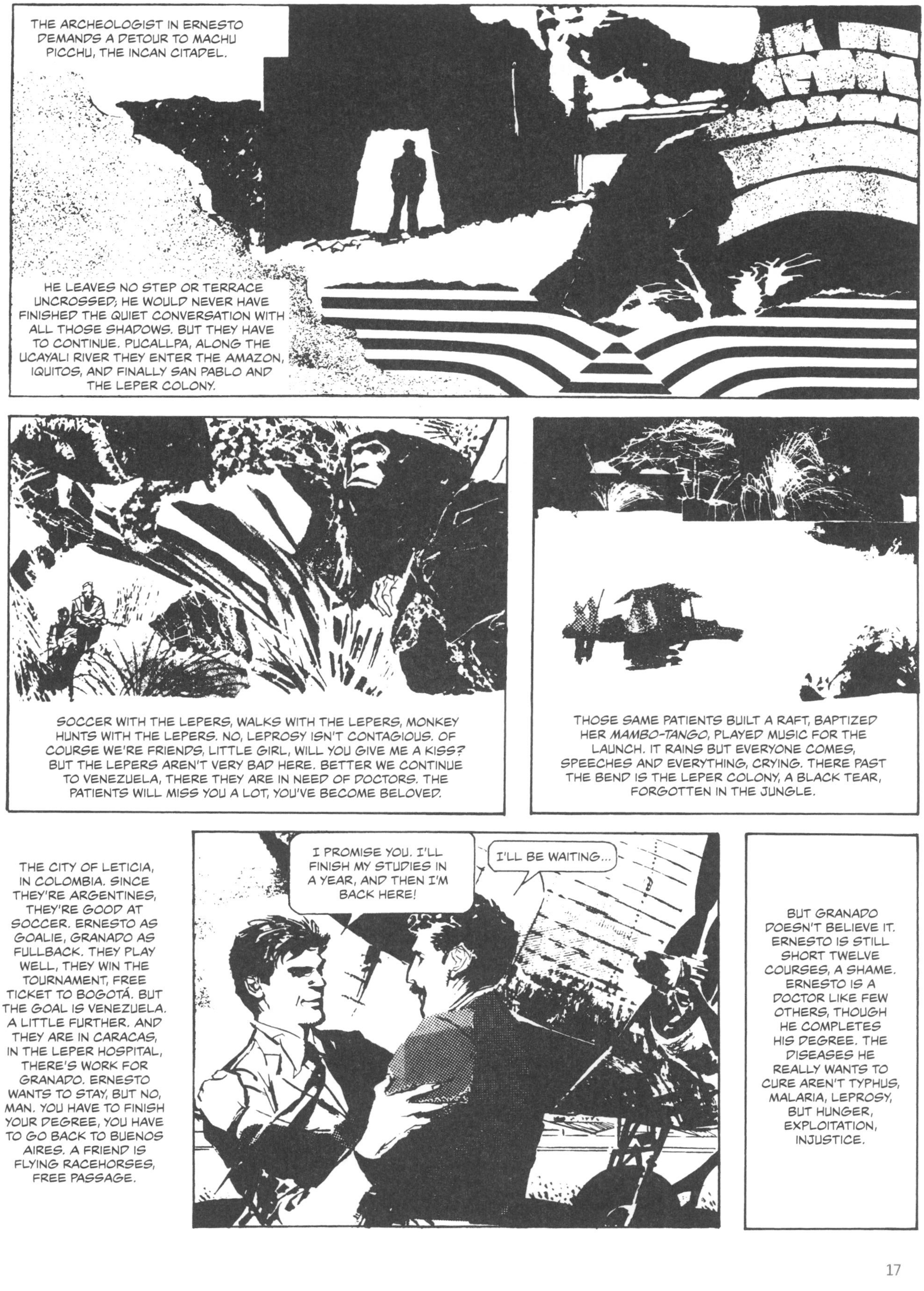
THE ARCHEOLOGIST IN ERNESTO DEMANDS A DETOUR TO MACHU PICCHU, THE INCAN CITADEL.
HE LEAVES NO STEP OR TERRACE UNCROSSED; HE WOULD NEVER HAVE FINISHED THE QUIET CONVERSATION WITH ALL THOSE SHADOWS. BUT THEY HAVE TO CONTINUE. PUCALLPA, ALONG THE UCAYALI RIVER THEY ENTER THE AMAZON, IQUITOS, AND FINALLY SAN PABLO AND THE LEPER COLONY.
SOCCER WITH THE LEPERS, WALKS WITH THE LEPERS, MONKEY HUNTS WITH THE LEPERS. NO, LEPROSY ISN'T CONTAGIOUS. OF COURSE WE'RE FRIENDS, LITTLE GIRL, WILL YOU GIVE ME A KISS? BUT THE LEPERS AREN'T VERY BAD HERE. BETTER WE CONTINUE TO VENEZUELA, THERE THEY ARE IN NEED OF DOCTORS. THE PATIENTS WILL MISS YOU A LOT, YOU'VE BECOME BELOVED.
THOSE SAME PATIENTS BUILT A RAFT, BAPTIZED HER *MAMBO-TANGO*, PLAYED MUSIC FOR THE LAUNCH. IT RAINS BUT EVERYONE COMES, SPEECHES AND EVERYTHING, CRYING. THERE PAST THE BEND IS THE LEPER COLONY, A BLACK TEAR, FORGOTTEN IN THE JUNGLE.
THE CITY OF LETICIA, IN COLOMBIA. SINCE THEY'RE ARGENTINES, THEY'RE GOOD AT SOCCER. ERNESTO AS GOALIE, GRANADO AS FULLBACK. THEY PLAY WELL, THEY WIN THE TOURNAMENT, FREE TICKET TO BOGOTÁ. BUT THE GOAL IS VENEZUELA. A LITTLE FURTHER. AND THEY ARE IN CARACAS, IN THE LEPER HOSPITAL, THERE'S WORK FOR GRANADO. ERNESTO WANTS TO STAY, BUT NO, MAN. YOU HAVE TO FINISH YOUR DEGREE, YOU HAVE TO GO BACK TO BUENOS AIRES. A FRIEND IS FLYING RACEHORSES, FREE PASSAGE.
I PROMISE YOU. I'LL FINISH MY STUDIES IN A YEAR, AND THEN I'M BACK HERE!
I'LL BE WAITING...
BUT GRANADO DOESN'T BELIEVE IT. ERNESTO IS STILL SHORT TWELVE COURSES, A SHAME. ERNESTO IS A DOCTOR LIKE FEW OTHERS, THOUGH HE COMPLETES HIS DEGREE. THE DISEASES HE REALLY WANTS TO CURE AREN'T TYPHUS, MALARIA, LEPROSY, BUT HUNGER, EXPLOITATION, INJUSTICE.

FOURTEENTH OF MAY

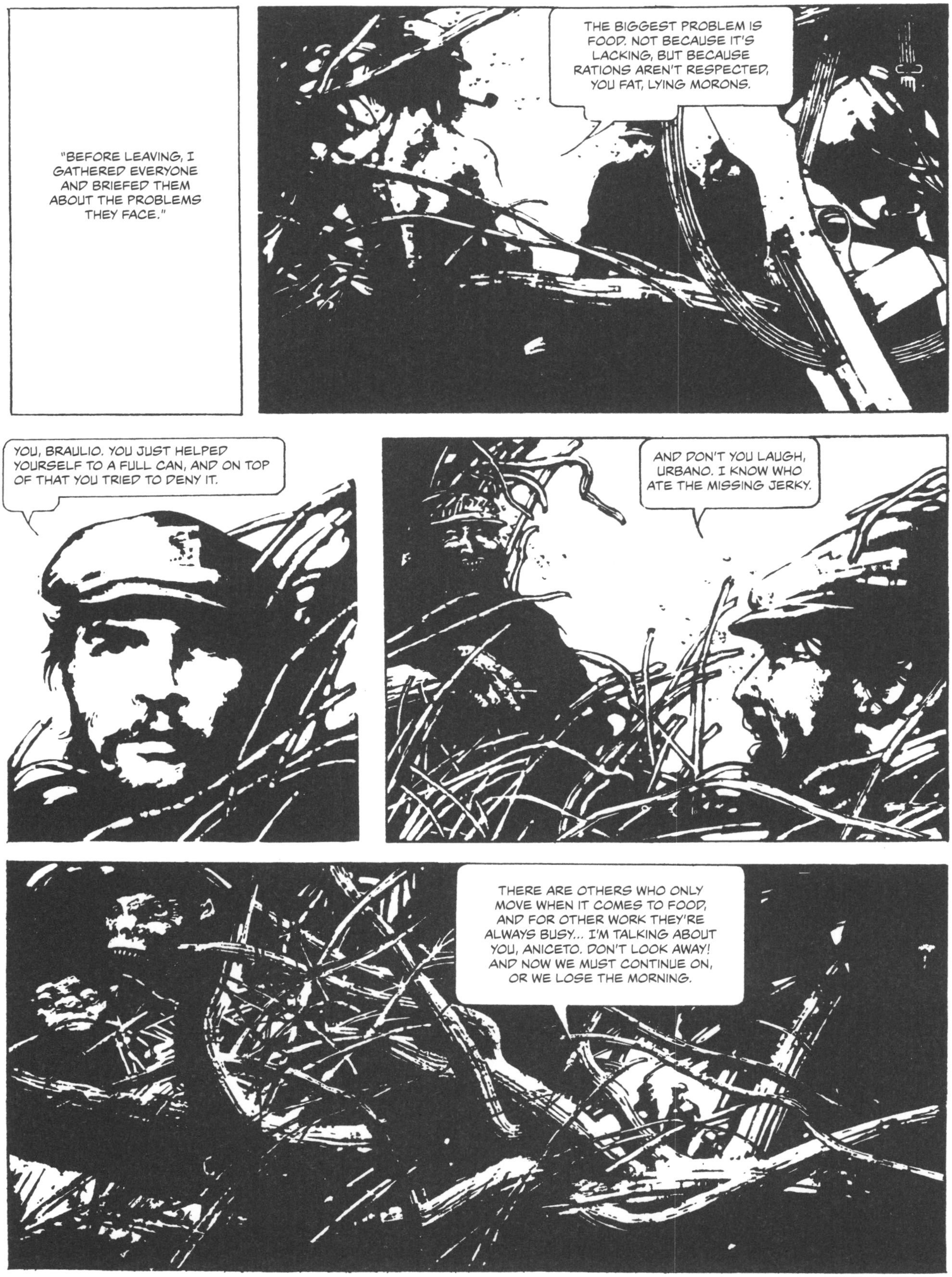
"BEFORE LEAVING, I GATHERED EVERYONE AND BRIEFED THEM ABOUT THE PROBLEMS THEY FACE."
THE BIGGEST PROBLEM IS FOOD. NOT BECAUSE IT'S LACKING, BUT BECAUSE RATIONS AREN'T RESPECTED, YOU FAT, LYING MORONS.
YOU, BRAULIO. YOU JUST HELPED YOURSELF TO A FULL CAN, AND ON TOP OF THAT YOU TRIED TO DENY IT.
AND DON'T YOU LAUGH, URBANO. I KNOW WHO ATE THE MISSING JERKY.
THERE ARE OTHERS WHO ONLY MOVE WHEN IT COMES TO FOOD, AND FOR OTHER WORK THEY'RE ALWAYS BUSY... I'M TALKING ABOUT YOU, ANICETO. DON'T LOOK AWAY! AND NOW WE MUST CONTINUE ON, OR WE LOSE THE MORNING.

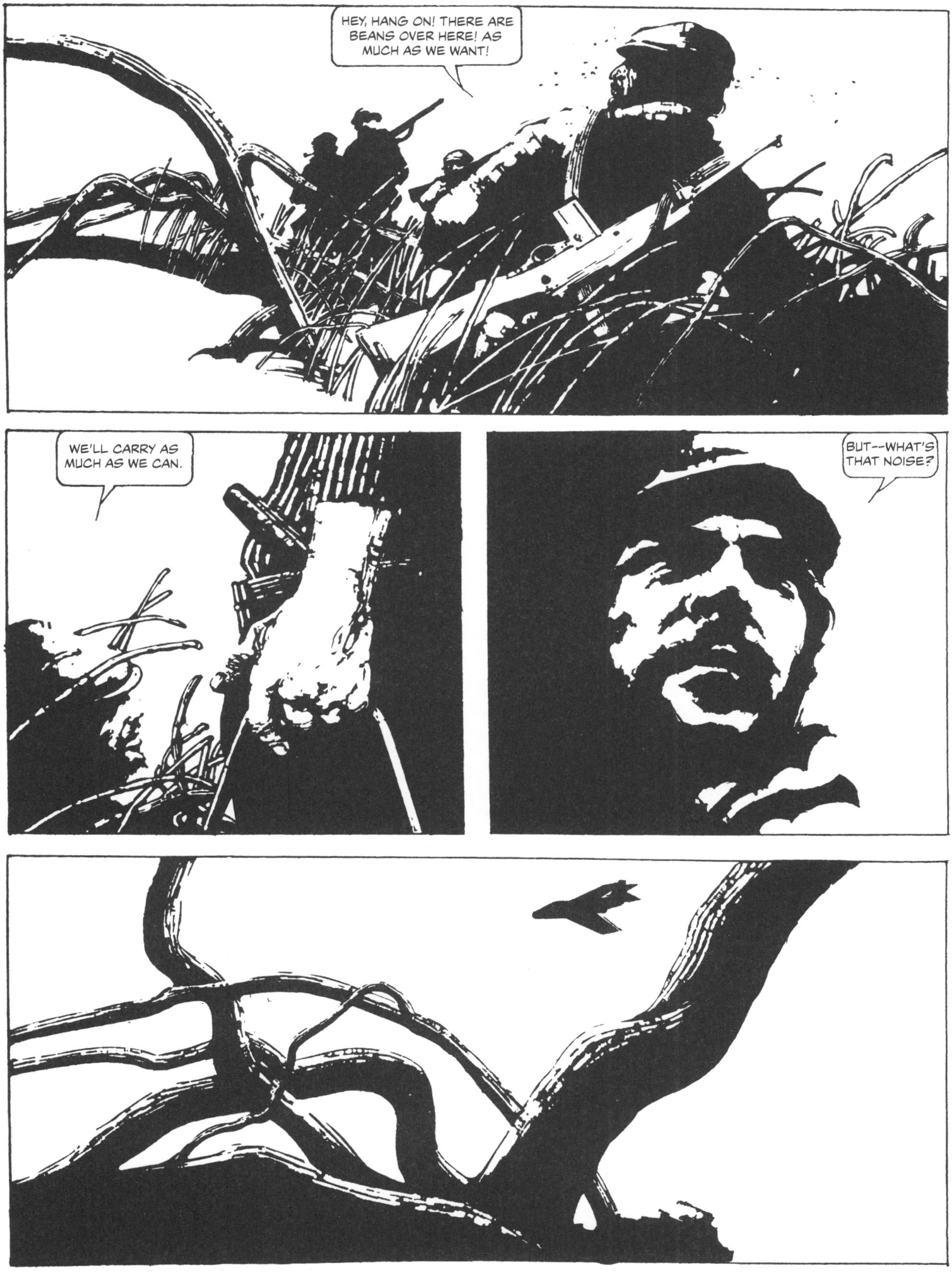
HEY, HANG ON! THERE ARE BEANS OVER HERE! AS MUCH AS WE WANT!
WE'LL CARRY AS MUCH AS WE CAN.
BUT--WHAT'S THAT NOISE?

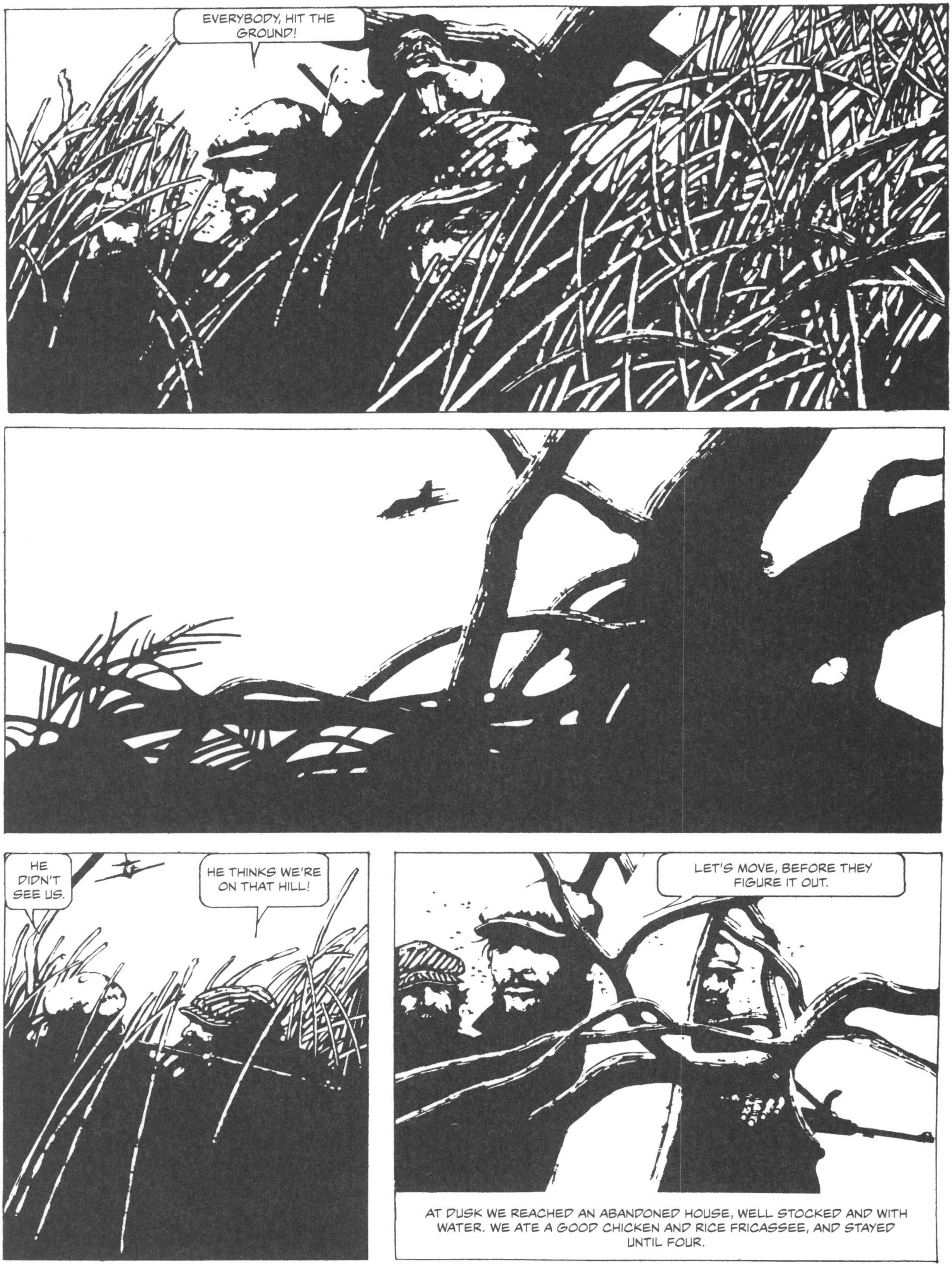
EVERYBODY, HIT THE GROUND!
HE DIDN'T SEE US.
HE THINKS WE'RE ON THAT HILL!
LET'S MOVE, BEFORE THEY FIGURE IT OUT.
AT DUSK WE REACHED AN ABANDONED HOUSE, WELL STOCKED AND WITH WATER. WE ATE A GOOD CHICKEN AND RICE FRICASSEE, AND STAYED UNTIL FOUR.

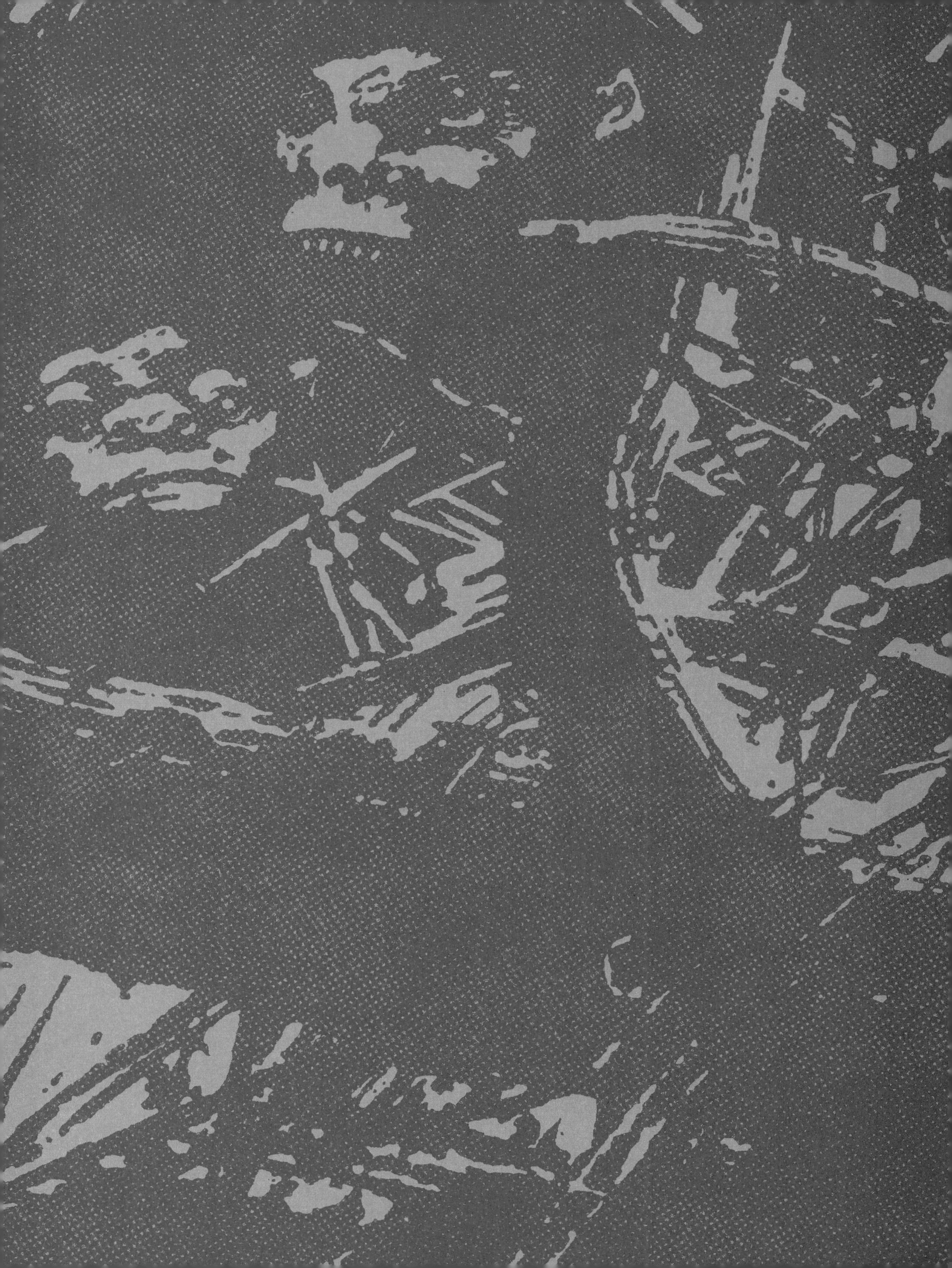

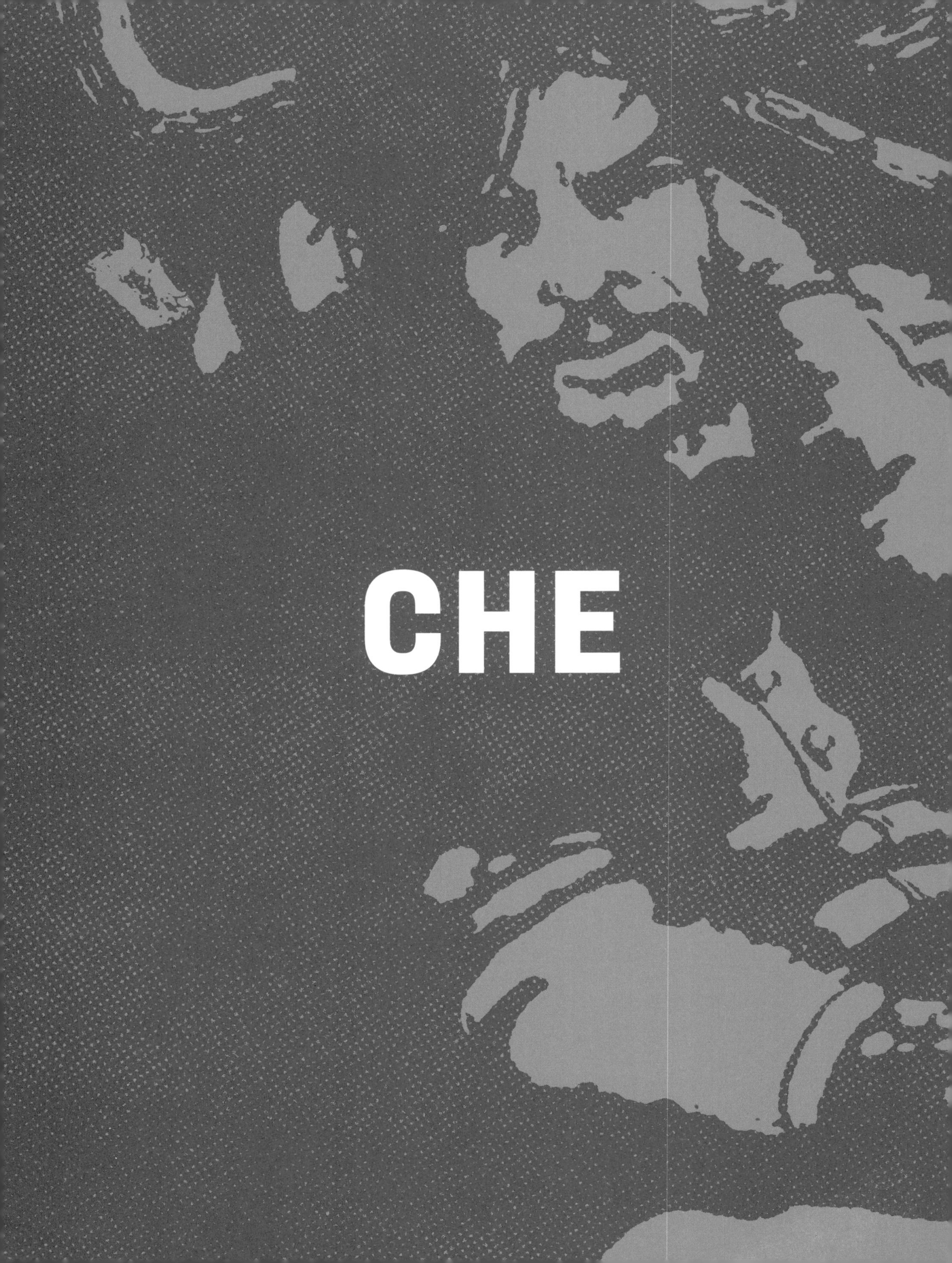
CHE

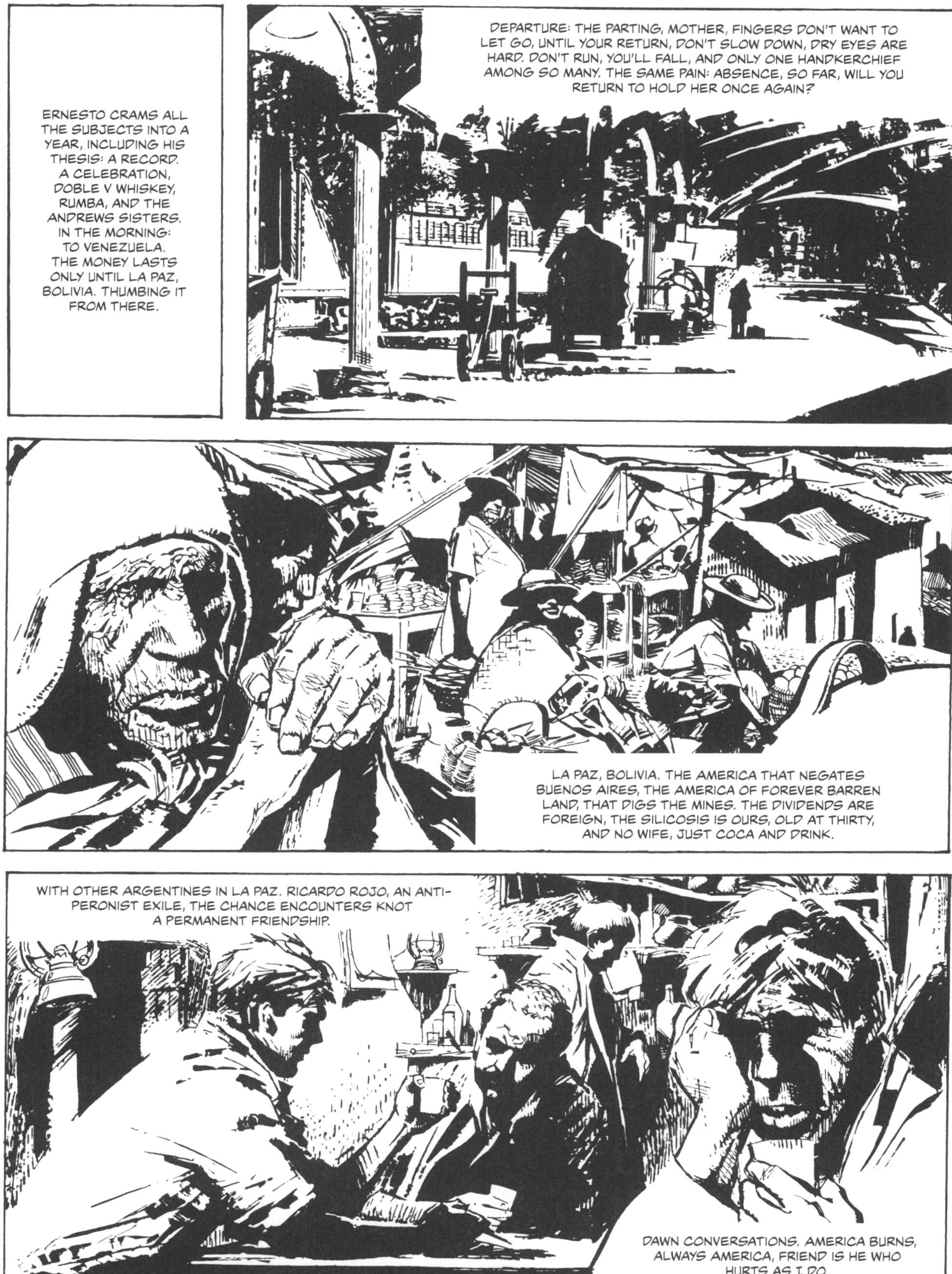
ERNESTO CRAMS ALL THE SUBJECTS INTO A YEAR, INCLUDING HIS THESIS: A RECORD. A CELEBRATION, DOBLE V WHISKEY, RUMBA, AND THE ANDREWS SISTERS. IN THE MORNING: TO VENEZUELA. THE MONEY LASTS ONLY UNTIL LA PAZ, BOLIVIA. THUMBING IT FROM THERE.
DEPARTURE: THE PARTING, MOTHER, FINGERS DON'T WANT TO LET GO, UNTIL YOUR RETURN, DON'T SLOW DOWN, DRY EYES ARE HARD. DON'T RUN, YOU'LL FALL, AND ONLY ONE HANDKERCHIEF AMONG SO MANY. THE SAME PAIN: ABSENCE, SO FAR, WILL YOU RETURN TO HOLD HER ONCE AGAIN?
LA PAZ, BOLIVIA. THE AMERICA THAT NEGATES BUENOS AIRES, THE AMERICA OF FOREVER BARREN LAND, THAT DIGS THE MINES. THE DIVIDENDS ARE FOREIGN, THE SILICOSIS IS OURS, OLD AT THIRTY, AND NO WIFE, JUST COCA AND DRINK.
WITH OTHER ARGENTINES IN LA PAZ. RICARDO ROJO, AN ANTI-PERONIST EXILE, THE CHANCE ENCOUNTERS KNOT A PERMANENT FRIENDSHIP.
DAWN CONVERSATIONS. AMERICA BURNS, ALWAYS AMERICA, FRIEND IS HE WHO HURTS AS I DO.

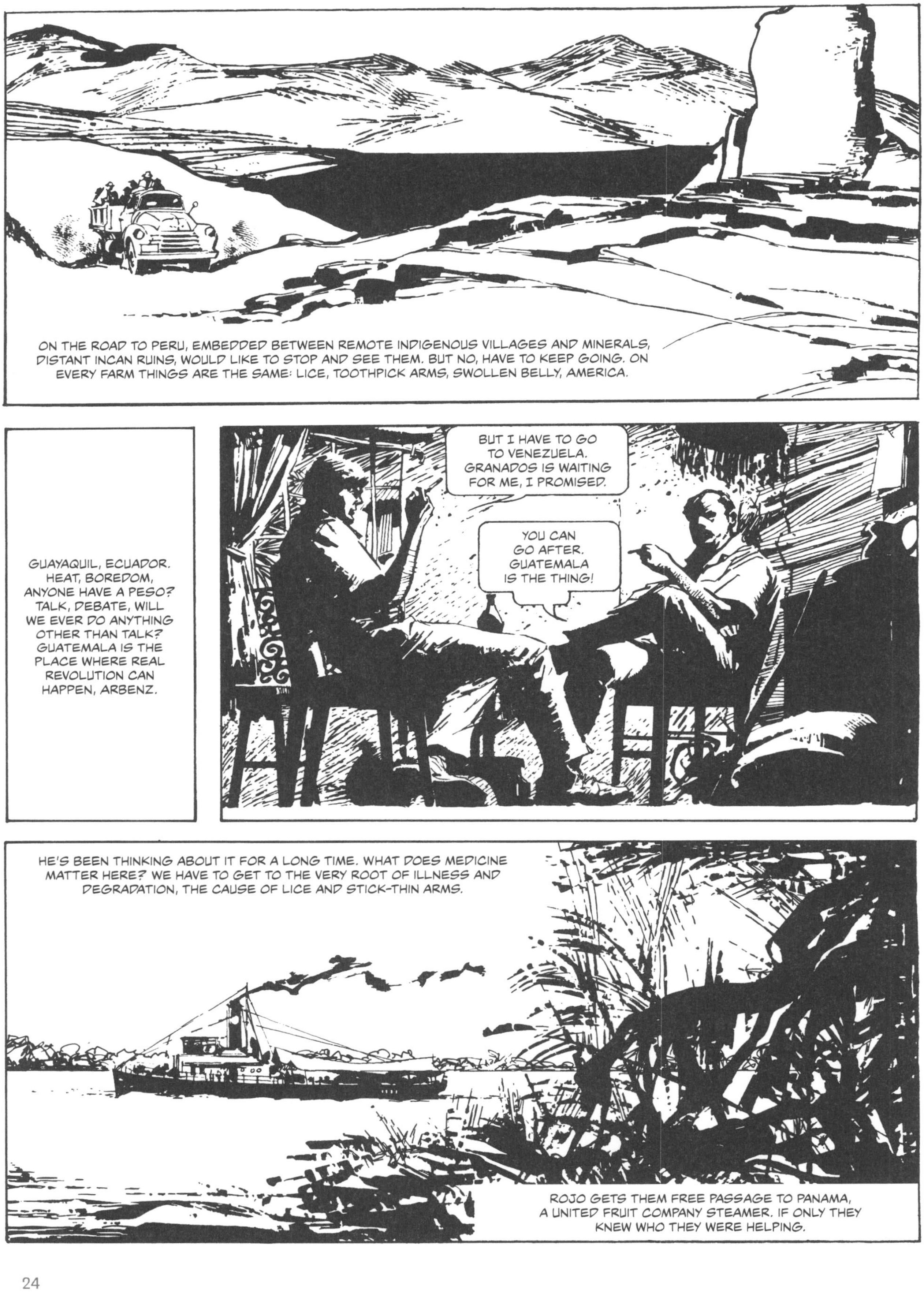
ON THE ROAD TO PERU, EMBEDDED BETWEEN REMOTE INDIGENOUS VILLAGES AND MINERALS, DISTANT INCAN RUINS, WOULD LIKE TO STOP AND SEE THEM. BUT NO, HAVE TO KEEP GOING. ON EVERY FARM THINGS ARE THE SAME: LICE, TOOTHPICK ARMS, SWOLLEN BELLY, AMERICA.
GUAYAQUIL, ECUADOR. HEAT, BOREDOM, ANYONE HAVE A PESO? TALK, DEBATE, WILL WE EVER DO ANYTHING OTHER THAN TALK? GUATEMALA IS THE PLACE WHERE REAL REVOLUTION CAN HAPPEN, ARBENZ.
BUT I HAVE TO GO TO VENEZUELA. GRANADOS IS WAITING FOR ME, I PROMISED.
YOU CAN GO AFTER. GUATEMALA IS THE THING!
HE'S BEEN THINKING ABOUT IT FOR A LONG TIME. WHAT DOES MEDICINE MATTER HERE? WE HAVE TO GET TO THE VERY ROOT OF ILLNESS AND DEGRADATION, THE CAUSE OF LICE AND STICK-THIN ARMS.
ROJO GETS THEM FREE PASSAGE TO PANAMA, A UNITED FRUIT COMPANY STEAMER. IF ONLY THEY KNEW WHO THEY WERE HELPING.

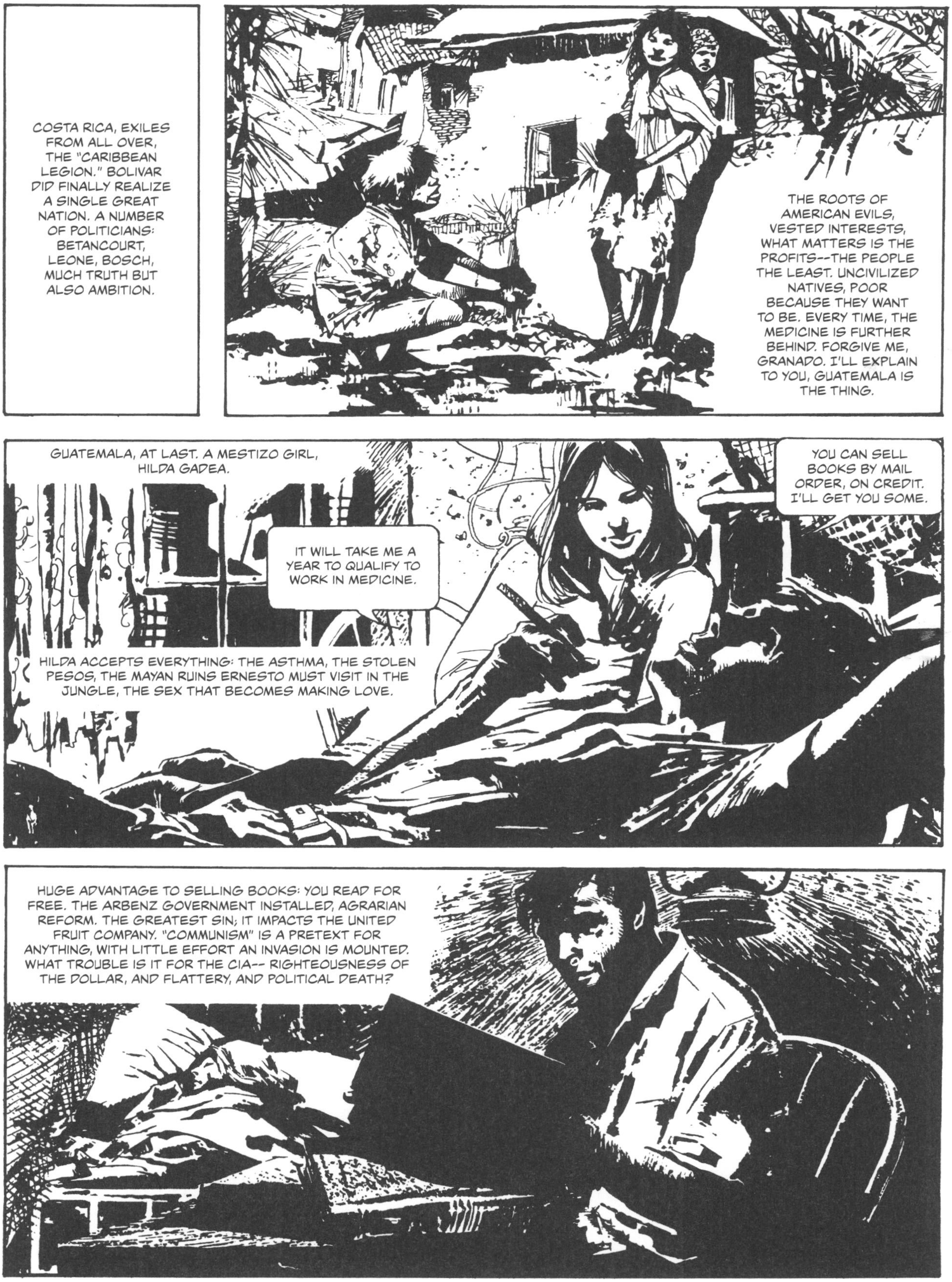
COSTA RICA, EXILES FROM ALL OVER, THE "CARIBBEAN LEGION." BOLIVAR DID FINALLY REALIZE A SINGLE GREAT NATION. A NUMBER OF POLITICIANS: BETANCOURT, LEONE, BOSCH, MUCH TRUTH BUT ALSO AMBITION.
THE ROOTS OF AMERICAN EVILS, VESTED INTERESTS, WHAT MATTERS IS THE PROFITS--THE PEOPLE THE LEAST. UNCIVILIZED NATIVES, POOR BECAUSE THEY WANT TO BE. EVERY TIME, THE MEDICINE IS FURTHER BEHIND. FORGIVE ME, GRANADO. I'LL EXPLAIN TO YOU, GUATEMALA IS THE THING.
GUATEMALA, AT LAST. A MESTIZO GIRL, HILDA GADEA.
YOU CAN SELL BOOKS BY MAIL ORDER, ON CREDIT. I'LL GET YOU SOME.
IT WILL TAKE ME A YEAR TO QUALIFY TO WORK IN MEDICINE.
HILDA ACCEPTS EVERYTHING: THE ASTHMA, THE STOLEN PESOS, THE MAYAN RUINS ERNESTO MUST VISIT IN THE JUNGLE, THE SEX THAT BECOMES MAKING LOVE.
HUGE ADVANTAGE TO SELLING BOOKS: YOU READ FOR FREE. THE ARBENZ GOVERNMENT INSTALLED, AGRARIAN REFORM. THE GREATEST SIN; IT IMPACTS THE UNITED FRUIT COMPANY. "COMMUNISM" IS A PRETEXT FOR ANYTHING, WITH LITTLE EFFORT AN INVASION IS MOUNTED. WHAT TROUBLE IS IT FOR THE CIA-- RIGHTEOUSNESS OF THE DOLLAR, AND FLATTERY, AND POLITICAL DEATH?

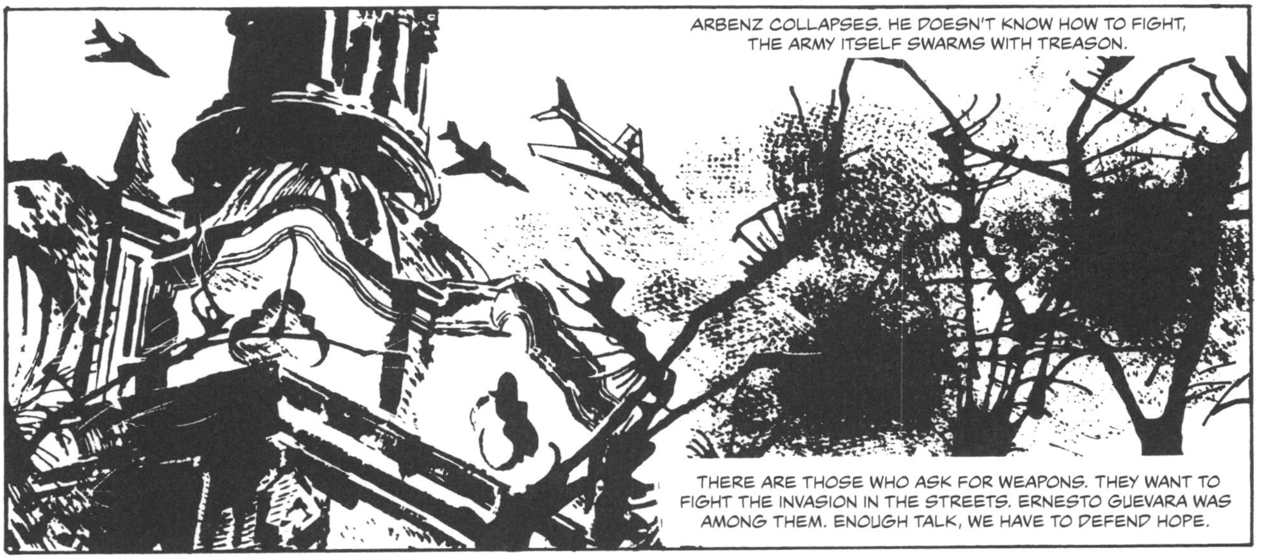
ARBENZ COLLAPSES. HE DOESN'T KNOW HOW TO FIGHT, THE ARMY ITSELF SWARMS WITH TREASON.
THERE ARE THOSE WHO ASK FOR WEAPONS. THEY WANT TO FIGHT THE INVASION IN THE STREETS. ERNESTO GUEVARA WAS AMONG THEM. ENOUGH TALK, WE HAVE TO DEFEND HOPE.

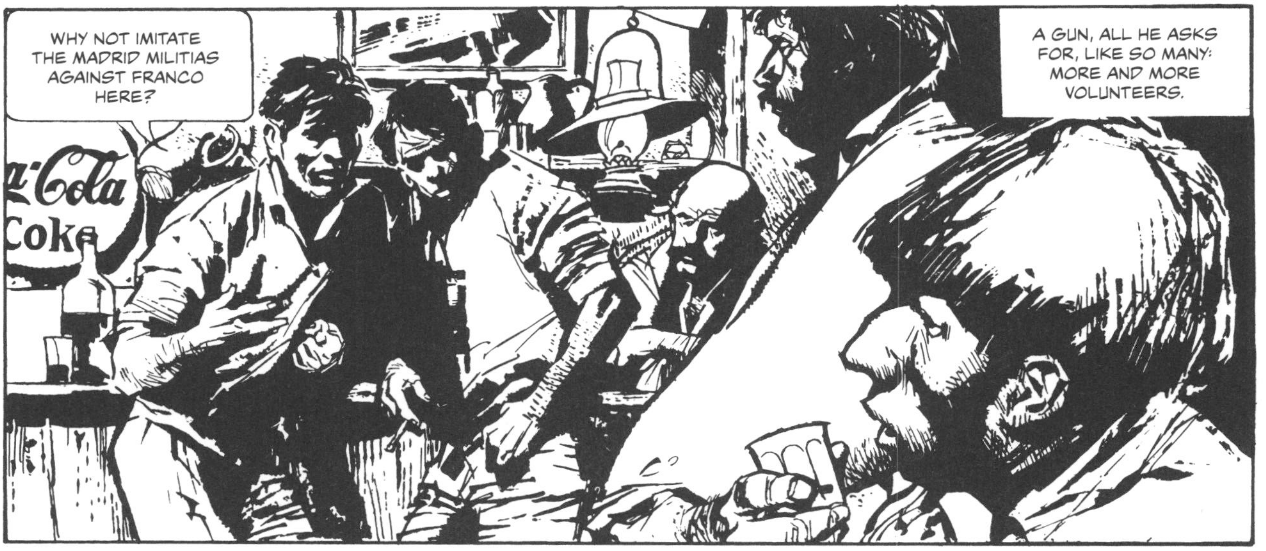
WHY NOT IMITATE THE MADRID MILITIAS AGAINST FRANCO HERE?
A GUN, ALL HE ASKS FOR, LIKE SO MANY: MORE AND MORE VOLUNTEERS.
Coke

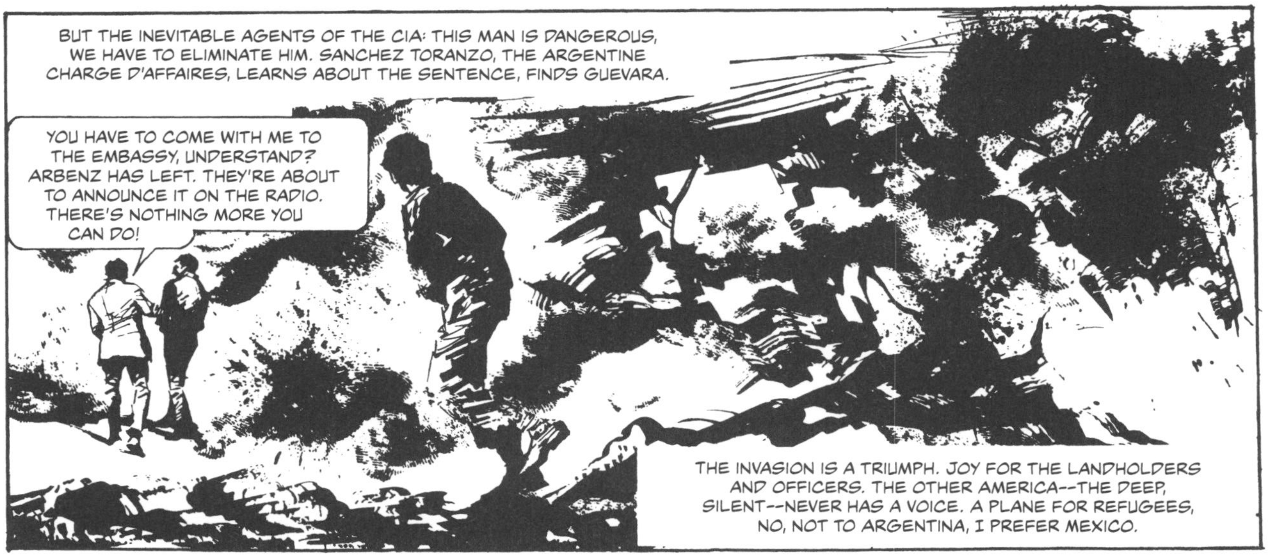
BUT THE INEVITABLE AGENTS OF THE CIA: THIS MAN IS DANGEROUS, WE HAVE TO ELIMINATE HIM. SANCHEZ TORANZO, THE ARGENTINE CHARGE D'AFFAIRES, LEARNS ABOUT THE SENTENCE, FINDS GUEVARA.
YOU HAVE TO COME WITH ME TO THE EMBASSY, UNDERSTAND? ARBENZ HAS LEFT. THEY'RE ABOUT TO ANNOUNCE IT ON THE RADIO. THERE'S NOTHING MORE YOU CAN DO!
THE INVASION IS A TRIUMPH. JOY FOR THE LANDHOLDERS AND OFFICERS. THE OTHER AMERICA--THE DEEP, SILENT--NEVER HAS A VOICE. A PLANE FOR REFUGEES, NO, NOT TO ARGENTINA, I PREFER MEXICO.

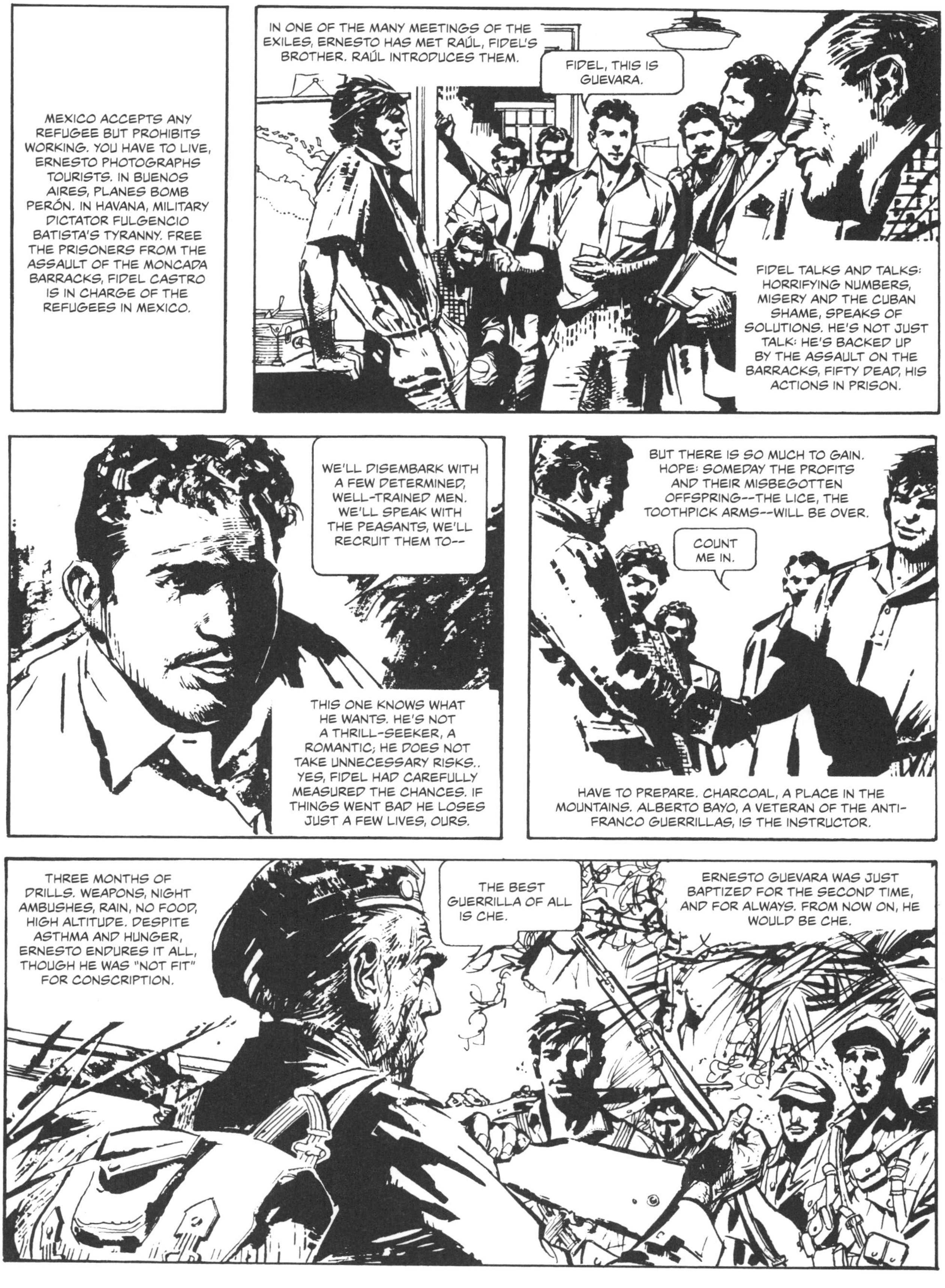
MEXICO ACCEPTS ANY REFUGEE BUT PROHIBITS WORKING. YOU HAVE TO LIVE, ERNESTO PHOTOGRAPHS TOURISTS. IN BUENOS AIRES, PLANES BOMB PERÓN. IN HAVANA, MILITARY DICTATOR FULGENCIO BATISTA'S TYRANNY. FREE THE PRISONERS FROM THE ASSAULT OF THE MONCADA BARRACKS, FIDEL CASTRO IS IN CHARGE OF THE REFUGEES IN MEXICO.
IN ONE OF THE MANY MEETINGS OF THE EXILES, ERNESTO HAS MET RAÚL, FIDEL'S BROTHER. RAÚL INTRODUCES THEM.
FIDEL, THIS IS GUEVARA.
FIDEL TALKS AND TALKS: HORRIFYING NUMBERS, MISERY AND THE CUBAN SHAME, SPEAKS OF SOLUTIONS. HE'S NOT JUST TALK: HE'S BACKED UP BY THE ASSAULT ON THE BARRACKS, FIFTY DEAD, HIS ACTIONS IN PRISON.
WE'LL DISEMBARK WITH A FEW DETERMINED, WELL-TRAINED MEN. WE'LL SPEAK WITH THE PEASANTS, WE'LL RECRUIT THEM TO--
THIS ONE KNOWS WHAT HE WANTS. HE'S NOT A THRILL-SEEKER, A ROMANTIC; HE DOES NOT TAKE UNNECESSARY RISKS.. YES, FIDEL HAD CAREFULLY MEASURED THE CHANCES. IF THINGS WENT BAD HE LOSES JUST A FEW LIVES, OURS.
BUT THERE IS SO MUCH TO GAIN. HOPE: SOMEDAY THE PROFITS AND THEIR MISBEGOTTEN OFFSPRING--THE LICE, THE TOOTHPICK ARMS--WILL BE OVER.
COUNT ME IN.
HAVE TO PREPARE. CHARCOAL, A PLACE IN THE MOUNTAINS. ALBERTO BAYO, A VETERAN OF THE ANTI-FRANCO GUERRILLAS, IS THE INSTRUCTOR.
THREE MONTHS OF DRILLS. WEAPONS, NIGHT AMBUSHES, RAIN, NO FOOD, HIGH ALTITUDE. DESPITE ASTHMA AND HUNGER, ERNESTO ENDURES IT ALL, THOUGH HE WAS "NOT FIT" FOR CONSCRIPTION.
THE BEST GUERRILLA OF ALL IS CHE.
ERNESTO GUEVARA WAS JUST BAPTIZED FOR THE SECOND TIME, AND FOR ALWAYS. FROM NOW ON, HE WOULD BE CHE.

SIXTEENTH OF MAY

"AT THE START OF THE MARCH, I GOT VERY SICK, VOMITING AND DIARRHEA."

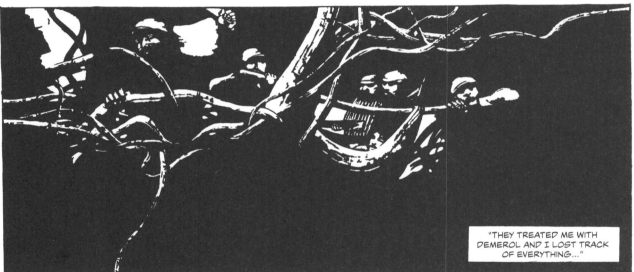

"THEY TREATED ME WITH DEMEROL AND I LOST TRACK OF EVERYTHING..."

"...WHEN I WOKE I WAS MUCH BETTER, BUT AS DIRTY AS A BABY. I WAS LENT PANTS, BUT WITHOUT WATER, I STUNK FOR KILOMETERS."

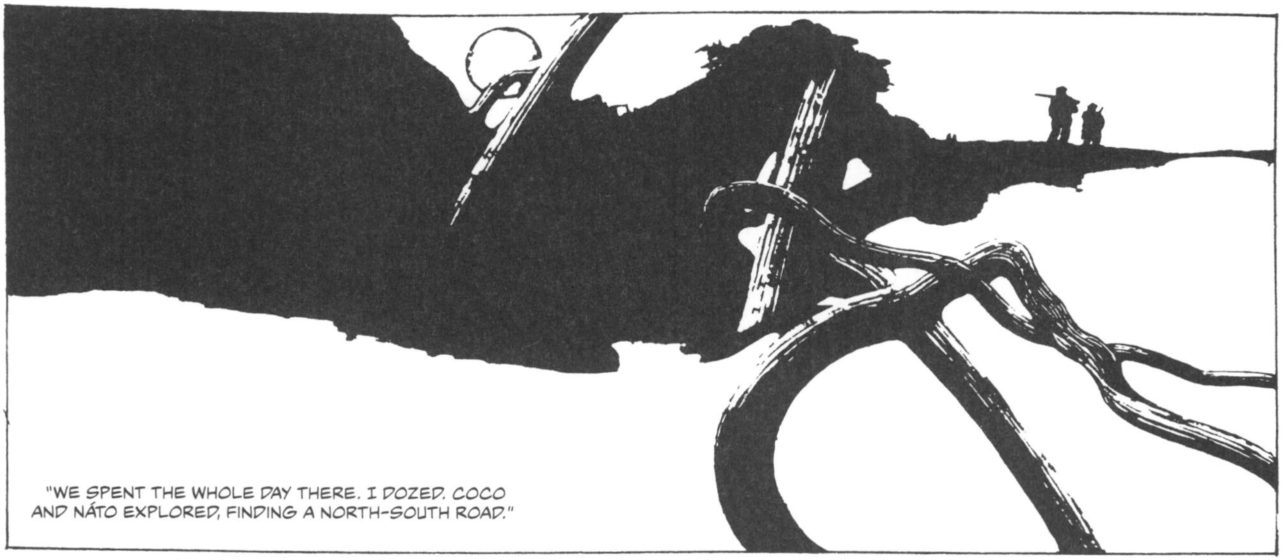
"WE SPENT THE WHOLE DAY THERE. I DOZED. COCO AND NÁTO EXPLORED, FINDING A NORTH-SOUTH ROAD."

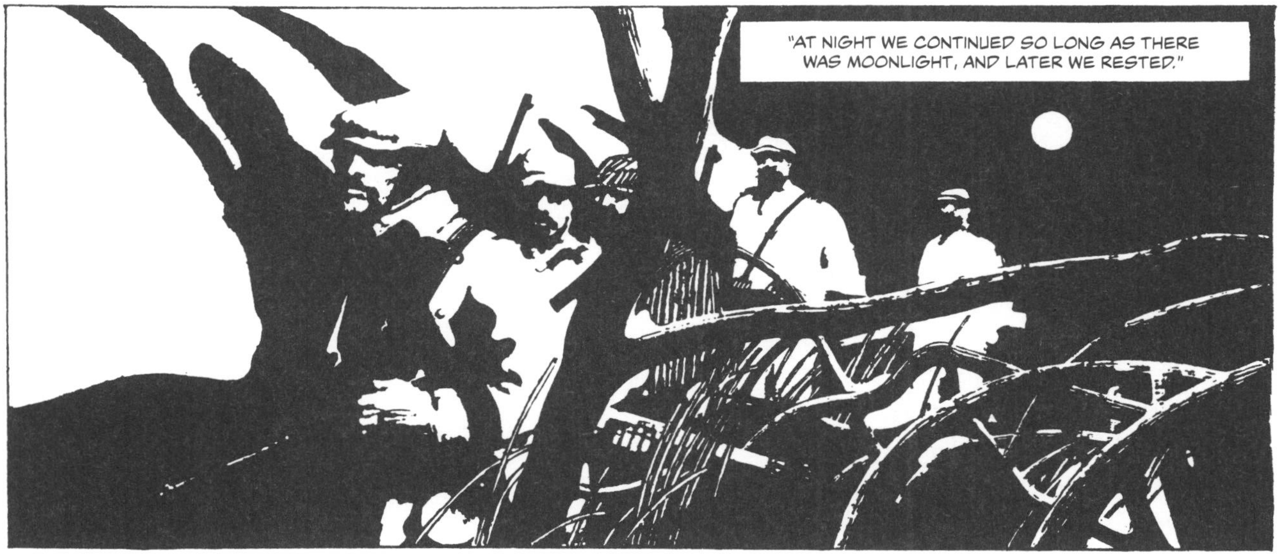
"AT NIGHT WE CONTINUED SO LONG AS THERE WAS MOONLIGHT, AND LATER WE RESTED."

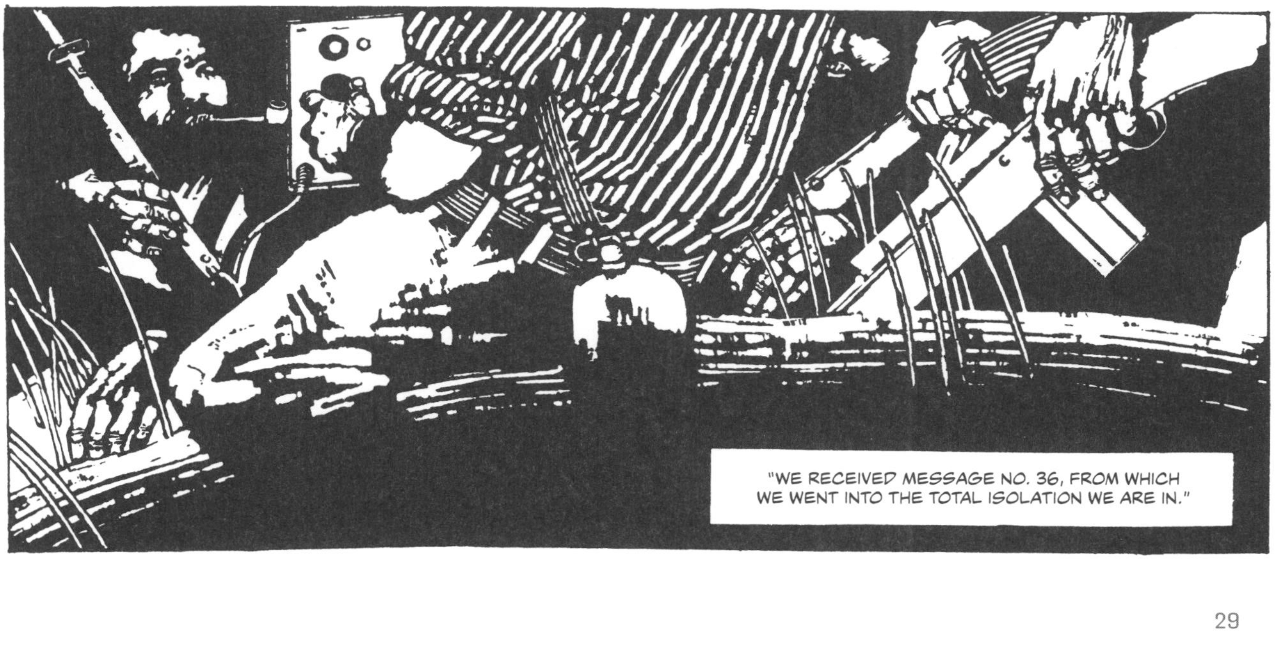
"WE RECEIVED MESSAGE NO. 36, FROM WHICH WE WENT INTO THE TOTAL ISOLATION WE ARE IN."

SIXTH OF JULY

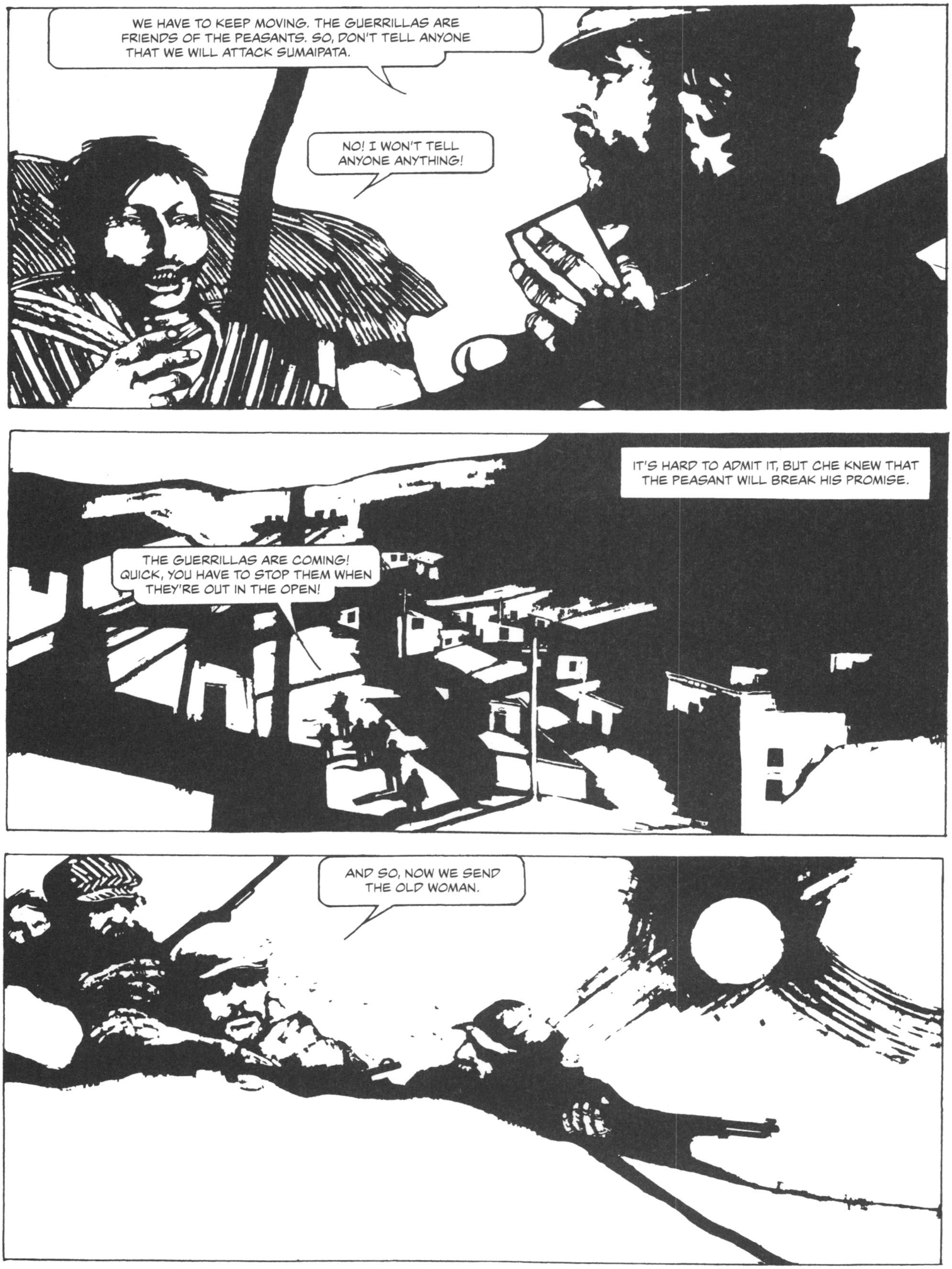

WE HAVE TO KEEP MOVING. THE GUERRILLAS ARE FRIENDS OF THE PEASANTS. SO, DON'T TELL ANYONE THAT WE WILL ATTACK SUMAIPATA.
NO! I WON'T TELL ANYONE ANYTHING!
IT'S HARD TO ADMIT IT, BUT CHE KNEW THAT THE PEASANT WILL BREAK HIS PROMISE.
THE GUERRILLAS ARE COMING! QUICK, YOU HAVE TO STOP THEM WHEN THEY'RE OUT IN THE OPEN!
AND SO, NOW WE SEND THE OLD WOMAN.

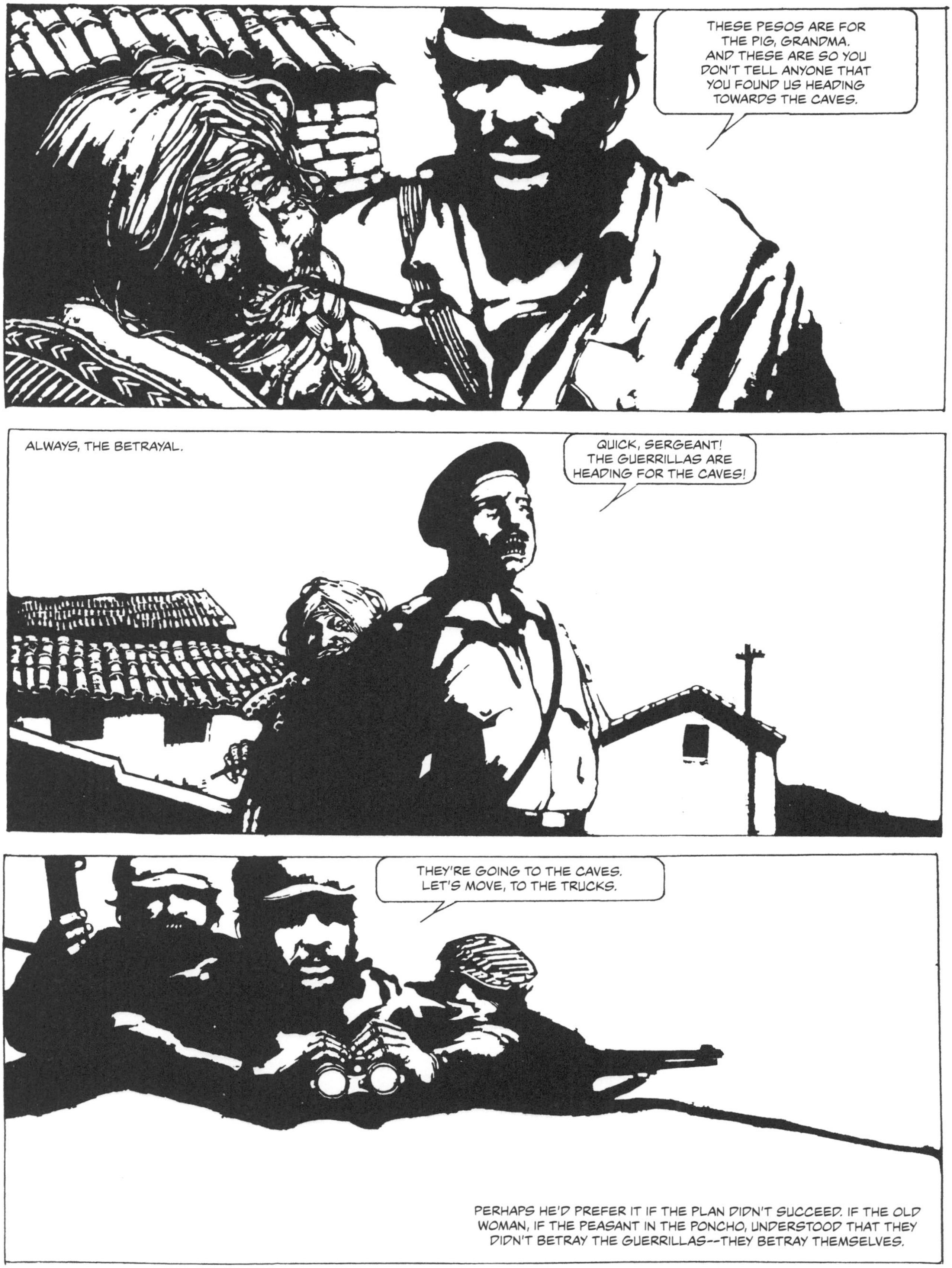
THESE PESOS ARE FOR THE PIG, GRANDMA. AND THESE ARE SO YOU DON'T TELL ANYONE THAT YOU FOUND US HEADING TOWARDS THE CAVES.
ALWAYS, THE BETRAYAL.
QUICK, SERGEANT! THE GUERRILLAS ARE HEADING FOR THE CAVES!
THEY'RE GOING TO THE CAVES. LET'S MOVE, TO THE TRUCKS.
PERHAPS HE'D PREFER IT IF THE PLAN DIDN'T SUCCEED. IF THE OLD WOMAN, IF THE PEASANT IN THE PONCHO, UNDERSTOOD THAT THEY DIDN'T BETRAY THE GUERRILLAS--THEY BETRAY THEMSELVES.

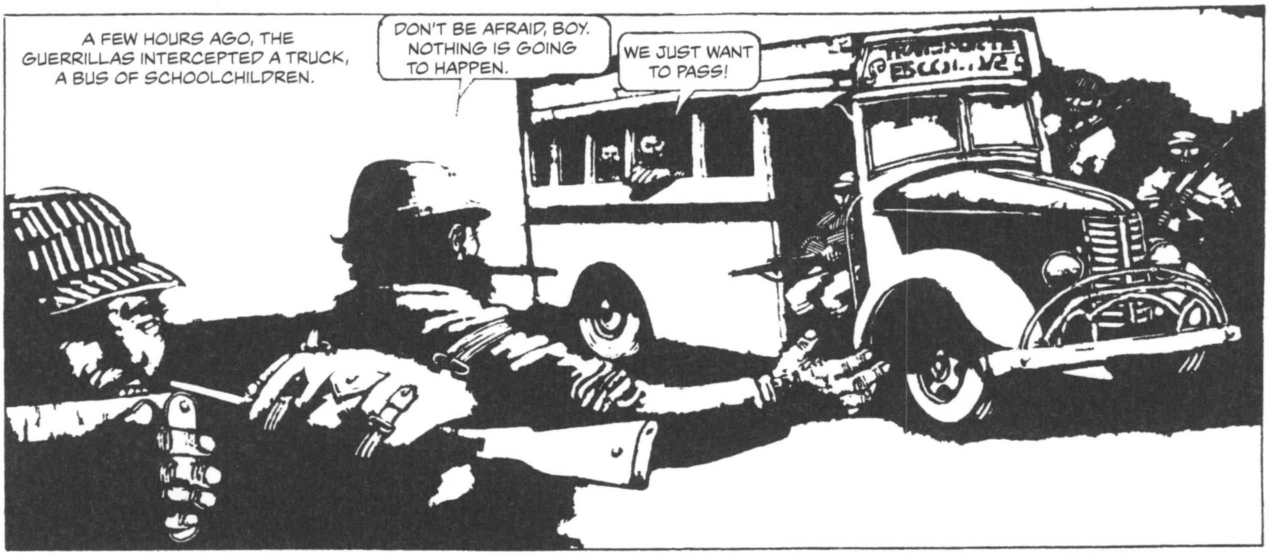
A FEW HOURS AGO, THE GUERRILLAS INTERCEPTED A TRUCK, A BUS OF SCHOOLCHILDREN.
DON'T BE AFRAID, BOY. NOTHING IS GOING TO HAPPEN.
WE JUST WANT TO PASS!

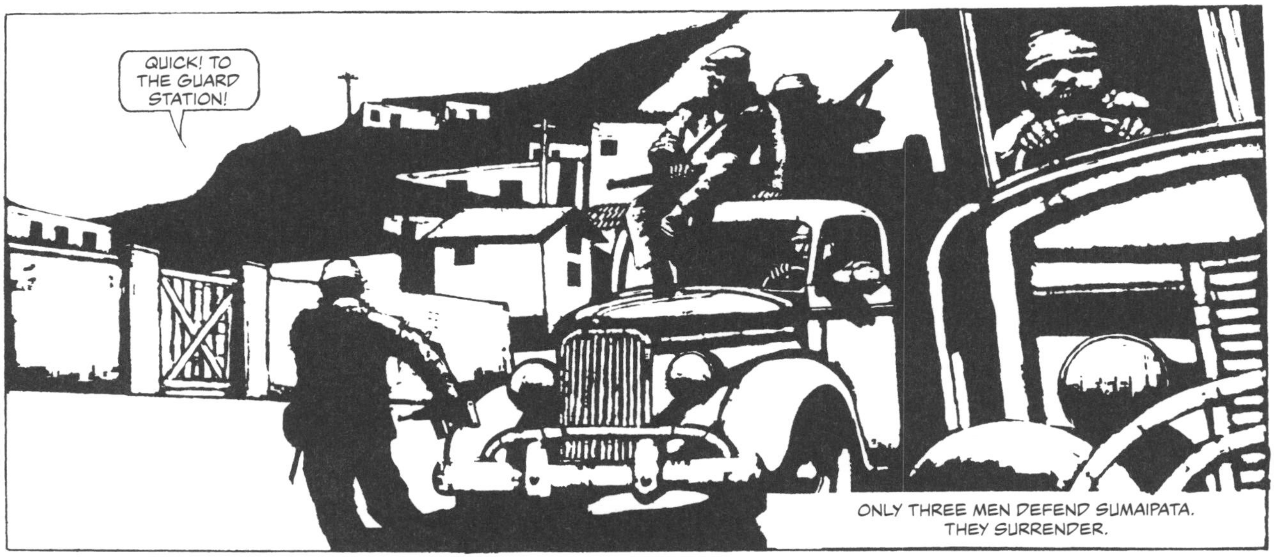
QUICK! TO THE GUARD STATION!
ONLY THREE MEN DEFEND SUMAIPATA. THEY SURRENDER.

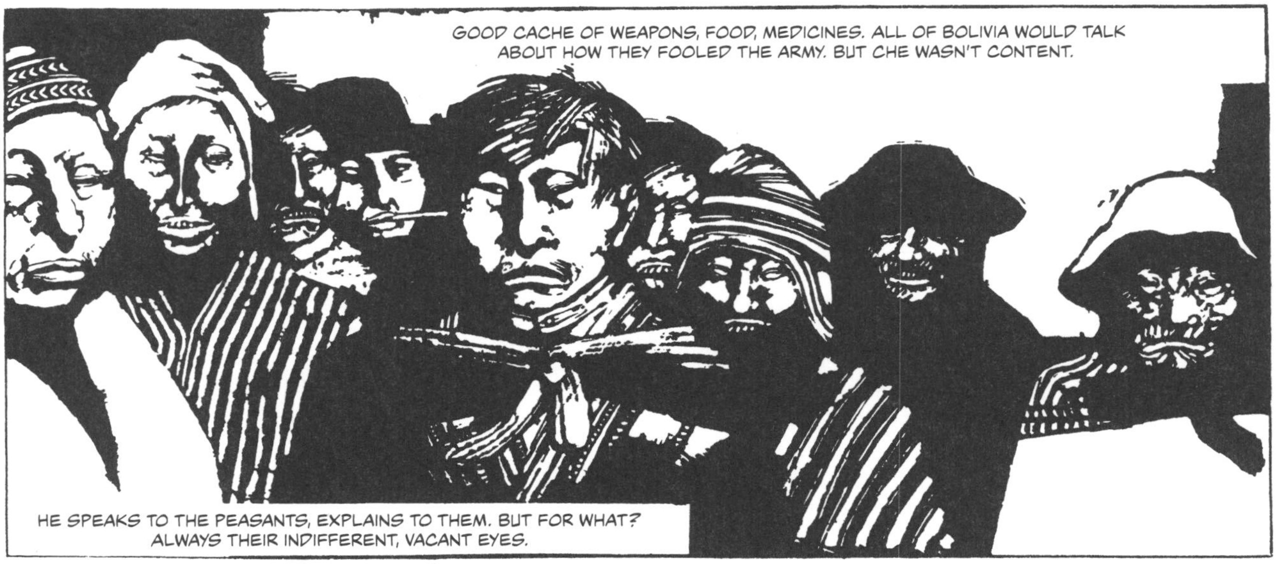
GOOD CACHE OF WEAPONS, FOOD, MEDICINES. ALL OF BOLIVIA WOULD TALK ABOUT HOW THEY FOOLED THE ARMY. BUT CHE WASN'T CONTENT.
HE SPEAKS TO THE PEASANTS, EXPLAINS TO THEM. BUT FOR WHAT? ALWAYS THEIR INDIFFERENT, VACANT EYES.

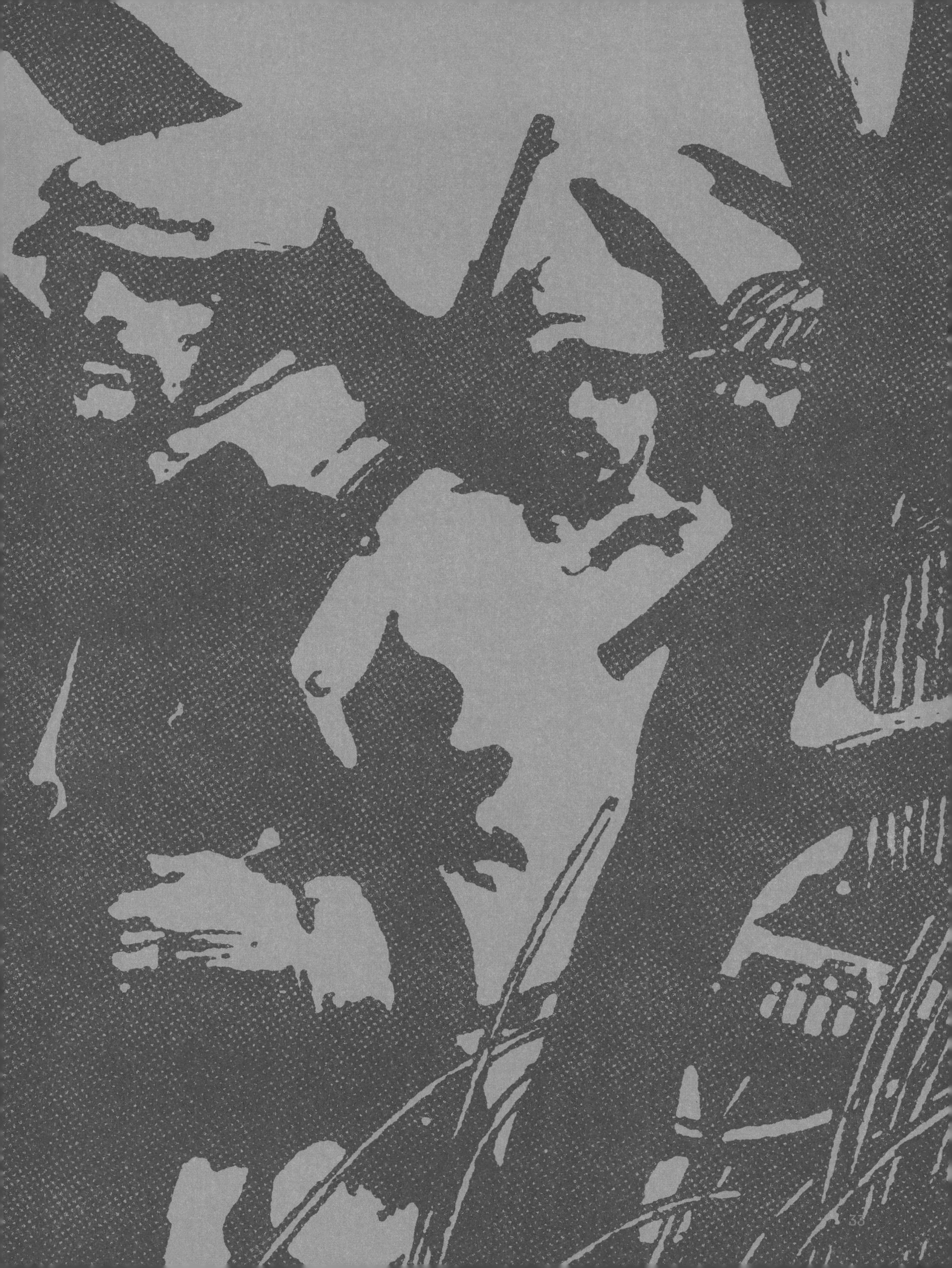

SIERRA MAESTRA

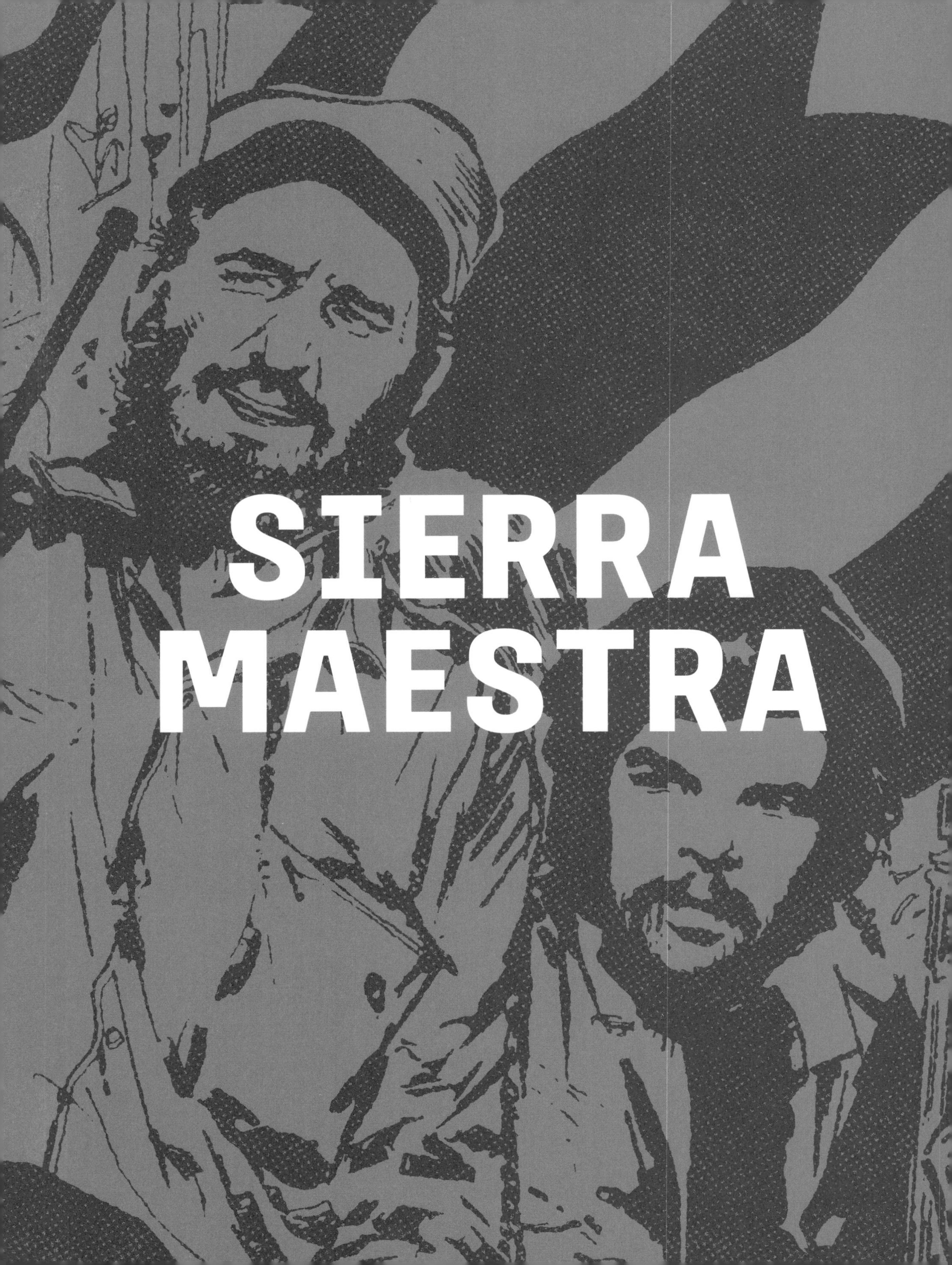

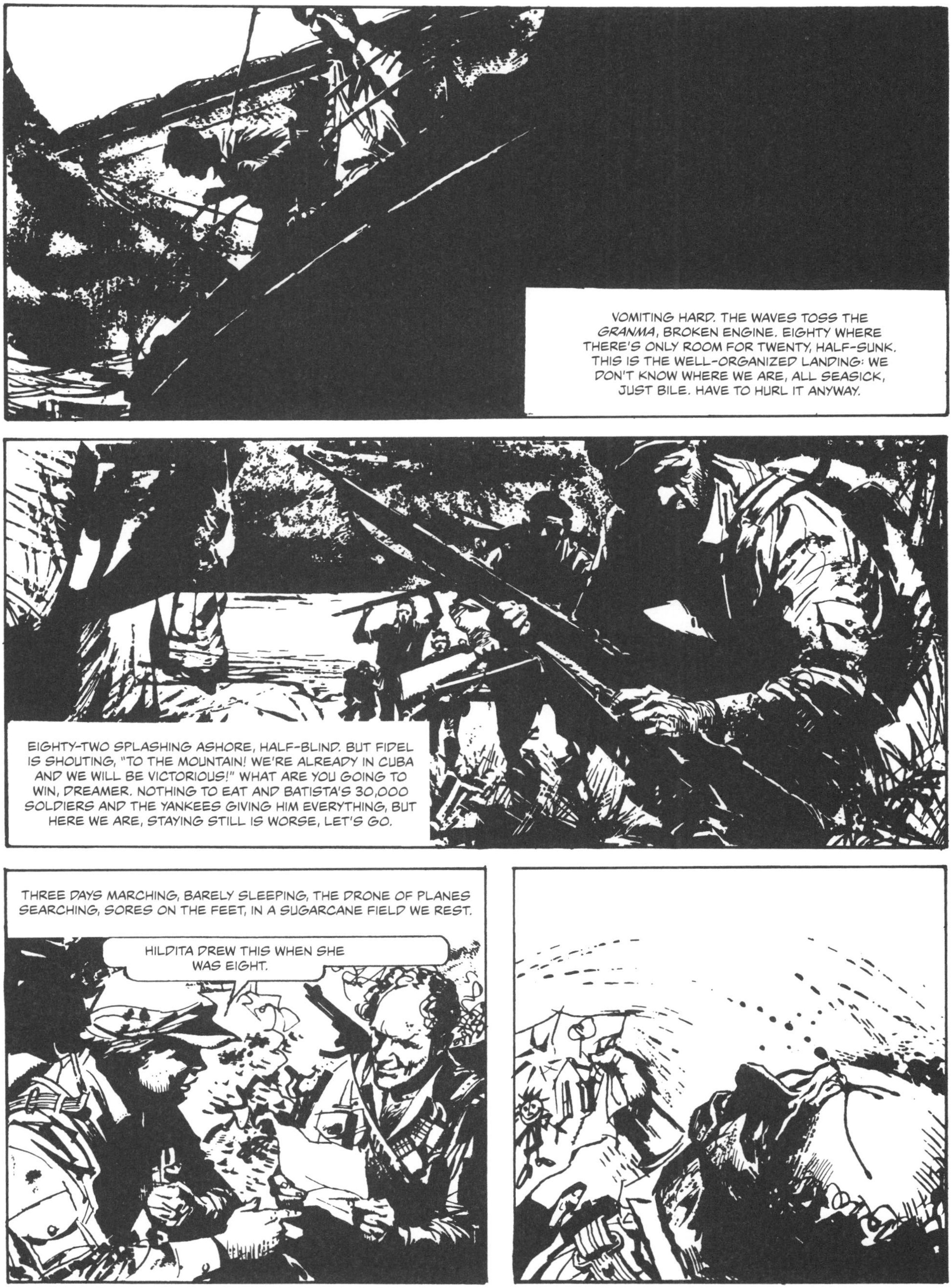
VOMITING HARD. THE WAVES TOSS THE *GRANMA*, BROKEN ENGINE. EIGHTY WHERE THERE'S ONLY ROOM FOR TWENTY, HALF-SUNK. THIS IS THE WELL-ORGANIZED LANDING: WE DON'T KNOW WHERE WE ARE, ALL SEASICK, JUST BILE. HAVE TO HURL IT ANYWAY.
EIGHTY-TWO SPLASHING ASHORE, HALF-BLIND. BUT FIDEL IS SHOUTING, "TO THE MOUNTAIN! WE'RE ALREADY IN CUBA AND WE WILL BE VICTORIOUS!" WHAT ARE YOU GOING TO WIN, DREAMER. NOTHING TO EAT AND BATISTA'S 30,000 SOLDIERS AND THE YANKEES GIVING HIM EVERYTHING, BUT HERE WE ARE, STAYING STILL IS WORSE, LET'S GO.
THREE DAYS MARCHING, BARELY SLEEPING, THE DRONE OF PLANES SEARCHING, SORES ON THE FEET, IN A SUGARCANE FIELD WE REST.
HILDITA DREW THIS WHEN SHE WAS EIGHT.

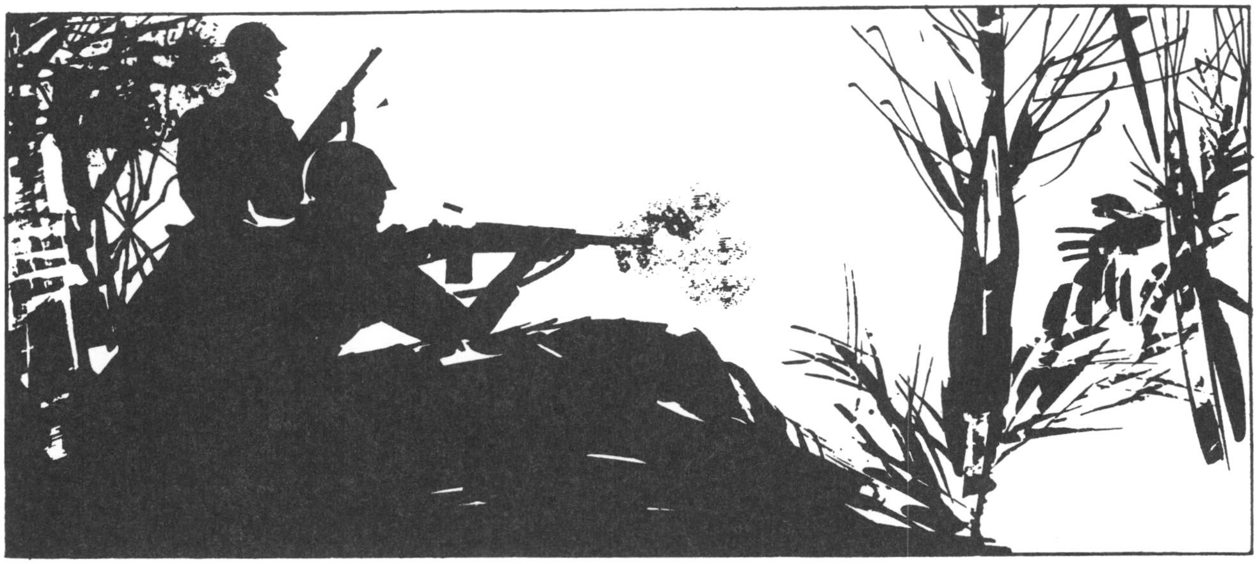

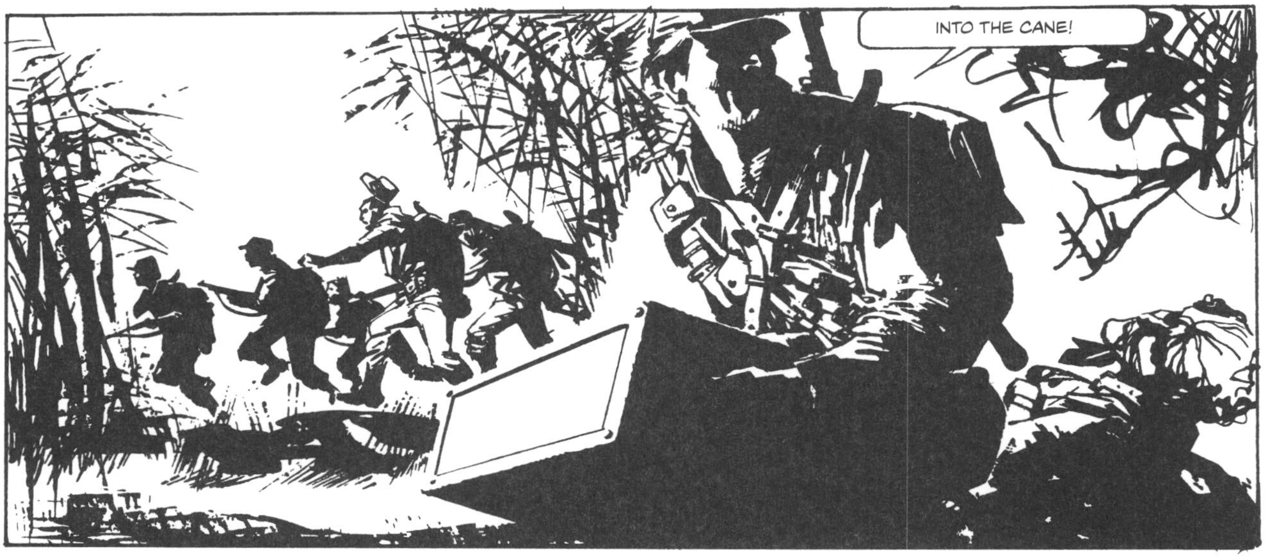
INTO THE CANE!

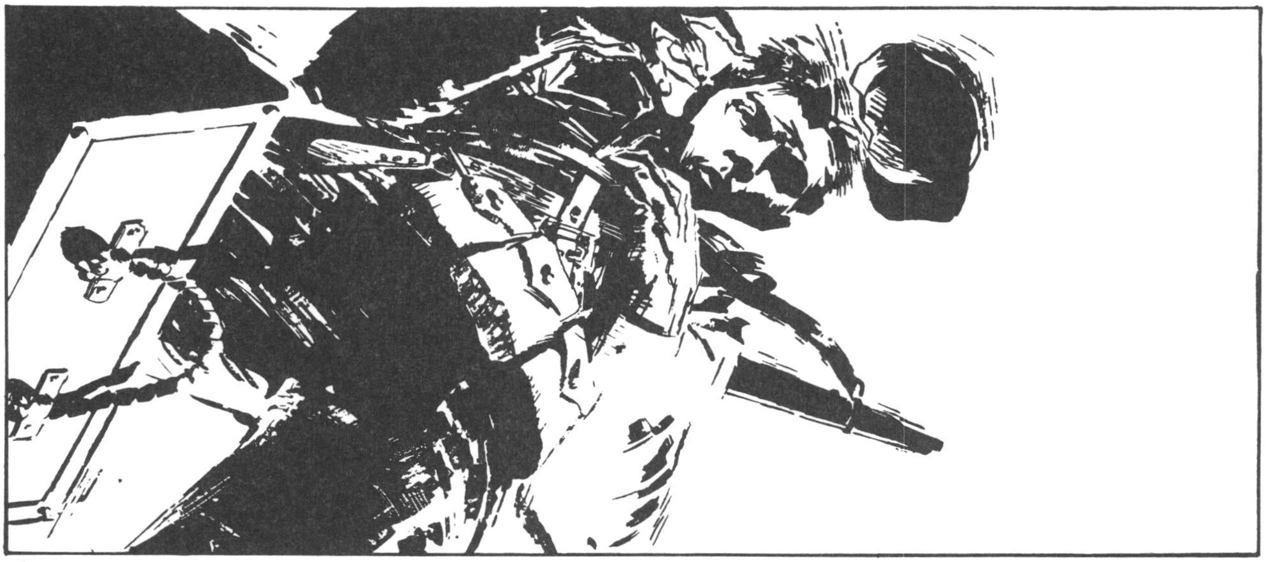

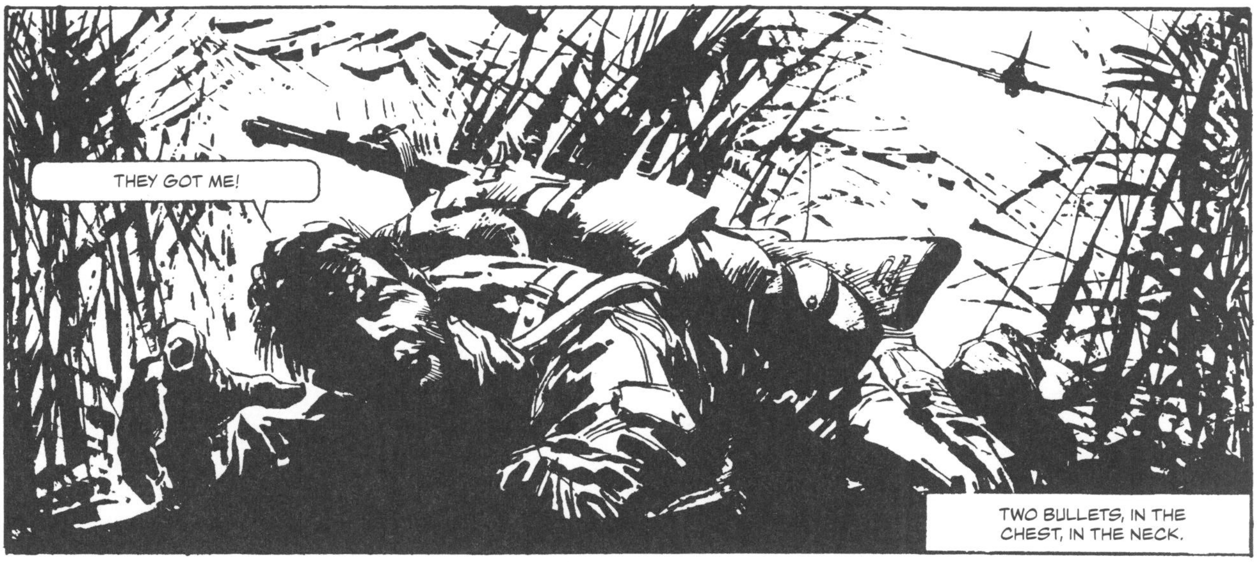
THEY GOT ME!
TWO BULLETS, IN THE CHEST, IN THE NECK.

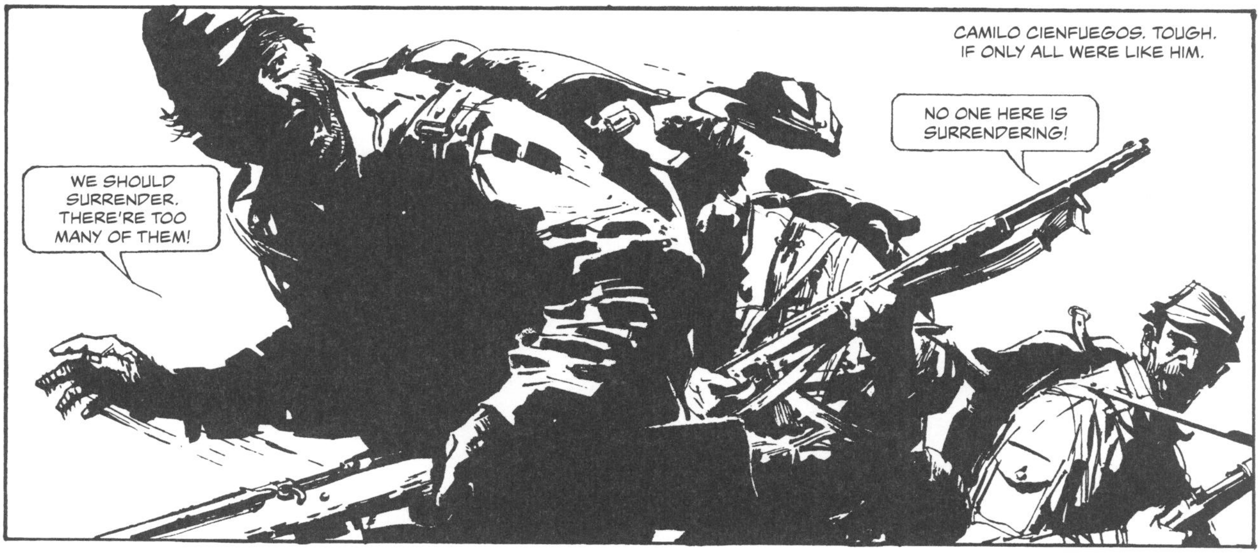
CAMILO CIENFUEGOS. TOUGH. IF ONLY ALL WERE LIKE HIM.
WE SHOULD SURRENDER. THERE'RE TOO MANY OF THEM!
NO ONE HERE IS SURRENDERING!

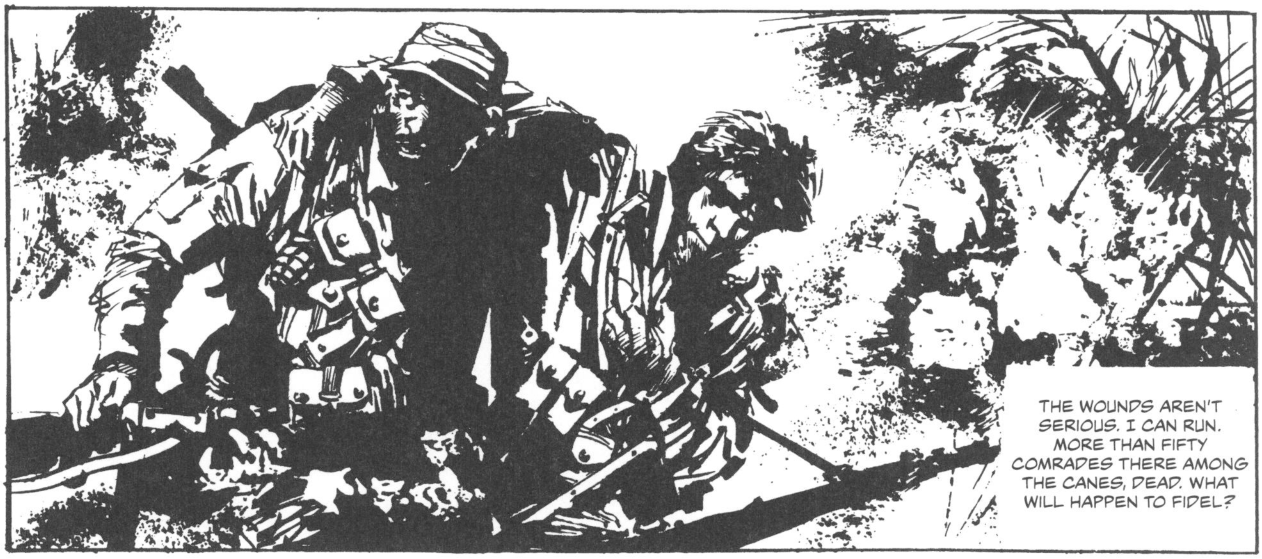
THE WOUNDS AREN'T SERIOUS. I CAN RUN. MORE THAN FIFTY COMRADES THERE AMONG THE CANES, DEAD. WHAT WILL HAPPEN TO FIDEL?

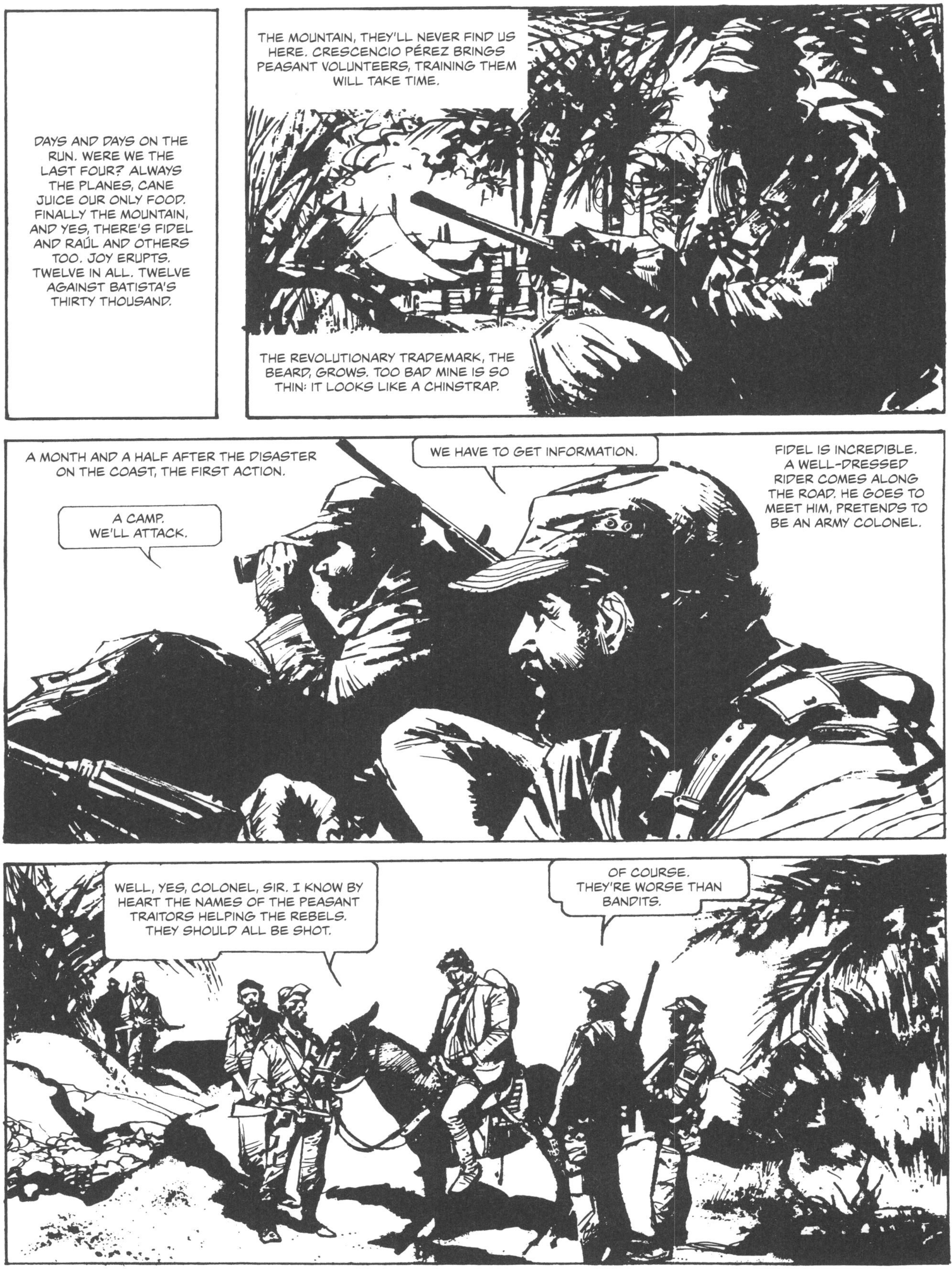
DAYS AND DAYS ON THE RUN. WERE WE THE LAST FOUR? ALWAYS THE PLANES, CANE JUICE OUR ONLY FOOD. FINALLY THE MOUNTAIN, AND YES, THERE'S FIDEL AND RAÚL AND OTHERS TOO. JOY ERUPTS. TWELVE IN ALL. TWELVE AGAINST BATISTA'S THIRTY THOUSAND.
THE MOUNTAIN, THEY'LL NEVER FIND US HERE. CRESCENCIO PÉREZ BRINGS PEASANT VOLUNTEERS, TRAINING THEM WILL TAKE TIME.
THE REVOLUTIONARY TRADEMARK, THE BEARD, GROWS. TOO BAD MINE IS SO THIN: IT LOOKS LIKE A CHINSTRAP.
A MONTH AND A HALF AFTER THE DISASTER ON THE COAST, THE FIRST ACTION.
A CAMP. WE'LL ATTACK.
WE HAVE TO GET INFORMATION.
FIDEL IS INCREDIBLE. A WELL-DRESSED RIDER COMES ALONG THE ROAD. HE GOES TO MEET HIM, PRETENDS TO BE AN ARMY COLONEL.
WELL, YES, COLONEL, SIR. I KNOW BY HEART THE NAMES OF THE PEASANT TRAITORS HELPING THE REBELS. THEY SHOULD ALL BE SHOT.
OF COURSE. THEY'RE WORSE THAN BANDITS.

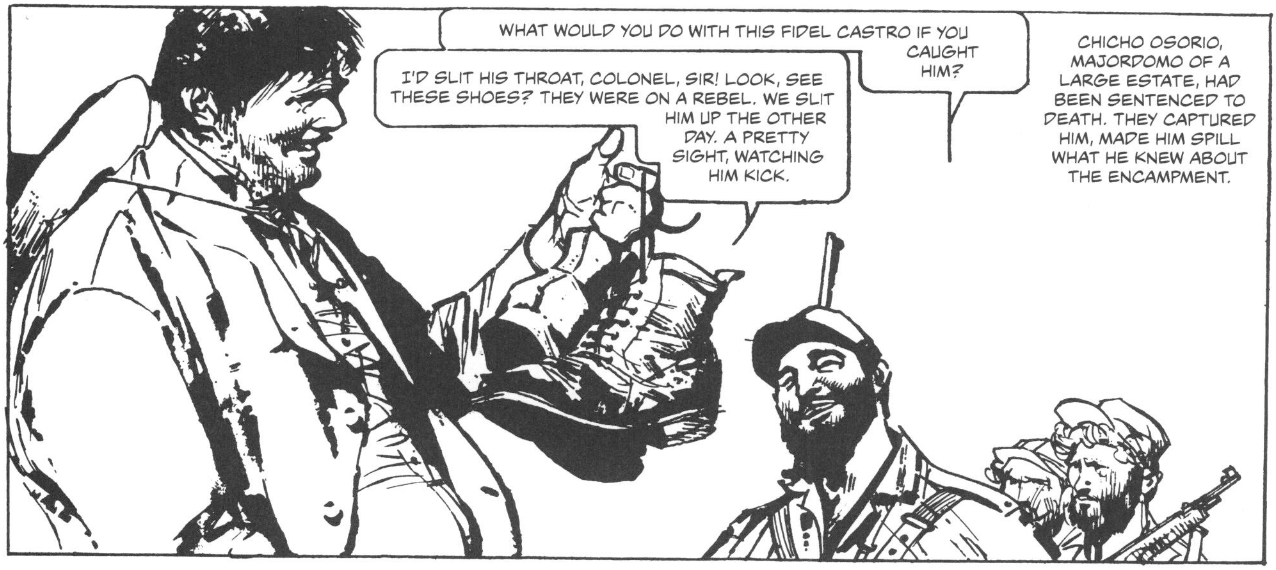
WHAT WOULD YOU DO WITH THIS FIDEL CASTRO IF YOU CAUGHT HIM?
I'D SLIT HIS THROAT, COLONEL, SIR! LOOK, SEE THESE SHOES? THEY WERE ON A REBEL. WE SLIT HIM UP THE OTHER DAY. A PRETTY SIGHT, WATCHING HIM KICK.
CHICHO OSORIO, MAJORDOMO OF A LARGE ESTATE, HAD BEEN SENTENCED TO DEATH. THEY CAPTURED HIM, MADE HIM SPILL WHAT HE KNEW ABOUT THE ENCAMPMENT.

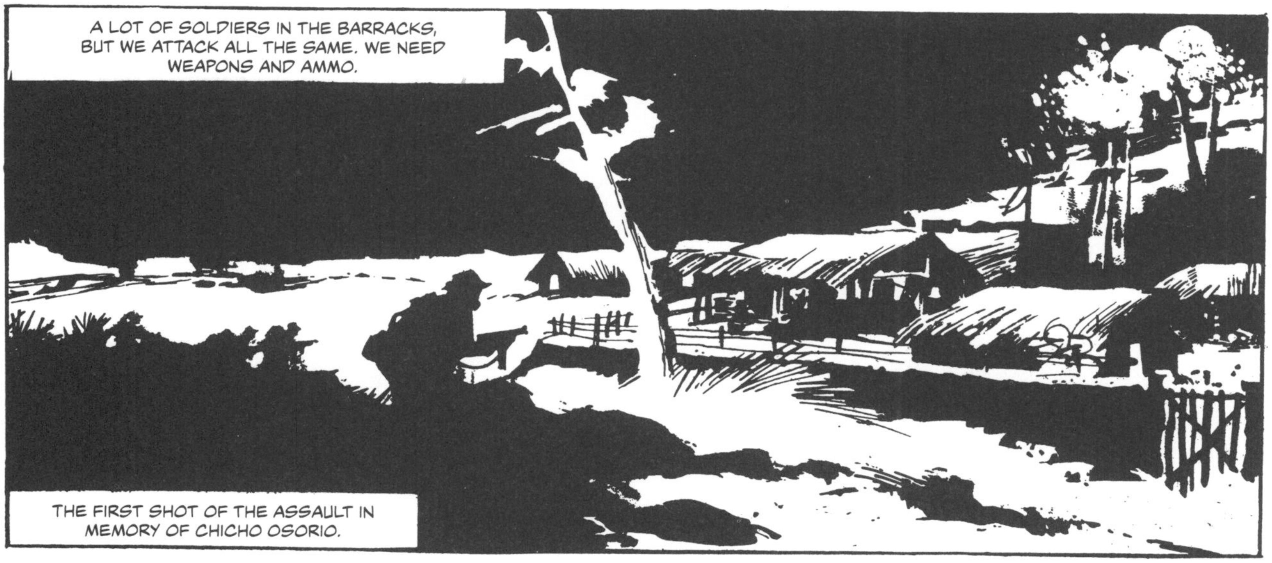
A LOT OF SOLDIERS IN THE BARRACKS, BUT WE ATTACK ALL THE SAME. WE NEED WEAPONS AND AMMO.
THE FIRST SHOT OF THE ASSAULT IN MEMORY OF CHICHO OSORIO.

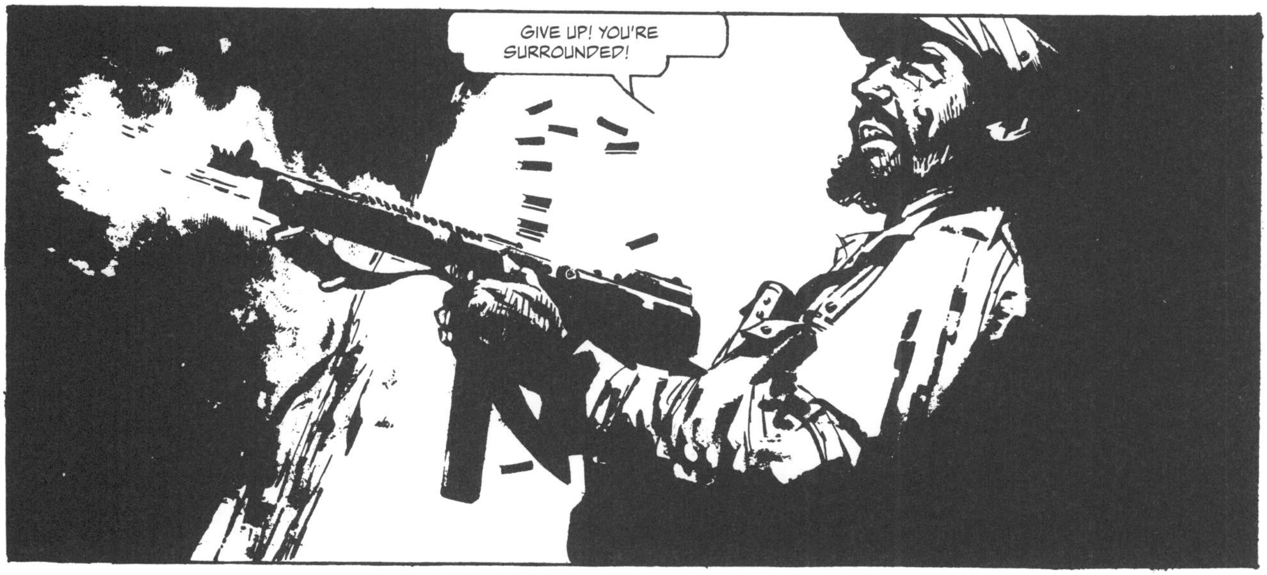
GIVE UP! YOU'RE SURROUNDED!

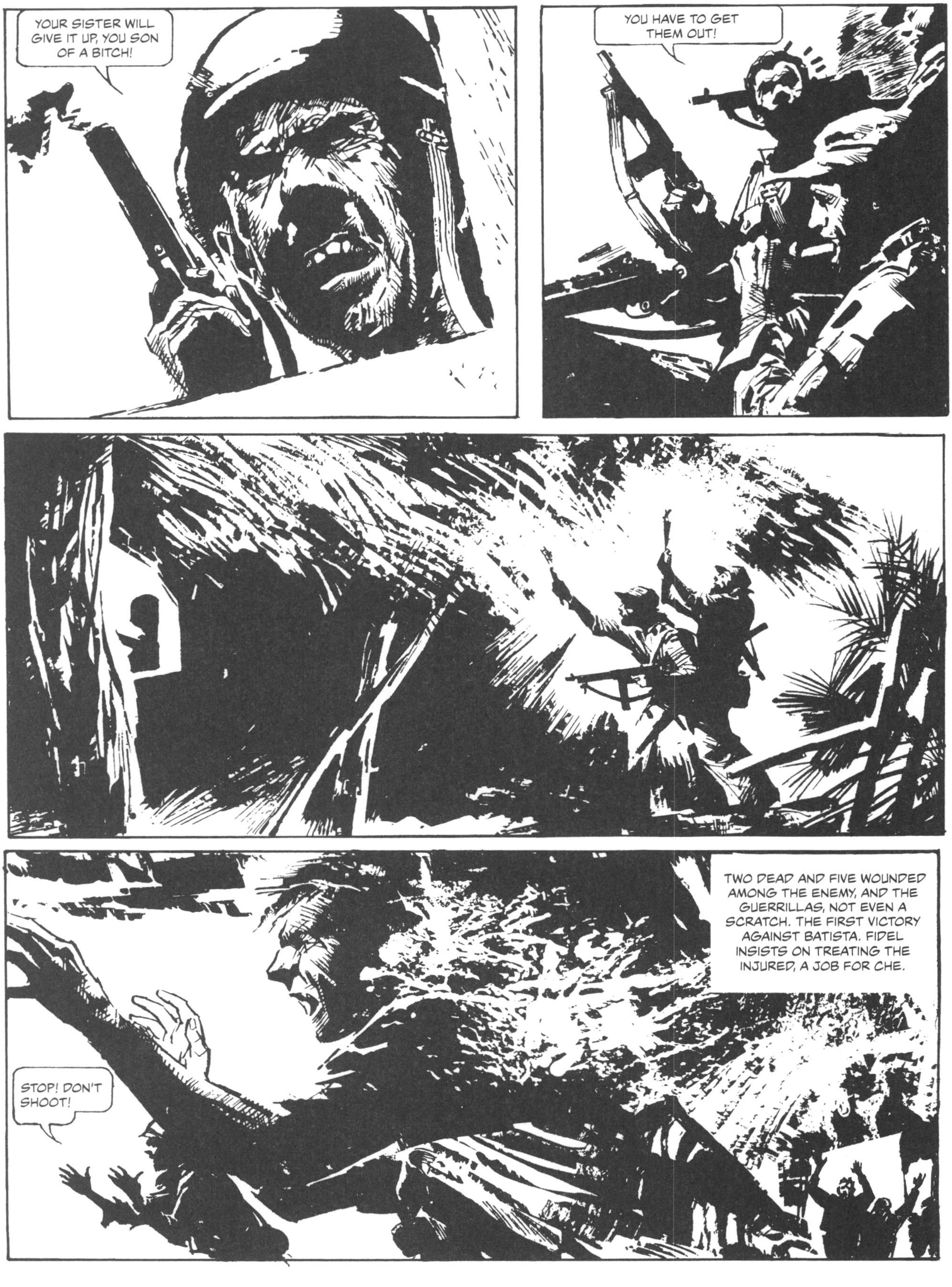
YOUR SISTER WILL GIVE IT UP, YOU SON OF A BITCH!
YOU HAVE TO GET THEM OUT!
TWO DEAD AND FIVE WOUNDED AMONG THE ENEMY, AND THE GUERRILLAS, NOT EVEN A SCRATCH. THE FIRST VICTORY AGAINST BATISTA. FIDEL INSISTS ON TREATING THE INJURED, A JOB FOR CHE.
STOP! DON'T SHOOT!

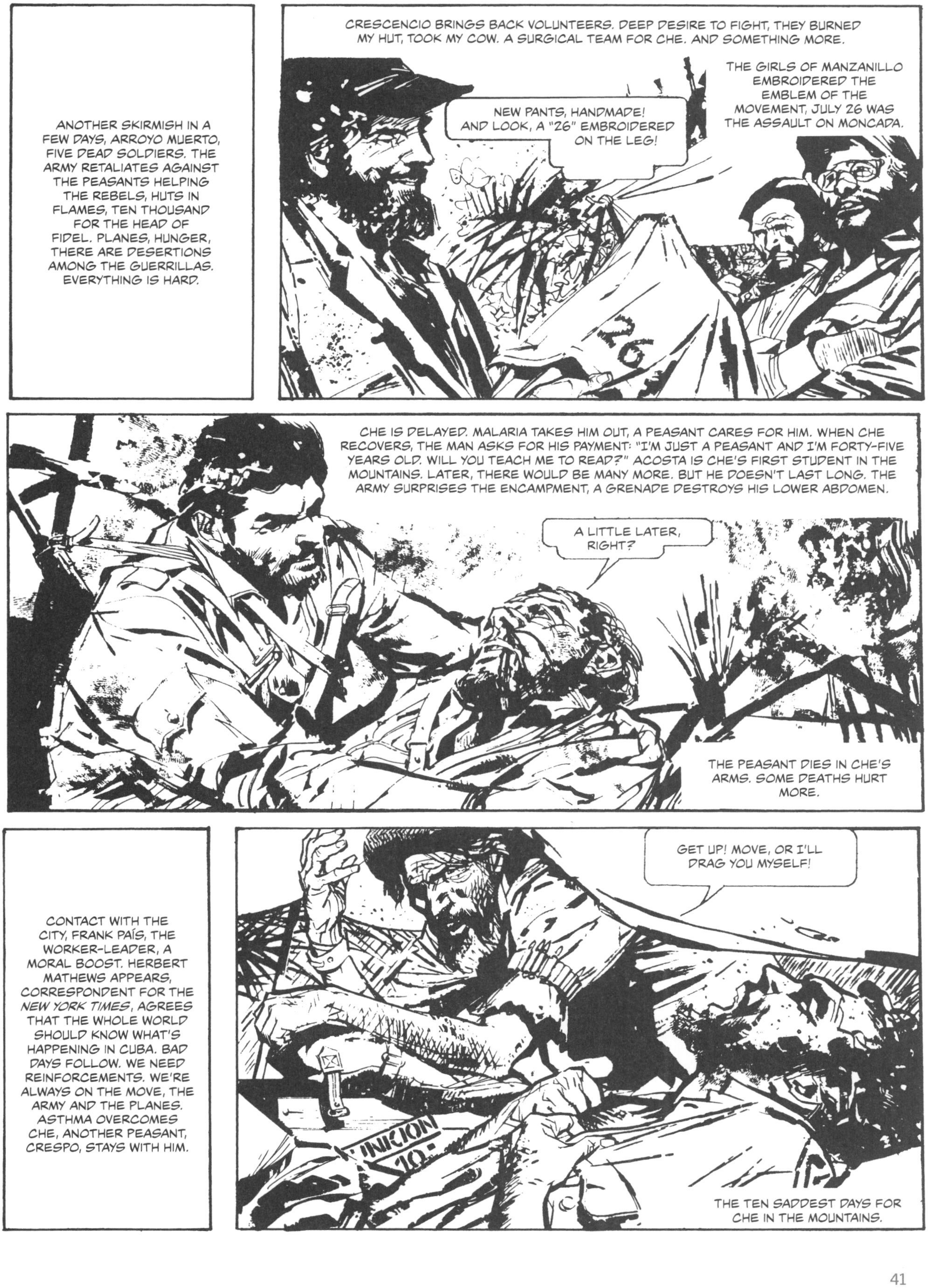
ANOTHER SKIRMISH IN A FEW DAYS, ARROYO MUERTO, FIVE DEAD SOLDIERS. THE ARMY RETALIATES AGAINST THE PEASANTS HELPING THE REBELS, HUTS IN FLAMES, TEN THOUSAND FOR THE HEAD OF FIDEL. PLANES, HUNGER, THERE ARE DESERTIONS AMONG THE GUERRILLAS. EVERYTHING IS HARD.
CRESCENCIO BRINGS BACK VOLUNTEERS. DEEP DESIRE TO FIGHT, THEY BURNED MY HUT, TOOK MY COW. A SURGICAL TEAM FOR CHE. AND SOMETHING MORE.
NEW PANTS, HANDMADE! AND LOOK, A "26" EMBROIDERED ON THE LEG!
THE GIRLS OF MANZANILLO EMBROIDERED THE EMBLEM OF THE MOVEMENT, JULY 26 WAS THE ASSAULT ON MONCADA.
26
CHE IS DELAYED. MALARIA TAKES HIM OUT, A PEASANT CARES FOR HIM. WHEN CHE RECOVERS, THE MAN ASKS FOR HIS PAYMENT: "I'M JUST A PEASANT AND I'M FORTY-FIVE YEARS OLD. WILL YOU TEACH ME TO READ?" ACOSTA IS CHE'S FIRST STUDENT IN THE MOUNTAINS. LATER, THERE WOULD BE MANY MORE. BUT HE DOESN'T LAST LONG. THE ARMY SURPRISES THE ENCAMPMENT, A GRENADE DESTROYS HIS LOWER ABDOMEN.
A LITTLE LATER, RIGHT?
THE PEASANT DIES IN CHE'S ARMS. SOME DEATHS HURT MORE.
CONTACT WITH THE CITY, FRANK PAÍS, THE WORKER-LEADER, A MORAL BOOST. HERBERT MATHEWS APPEARS, CORRESPONDENT FOR THE *NEW YORK TIMES*, AGREES THAT THE WHOLE WORLD SHOULD KNOW WHAT'S HAPPENING IN CUBA. BAD DAYS FOLLOW. WE NEED REINFORCEMENTS. WE'RE ALWAYS ON THE MOVE, THE ARMY AND THE PLANES. ASTHMA OVERCOMES CHE, ANOTHER PEASANT, CRESPO, STAYS WITH HIM.
GET UP! MOVE, OR I'LL DRAG YOU MYSELF!
UNICION 10
THE TEN SADDEST DAYS FOR CHE IN THE MOUNTAINS.

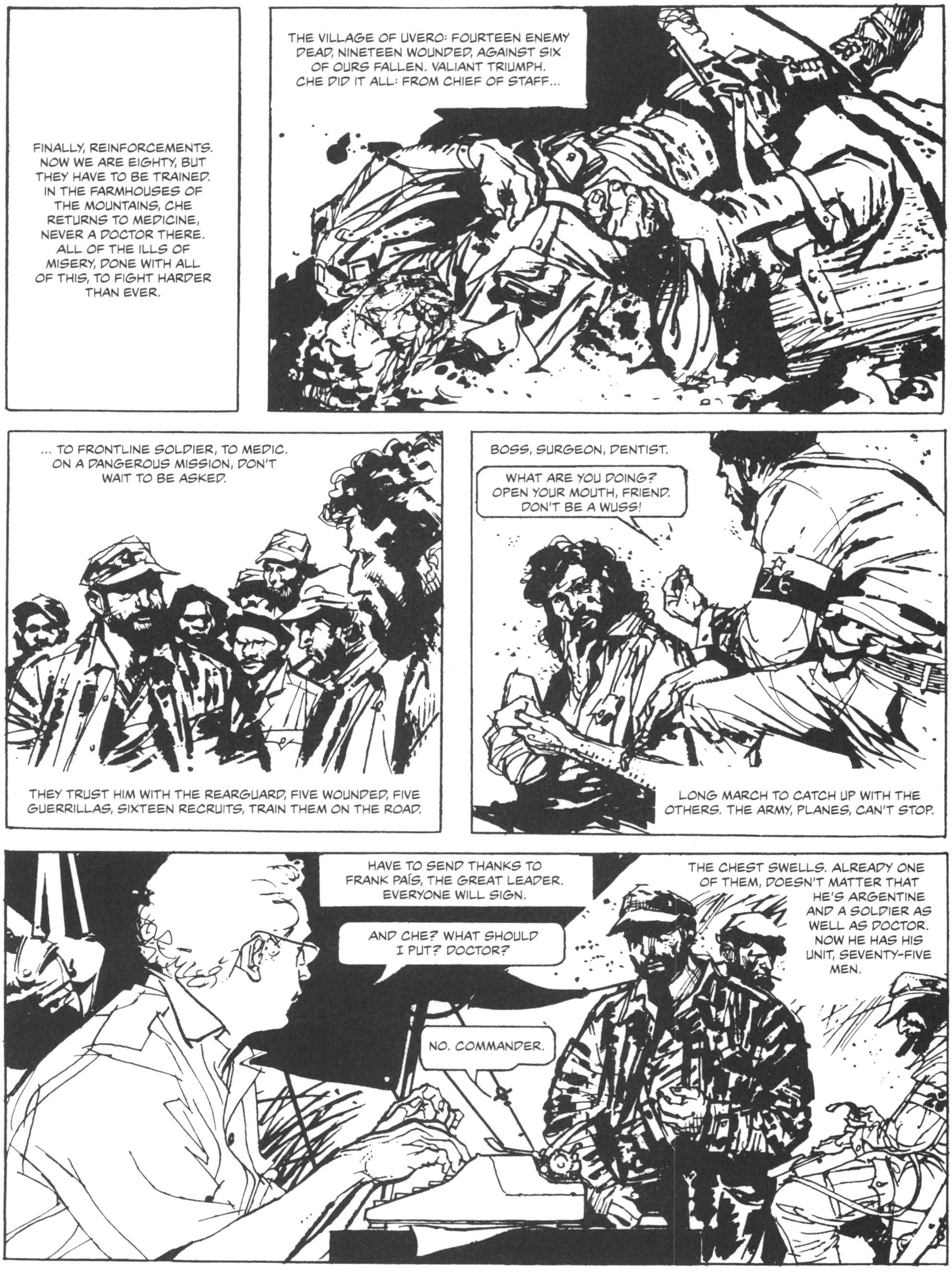
FINALLY, REINFORCEMENTS. NOW WE ARE EIGHTY, BUT THEY HAVE TO BE TRAINED. IN THE FARMHOUSES OF THE MOUNTAINS, CHE RETURNS TO MEDICINE, NEVER A DOCTOR THERE. ALL OF THE ILLS OF MISERY, DONE WITH ALL OF THIS, TO FIGHT HARDER THAN EVER.
THE VILLAGE OF UVERO: FOURTEEN ENEMY DEAD, NINETEEN WOUNDED, AGAINST SIX OF OURS FALLEN. VALIANT TRIUMPH. CHE DID IT ALL: FROM CHIEF OF STAFF...
... TO FRONTLINE SOLDIER, TO MEDIC. ON A DANGEROUS MISSION, DON'T WAIT TO BE ASKED.
THEY TRUST HIM WITH THE REARGUARD, FIVE WOUNDED, FIVE GUERRILLAS, SIXTEEN RECRUITS, TRAIN THEM ON THE ROAD.
BOSS, SURGEON, DENTIST.
WHAT ARE YOU DOING? OPEN YOUR MOUTH, FRIEND. DON'T BE A WUSS!
LONG MARCH TO CATCH UP WITH THE OTHERS. THE ARMY, PLANES, CAN'T STOP.
HAVE TO SEND THANKS TO FRANK PAÍS, THE GREAT LEADER. EVERYONE WILL SIGN.
AND CHE? WHAT SHOULD I PUT? DOCTOR?
NO. COMMANDER.
THE CHEST SWELLS. ALREADY ONE OF THEM, DOESN'T MATTER THAT HE'S ARGENTINE AND A SOLDIER AS WELL AS DOCTOR. NOW HE HAS HIS UNIT, SEVENTY-FIVE MEN.

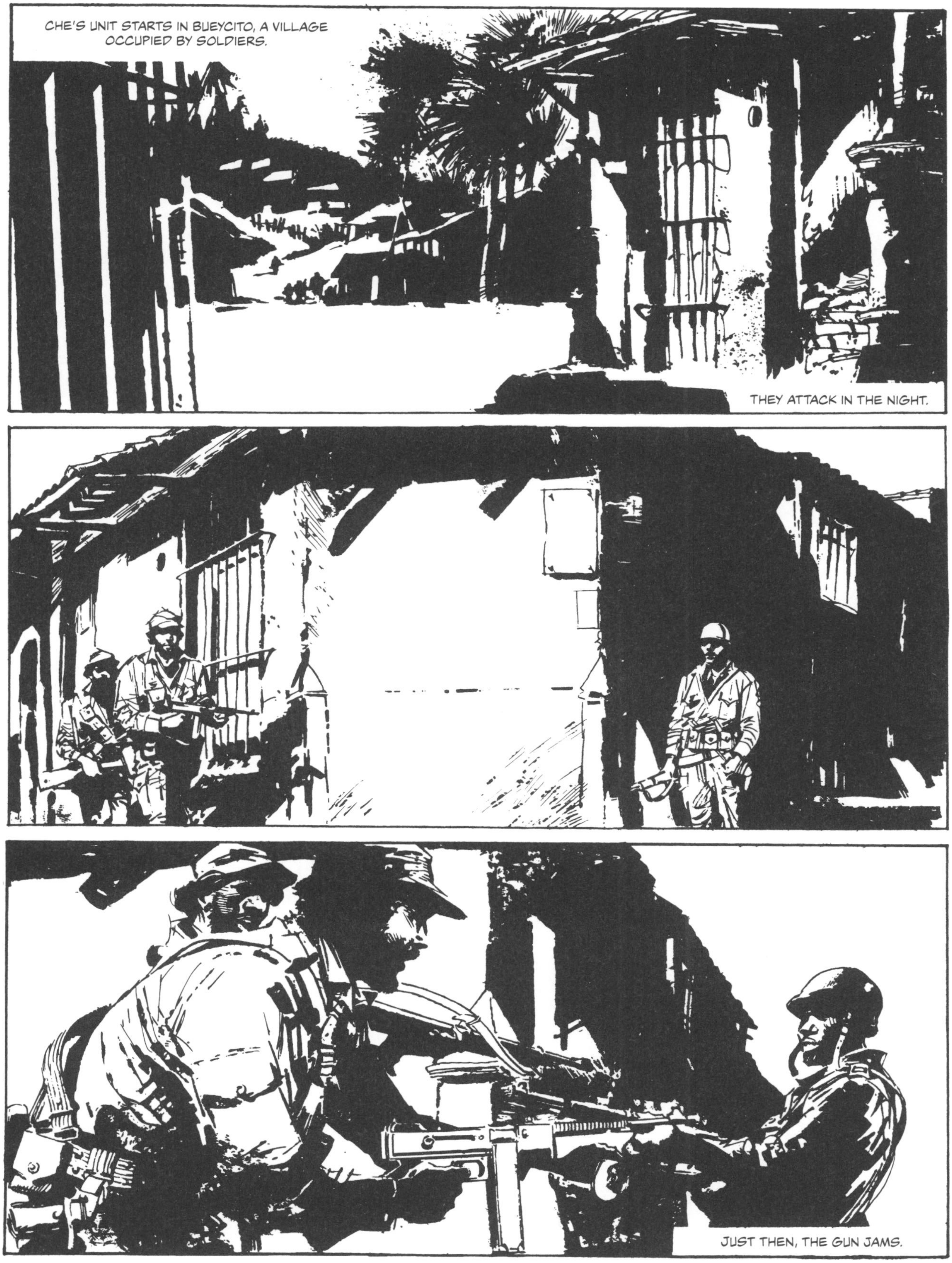
CHE'S UNIT STARTS IN BUEYCITO, A VILLAGE OCCUPIED BY SOLDIERS.
THEY ATTACK IN THE NIGHT.
JUST THEN, THE GUN JAMS.

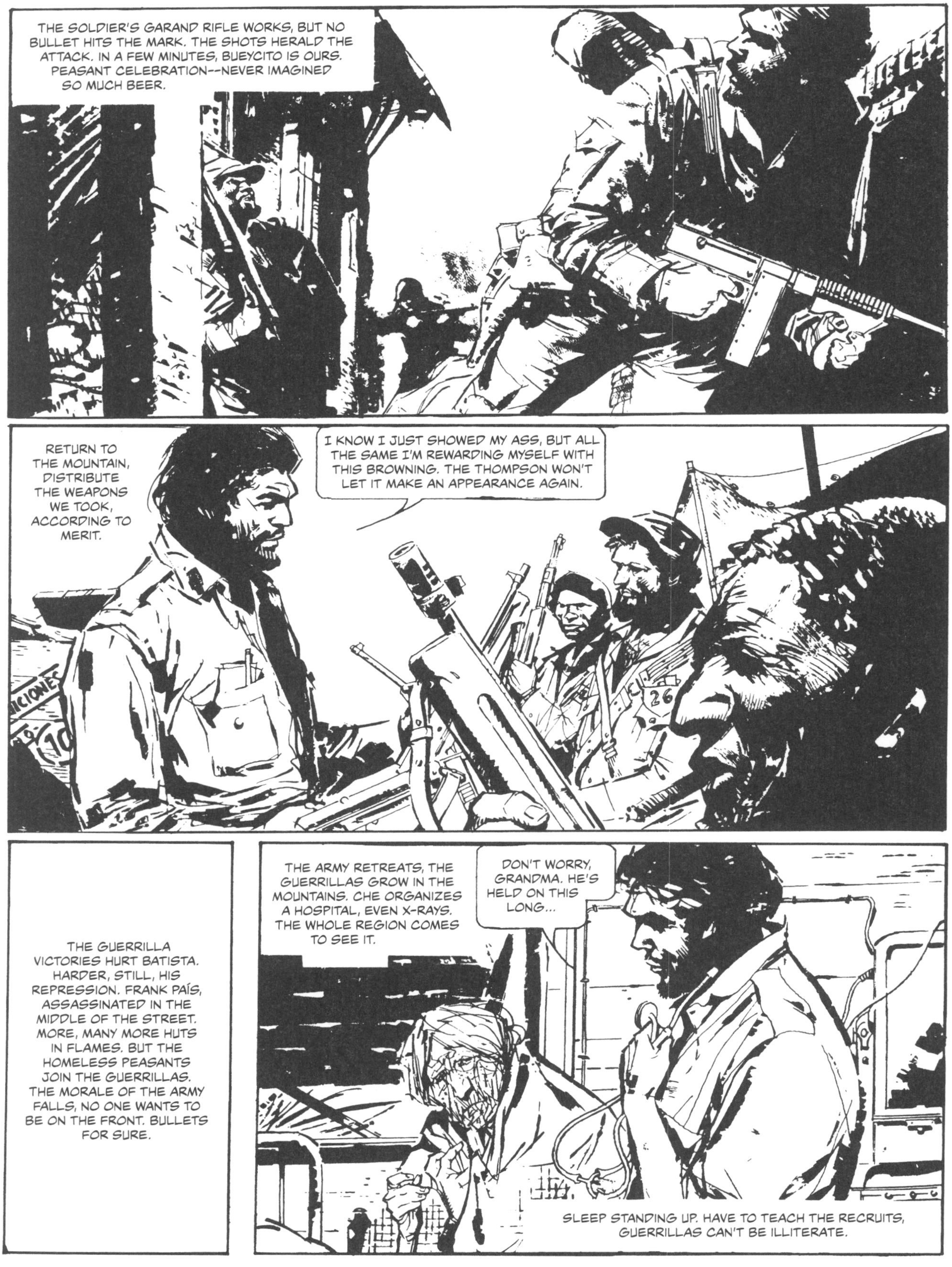
THE SOLDIER'S GARAND RIFLE WORKS, BUT NO BULLET HITS THE MARK. THE SHOTS HERALD THE ATTACK. IN A FEW MINUTES, BUEYCITO IS OURS. PEASANT CELEBRATION--NEVER IMAGINED SO MUCH BEER.
RETURN TO THE MOUNTAIN, DISTRIBUTE THE WEAPONS WE TOOK, ACCORDING TO MERIT.
I KNOW I JUST SHOWED MY ASS, BUT ALL THE SAME I'M REWARDING MYSELF WITH THIS BROWNING. THE THOMPSON WON'T LET IT MAKE AN APPEARANCE AGAIN.
26
THE GUERRILLA VICTORIES HURT BATISTA. HARDER, STILL, HIS REPRESSION. FRANK PAÍS, ASSASSINATED IN THE MIDDLE OF THE STREET. MORE, MANY MORE HUTS IN FLAMES. BUT THE HOMELESS PEASANTS JOIN THE GUERRILLAS. THE MORALE OF THE ARMY FALLS, NO ONE WANTS TO BE ON THE FRONT. BULLETS FOR SURE.
THE ARMY RETREATS, THE GUERRILLAS GROW IN THE MOUNTAINS. CHE ORGANIZES A HOSPITAL, EVEN X-RAYS. THE WHOLE REGION COMES TO SEE IT.
DON'T WORRY, GRANDMA. HE'S HELD ON THIS LONG...
SLEEP STANDING UP. HAVE TO TEACH THE RECRUITS, GUERRILLAS CAN'T BE ILLITERATE.

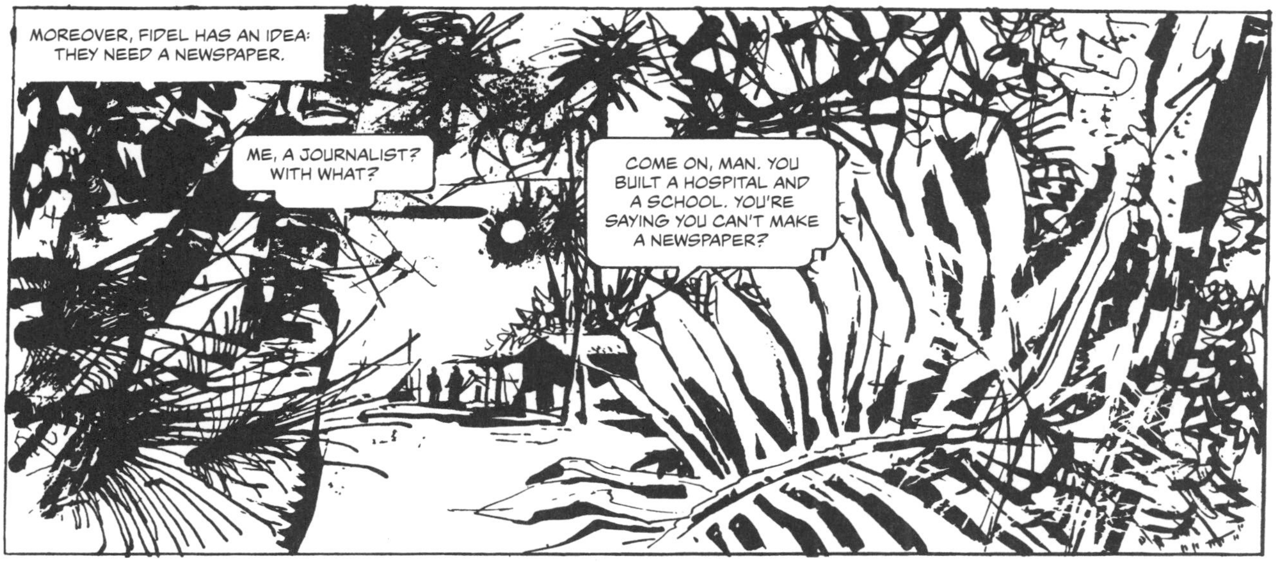
MOREOVER, FIDEL HAS AN IDEA: THEY NEED A NEWSPAPER.
ME, A JOURNALIST? WITH WHAT?
COME ON, MAN. YOU BUILT A HOSPITAL AND A SCHOOL. YOU'RE SAYING YOU CAN'T MAKE A NEWSPAPER?

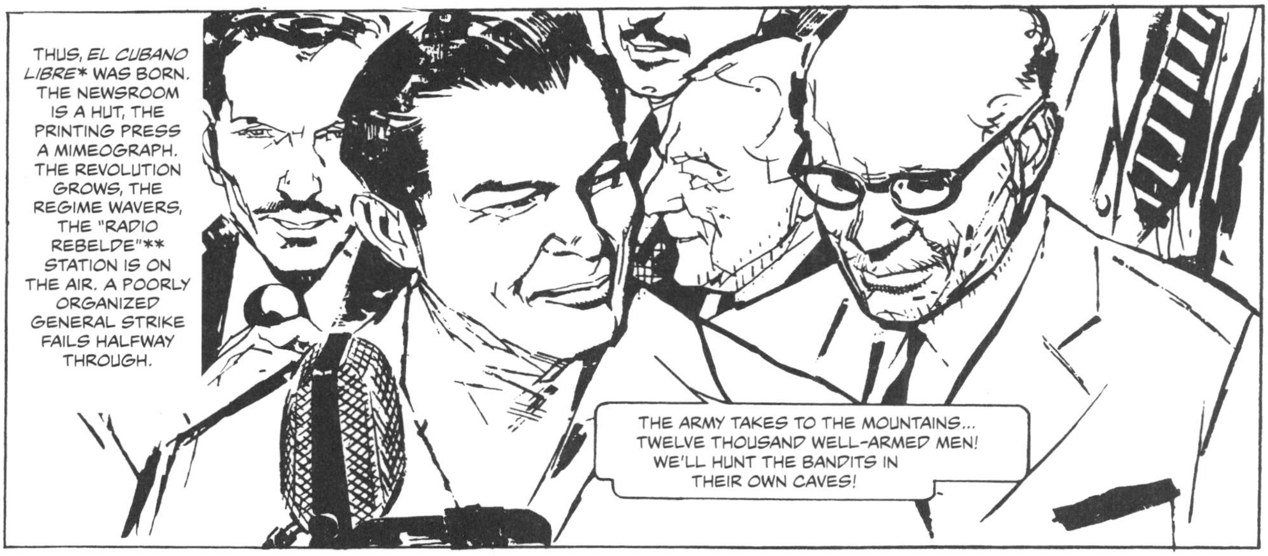
THUS, *EL CUBANO LIBRE** WAS BORN. THE NEWSROOM IS A HUT, THE PRINTING PRESS A MIMEOGRAPH. THE REVOLUTION GROWS, THE REGIME WAVERS, THE "RADIO REBELDE"** STATION IS ON THE AIR. A POORLY ORGANIZED GENERAL STRIKE FAILS HALFWAY THROUGH.
THE ARMY TAKES TO THE MOUNTAINS... TWELVE THOUSAND WELL-ARMED MEN! WE'LL HUNT THE BANDITS IN THEIR OWN CAVES!

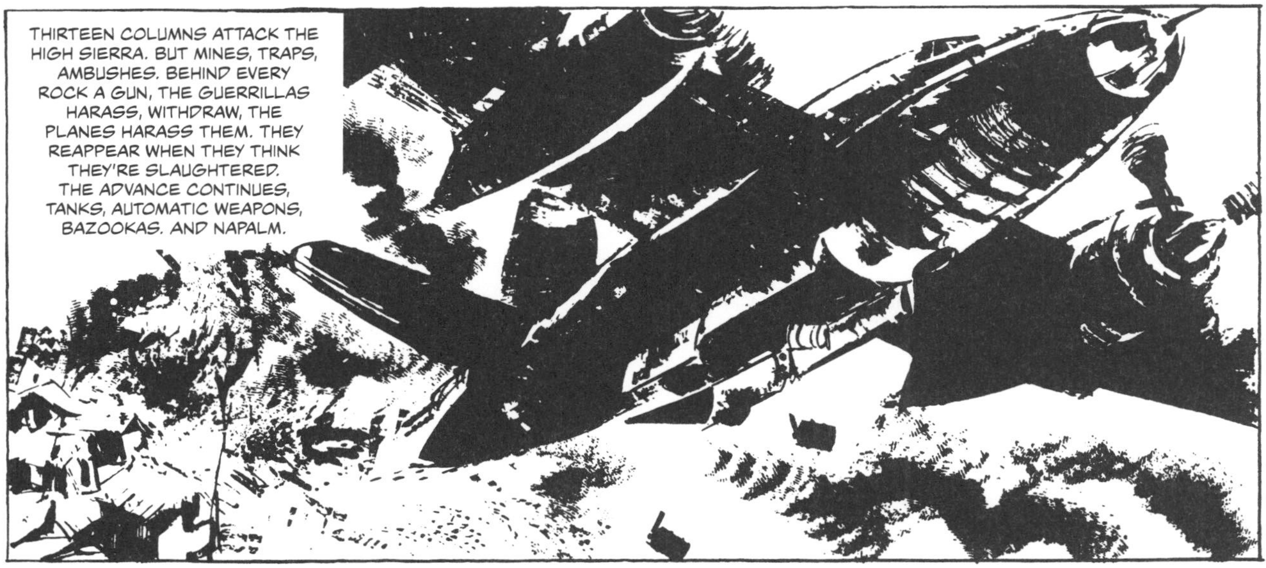
THIRTEEN COLUMNS ATTACK THE HIGH SIERRA. BUT MINES, TRAPS, AMBUSHES. BEHIND EVERY ROCK A GUN, THE GUERRILLAS HARASS, WITHDRAW, THE PLANES HARASS THEM. THEY REAPPEAR WHEN THEY THINK THEY'RE SLAUGHTERED. THE ADVANCE CONTINUES, TANKS, AUTOMATIC WEAPONS, BAZOOKAS. AND NAPALM.

*THE FREE CUBAN **RADIO REBEL

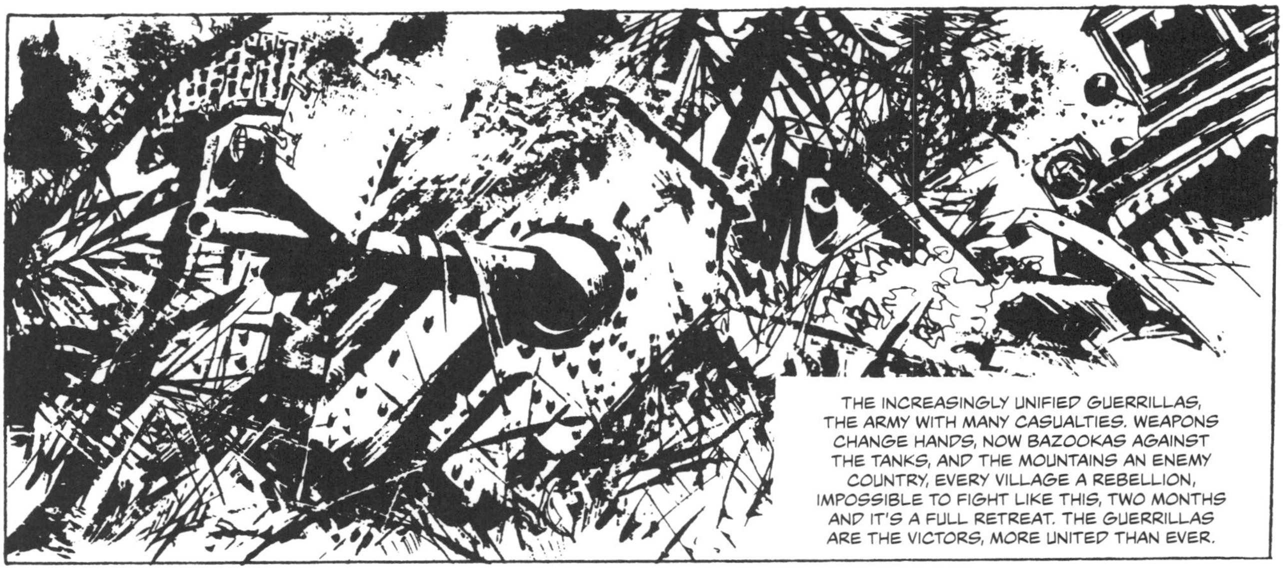
THE INCREASINGLY UNIFIED GUERRILLAS, THE ARMY WITH MANY CASUALTIES. WEAPONS CHANGE HANDS, NOW BAZOOKAS AGAINST THE TANKS, AND THE MOUNTAINS AN ENEMY COUNTRY, EVERY VILLAGE A REBELLION, IMPOSSIBLE TO FIGHT LIKE THIS, TWO MONTHS AND IT'S A FULL RETREAT. THE GUERRILLAS ARE THE VICTORS, MORE UNITED THAN EVER.

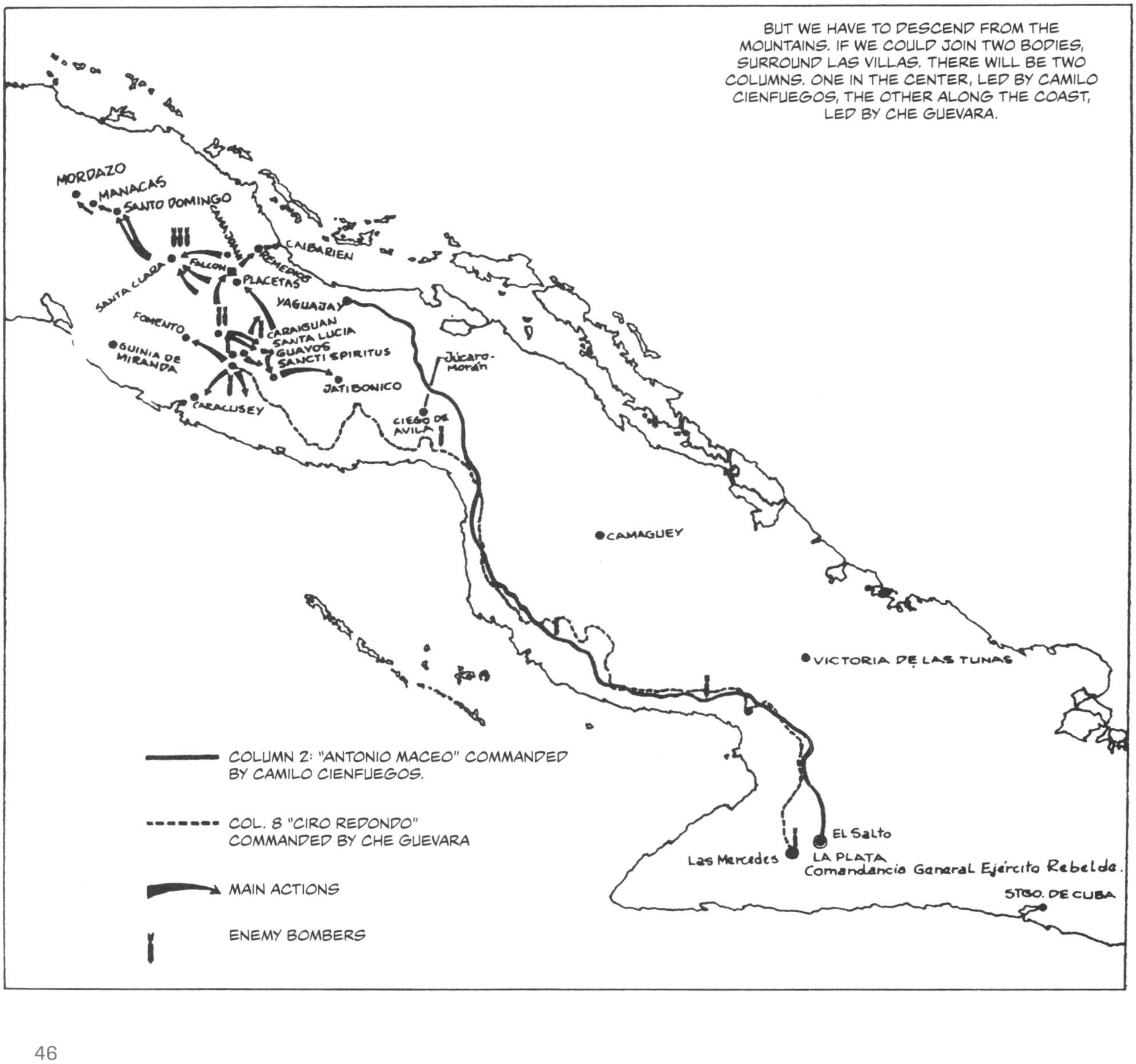
BUT WE HAVE TO DESCEND FROM THE MOUNTAINS. IF WE COULD JOIN TWO BODIES, SURROUND LAS VILLAS. THERE WILL BE TWO COLUMNS. ONE IN THE CENTER, LED BY CAMILO CIENFUEGOS, THE OTHER ALONG THE COAST, LED BY CHE GUEVARA.
MORDAZO
MANACAS
SANTO DOMINGO
SANTA CLARA
FALLON
CAIBARIEN
REMEDIOS
PLACETAS
YAGUAJAY
FOMENTO
CARAIGUAN
SANTA LUCIA
GUAYOS
SANCTI SPIRITUS
GUINIA DE MIRANDA
JATIBONICO
CARACUSEY
Júcaro-Morón
CIEGO DE AVILA
CAMAGUEY
VICTORIA DE LAS TUNAS
El Salto
Las Mercedes
LA PLATA
Comandancia General Ejército Rebelde.
STGO. DE CUBA
COLUMN 2: "ANTONIO MACEO" COMMANDED BY CAMILO CIENFUEGOS.
COL. 8 "CIRO REDONDO" COMMANDED BY CHE GUEVARA
MAIN ACTIONS
ENEMY BOMBERS

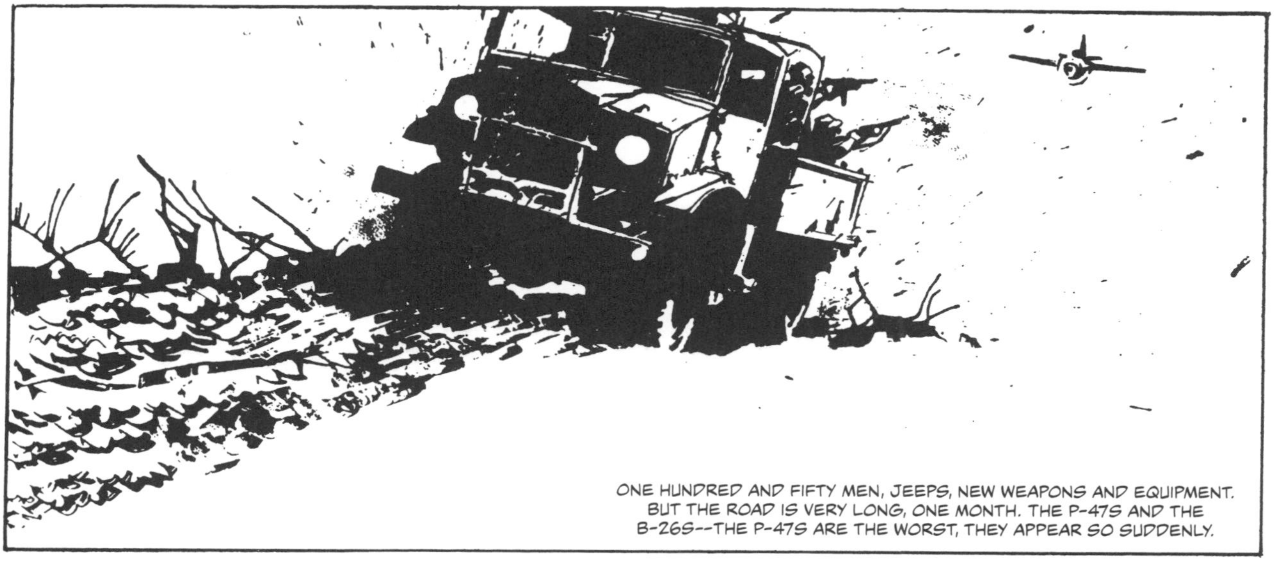
ONE HUNDRED AND FIFTY MEN, JEEPS, NEW WEAPONS AND EQUIPMENT. BUT THE ROAD IS VERY LONG, ONE MONTH. THE P-47S AND THE B-26S--THE P-47S ARE THE WORST, THEY APPEAR SO SUDDENLY.

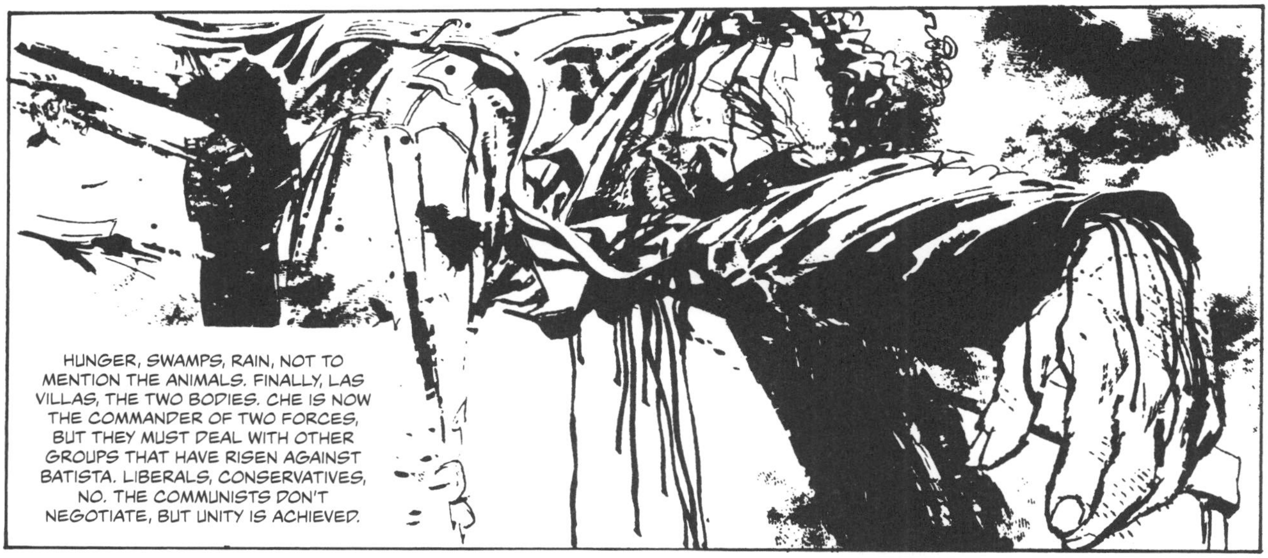
HUNGER, SWAMPS, RAIN, NOT TO MENTION THE ANIMALS. FINALLY, LAS VILLAS, THE TWO BODIES. CHE IS NOW THE COMMANDER OF TWO FORCES, BUT THEY MUST DEAL WITH OTHER GROUPS THAT HAVE RISEN AGAINST BATISTA. LIBERALS, CONSERVATIVES, NO. THE COMMUNISTS DON'T NEGOTIATE, BUT UNITY IS ACHIEVED.

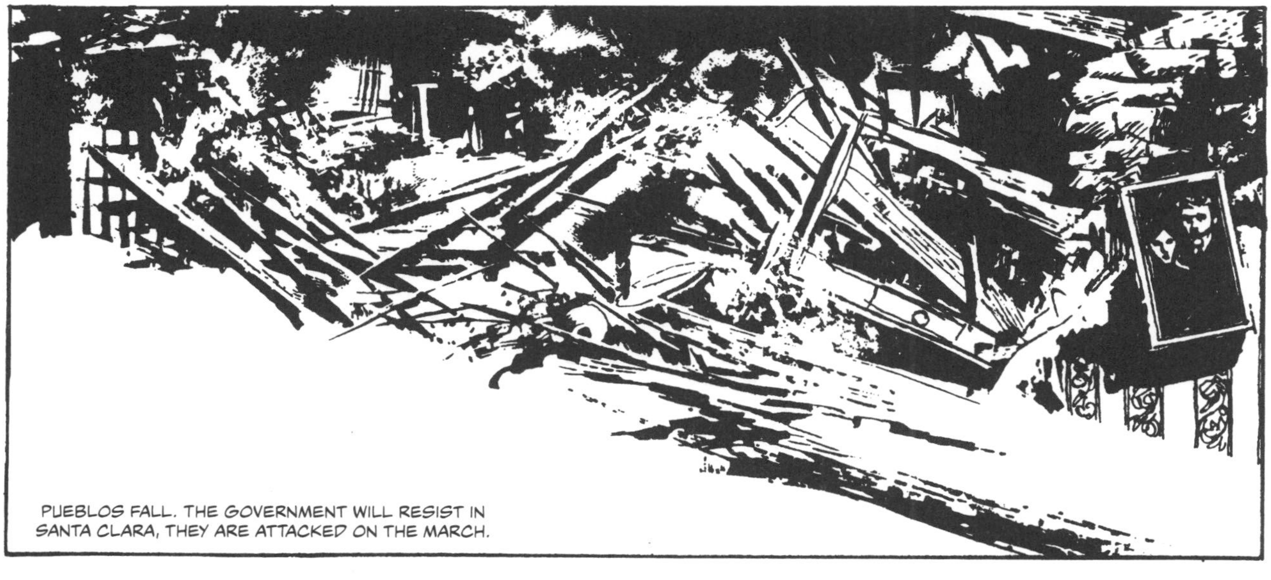
PUEBLOS FALL. THE GOVERNMENT WILL RESIST IN SANTA CLARA, THEY ARE ATTACKED ON THE MARCH.

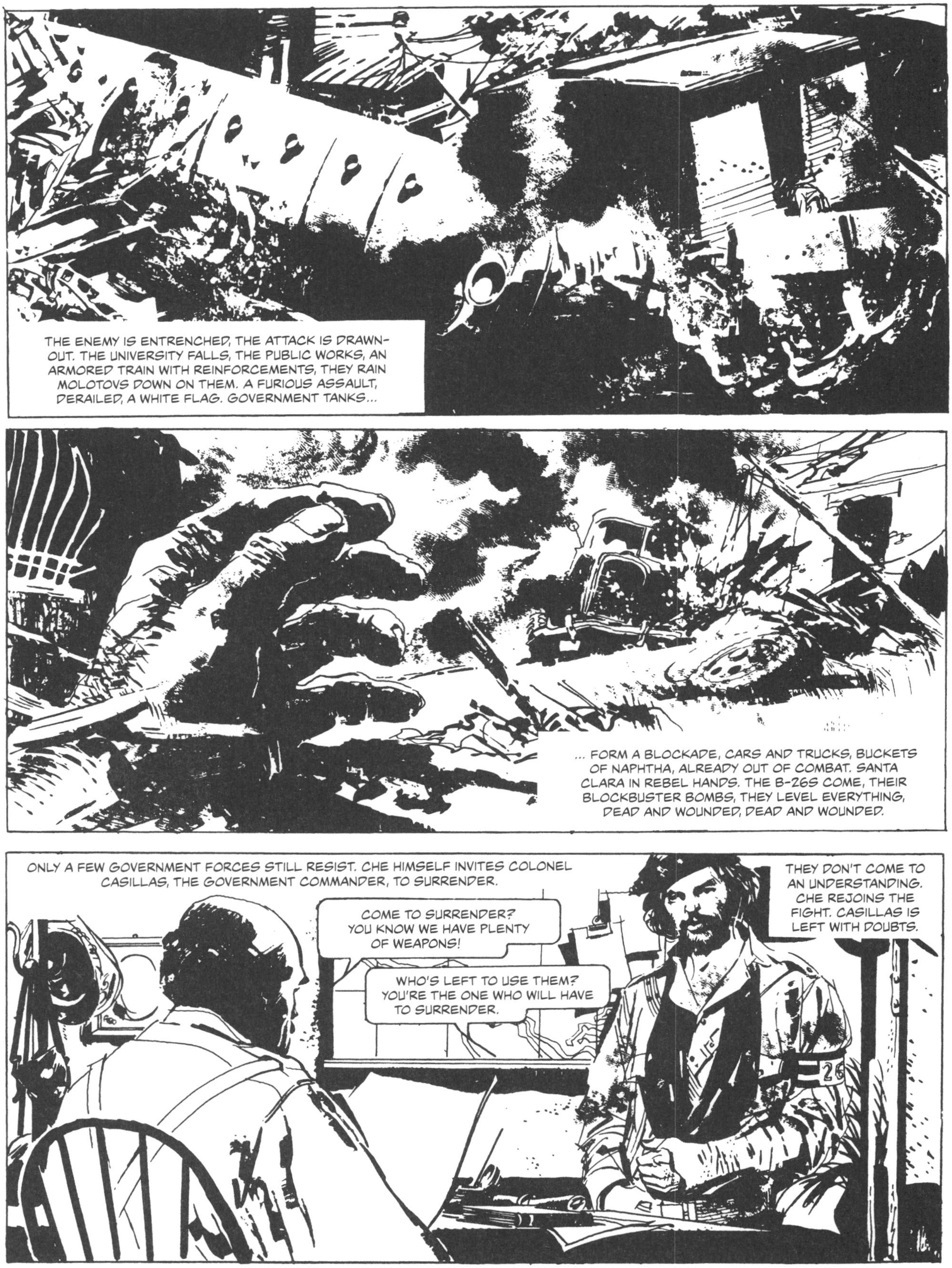
THE ENEMY IS ENTRENCHED, THE ATTACK IS DRAWN-OUT. THE UNIVERSITY FALLS, THE PUBLIC WORKS, AN ARMORED TRAIN WITH REINFORCEMENTS, THEY RAIN MOLOTOVS DOWN ON THEM. A FURIOUS ASSAULT, DERAILED, A WHITE FLAG. GOVERNMENT TANKS...
... FORM A BLOCKADE, CARS AND TRUCKS, BUCKETS OF NAPHTHA, ALREADY OUT OF COMBAT. SANTA CLARA IN REBEL HANDS. THE B-26S COME, THEIR BLOCKBUSTER BOMBS, THEY LEVEL EVERYTHING, DEAD AND WOUNDED, DEAD AND WOUNDED.
ONLY A FEW GOVERNMENT FORCES STILL RESIST. CHE HIMSELF INVITES COLONEL CASILLAS, THE GOVERNMENT COMMANDER, TO SURRENDER.
COME TO SURRENDER? YOU KNOW WE HAVE PLENTY OF WEAPONS!
WHO'S LEFT TO USE THEM? YOU'RE THE ONE WHO WILL HAVE TO SURRENDER.
THEY DON'T COME TO AN UNDERSTANDING. CHE REJOINS THE FIGHT. CASILLAS IS LEFT WITH DOUBTS.
26

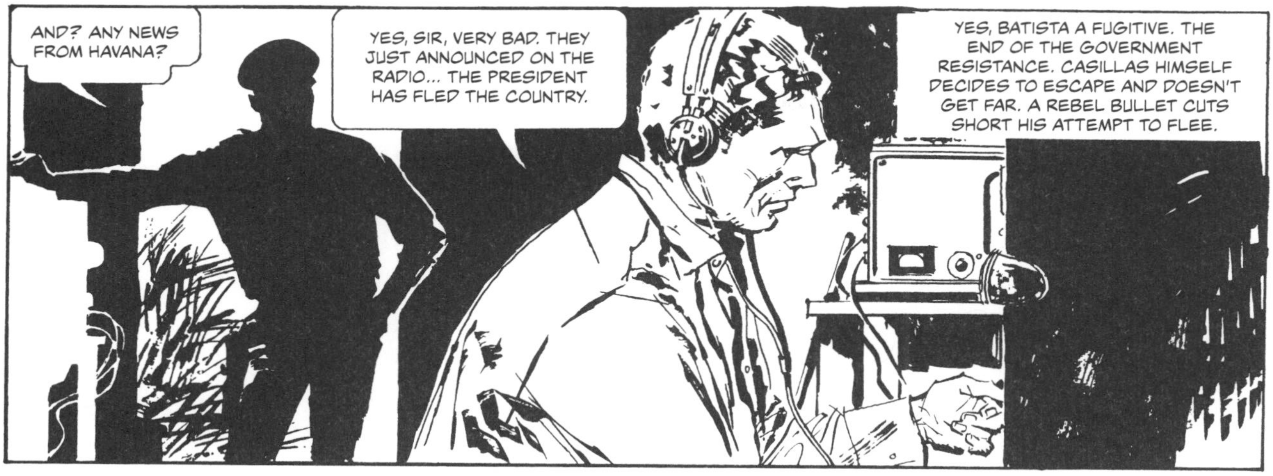
AND? ANY NEWS FROM HAVANA?
YES, SIR, VERY BAD. THEY JUST ANNOUNCED ON THE RADIO... THE PRESIDENT HAS FLED THE COUNTRY.
YES, BATISTA A FUGITIVE. THE END OF THE GOVERNMENT RESISTANCE. CASILLAS HIMSELF DECIDES TO ESCAPE AND DOESN'T GET FAR. A REBEL BULLET CUTS SHORT HIS ATTEMPT TO FLEE.

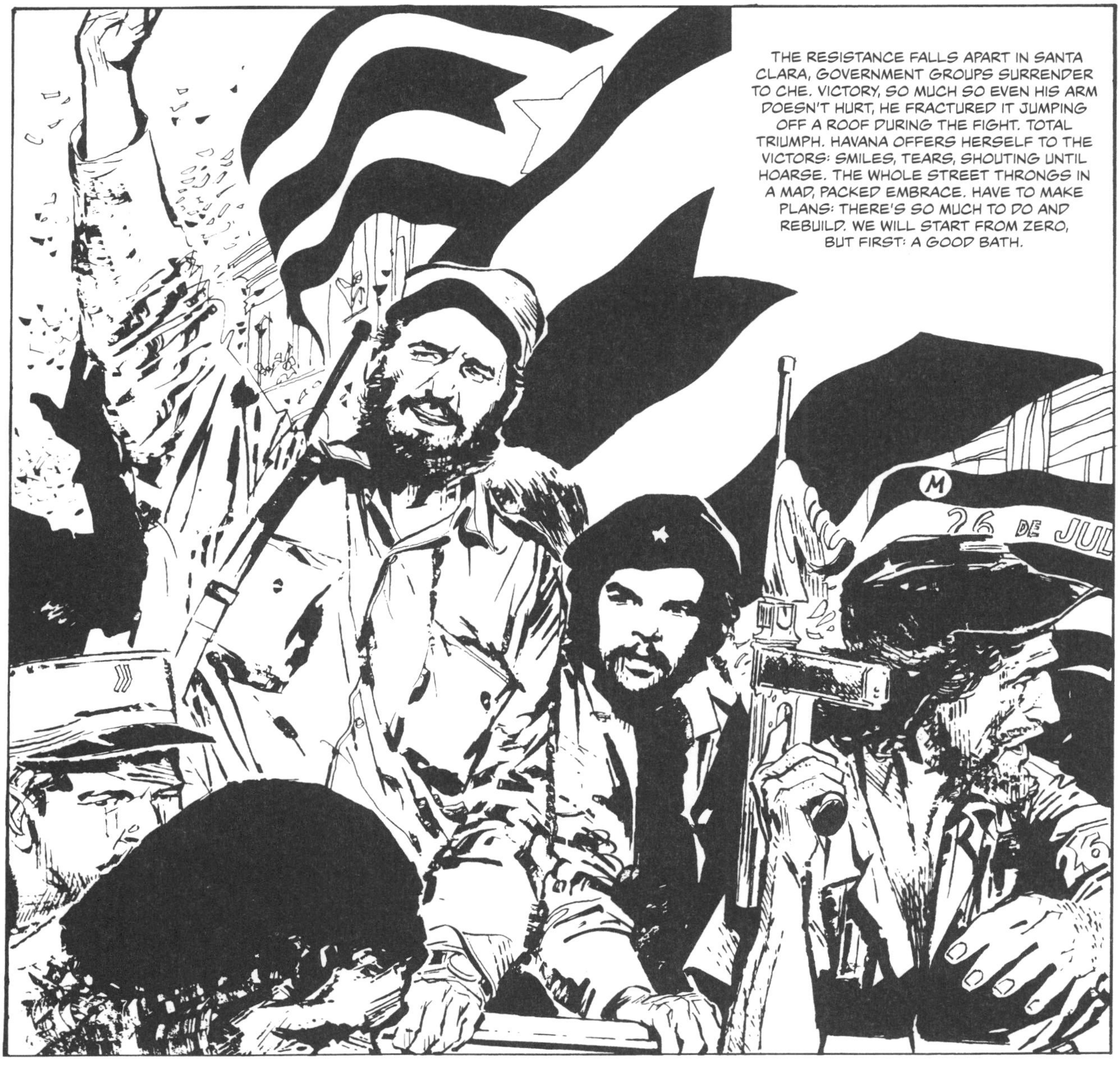
THE RESISTANCE FALLS APART IN SANTA CLARA, GOVERNMENT GROUPS SURRENDER TO CHE. VICTORY, SO MUCH SO EVEN HIS ARM DOESN'T HURT, HE FRACTURED IT JUMPING OFF A ROOF DURING THE FIGHT. TOTAL TRIUMPH. HAVANA OFFERS HERSELF TO THE VICTORS: SMILES, TEARS, SHOUTING UNTIL HOARSE. THE WHOLE STREET THRONGS IN A MAD, PACKED EMBRACE. HAVE TO MAKE PLANS: THERE'S SO MUCH TO DO AND REBUILD. WE WILL START FROM ZERO, BUT FIRST: A GOOD BATH.
M
26 DE JUL

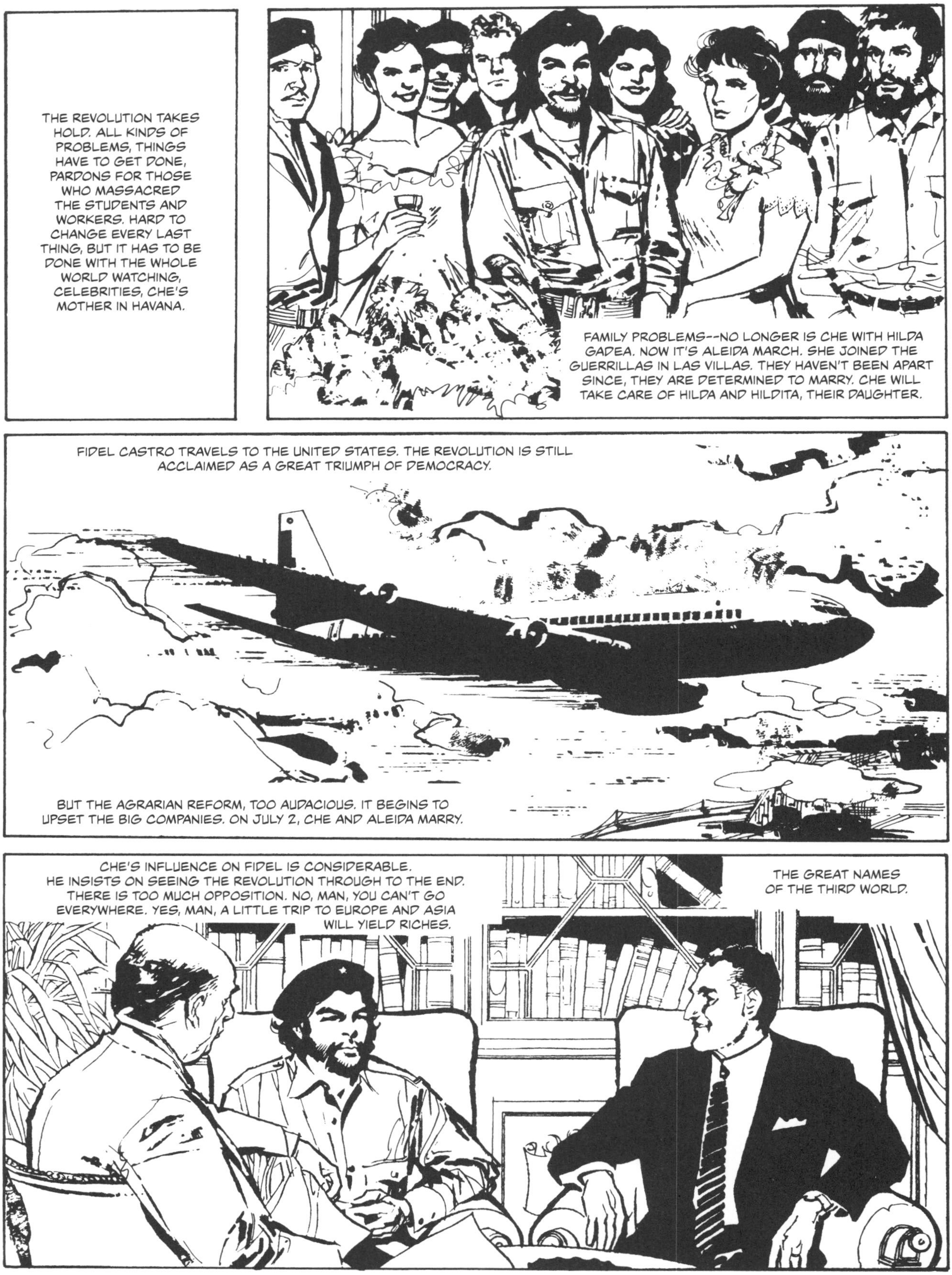
THE REVOLUTION TAKES HOLD. ALL KINDS OF PROBLEMS, THINGS HAVE TO GET DONE, PARDONS FOR THOSE WHO MASSACRED THE STUDENTS AND WORKERS. HARD TO CHANGE EVERY LAST THING, BUT IT HAS TO BE DONE WITH THE WHOLE WORLD WATCHING, CELEBRITIES, CHE'S MOTHER IN HAVANA.
FAMILY PROBLEMS--NO LONGER IS CHE WITH HILDA GADEA. NOW IT'S ALEIDA MARCH. SHE JOINED THE GUERRILLAS IN LAS VILLAS. THEY HAVEN'T BEEN APART SINCE, THEY ARE DETERMINED TO MARRY. CHE WILL TAKE CARE OF HILDA AND HILDITA, THEIR DAUGHTER.
FIDEL CASTRO TRAVELS TO THE UNITED STATES. THE REVOLUTION IS STILL ACCLAIMED AS A GREAT TRIUMPH OF DEMOCRACY.
BUT THE AGRARIAN REFORM, TOO AUDACIOUS. IT BEGINS TO UPSET THE BIG COMPANIES. ON JULY 2, CHE AND ALEIDA MARRY.
CHE'S INFLUENCE ON FIDEL IS CONSIDERABLE. HE INSISTS ON SEEING THE REVOLUTION THROUGH TO THE END. THERE IS TOO MUCH OPPOSITION. NO, MAN, YOU CAN'T GO EVERYWHERE. YES, MAN, A LITTLE TRIP TO EUROPE AND ASIA WILL YIELD RICHES.
THE GREAT NAMES OF THE THIRD WORLD.

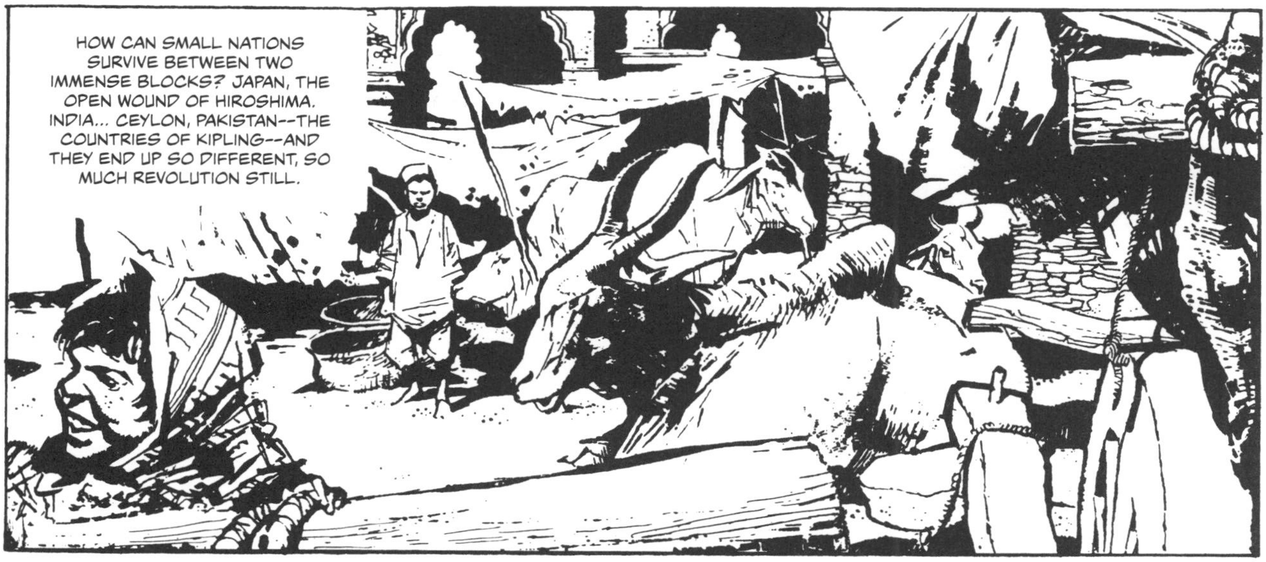
HOW CAN SMALL NATIONS SURVIVE BETWEEN TWO IMMENSE BLOCKS? JAPAN, THE OPEN WOUND OF HIROSHIMA. INDIA... CEYLON, PAKISTAN--THE COUNTRIES OF KIPLING--AND THEY END UP SO DIFFERENT, SO MUCH REVOLUTION STILL.
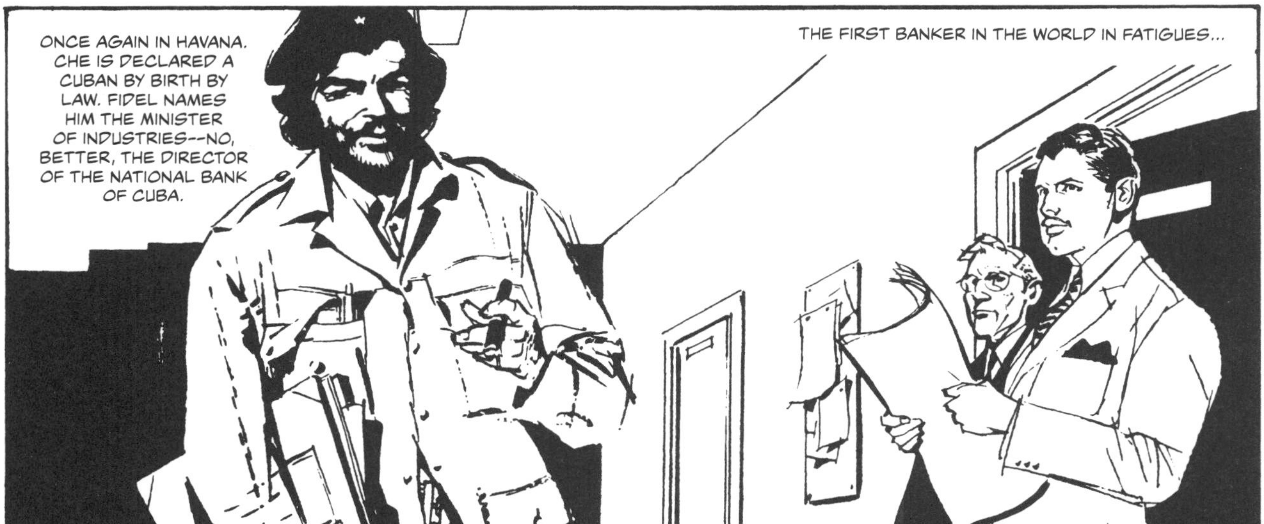
ONCE AGAIN IN HAVANA. CHE IS DECLARED A CUBAN BY BIRTH BY LAW. FIDEL NAMES HIM THE MINISTER OF INDUSTRIES--NO, BETTER, THE DIRECTOR OF THE NATIONAL BANK OF CUBA.
THE FIRST BANKER IN THE WORLD IN FATIGUES...
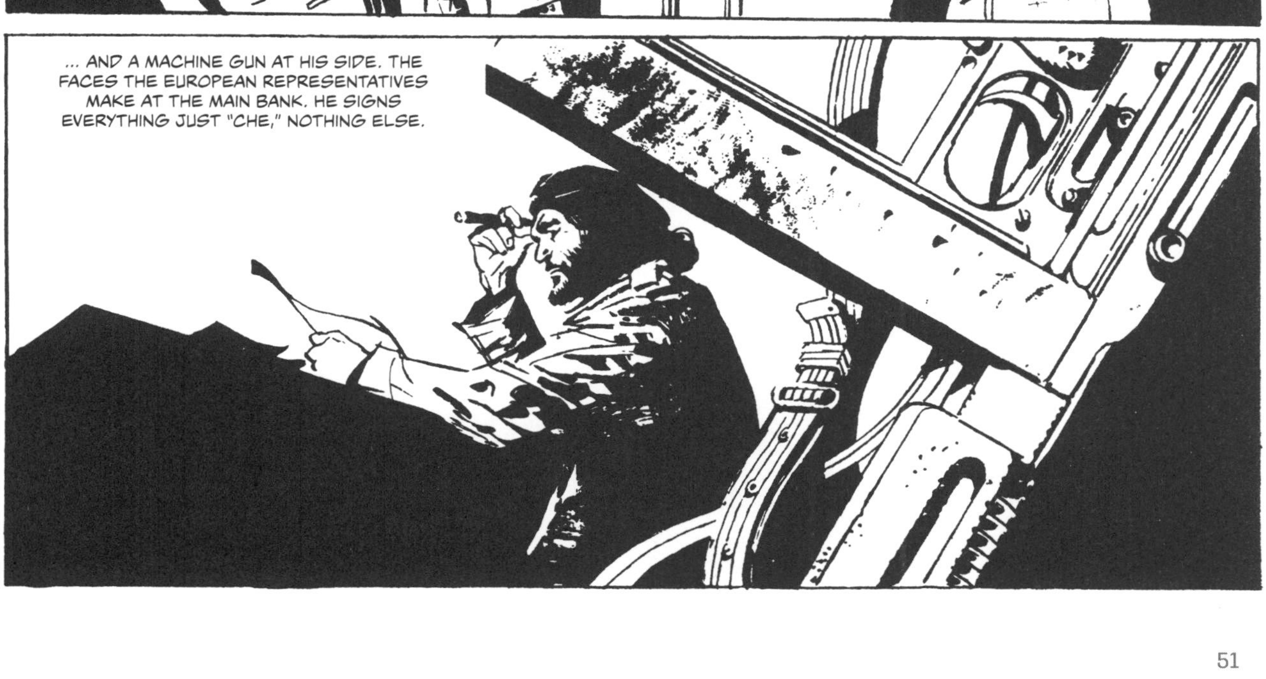
... AND A MACHINE GUN AT HIS SIDE. THE FACES THE EUROPEAN REPRESENTATIVES MAKE AT THE MAIN BANK. HE SIGNS EVERYTHING JUST "CHE," NOTHING ELSE.

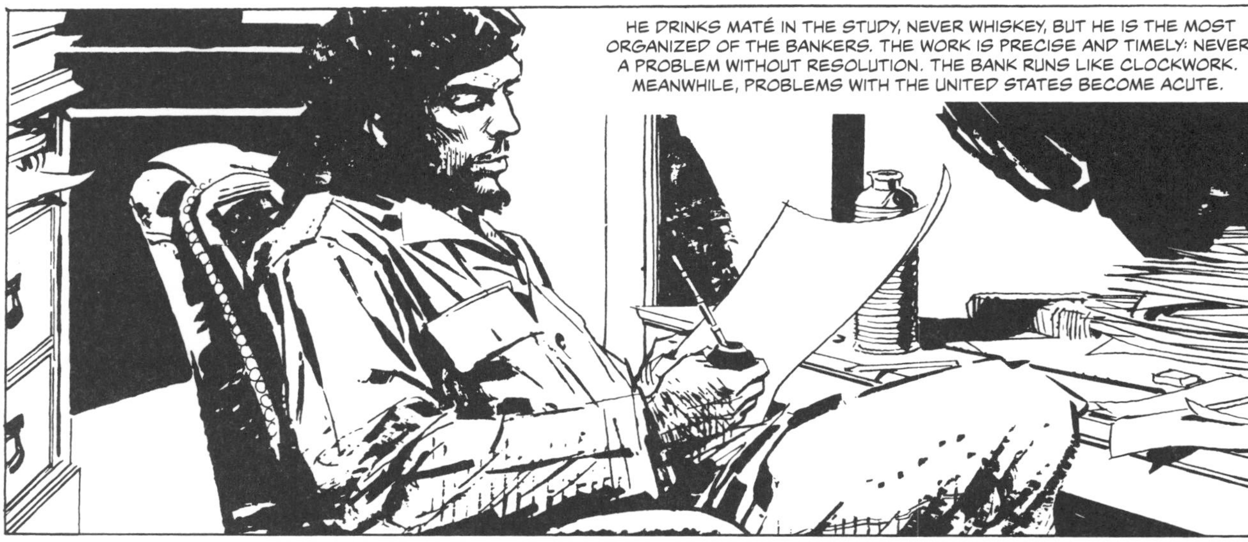
HE DRINKS MATÉ IN THE STUDY, NEVER WHISKEY, BUT HE IS THE MOST ORGANIZED OF THE BANKERS. THE WORK IS PRECISE AND TIMELY: NEVER A PROBLEM WITHOUT RESOLUTION. THE BANK RUNS LIKE CLOCKWORK. MEANWHILE, PROBLEMS WITH THE UNITED STATES BECOME ACUTE.

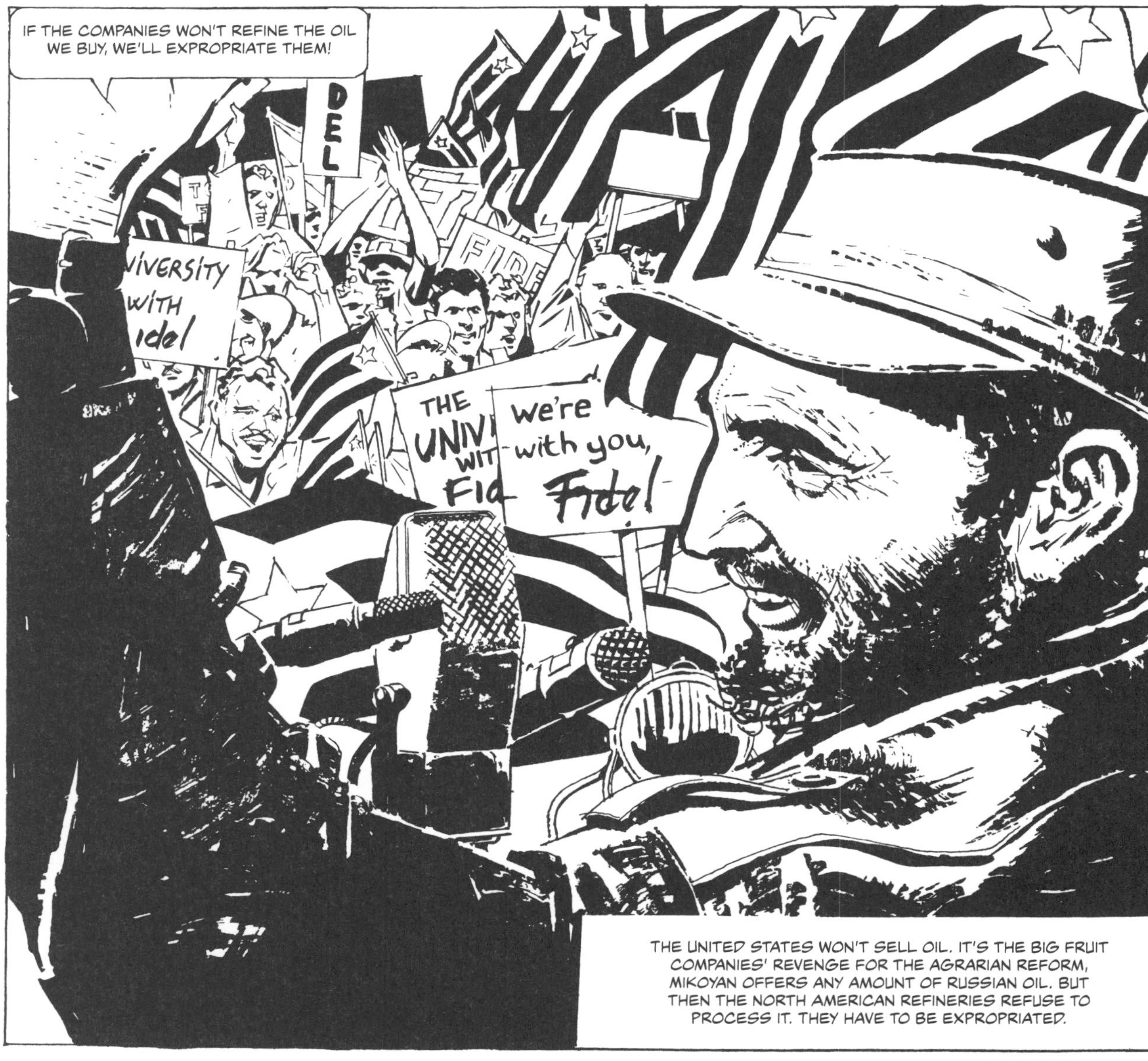
IF THE COMPANIES WON'T REFINE THE OIL WE BUY, WE'LL EXPROPRIATE THEM!
DEL
We're with you, Fidel
THE UNIVERSITY WITH FIDEL
THE UNITED STATES WON'T SELL OIL. IT'S THE BIG FRUIT COMPANIES' REVENGE FOR THE AGRARIAN REFORM. MIKOYAN OFFERS ANY AMOUNT OF RUSSIAN OIL. BUT THEN THE NORTH AMERICAN REFINERIES REFUSE TO PROCESS IT. THEY HAVE TO BE EXPROPRIATED.

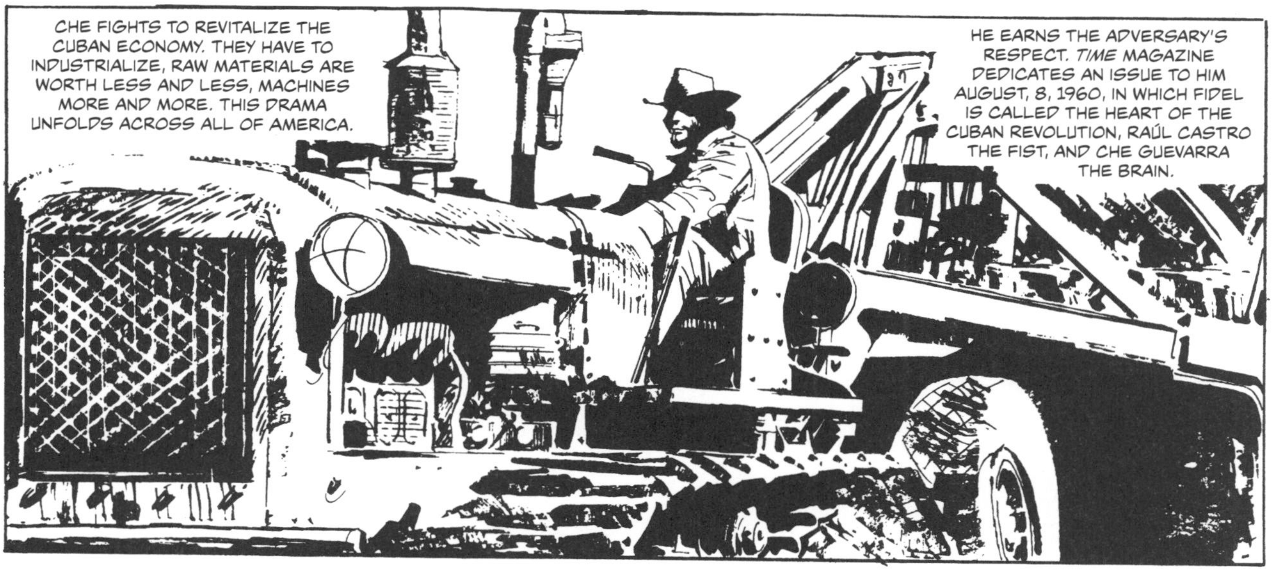
CHE FIGHTS TO REVITALIZE THE CUBAN ECONOMY. THEY HAVE TO INDUSTRIALIZE, RAW MATERIALS ARE WORTH LESS AND LESS, MACHINES MORE AND MORE. THIS DRAMA UNFOLDS ACROSS ALL OF AMERICA.
HE EARNS THE ADVERSARY'S RESPECT. *TIME MAGAZINE* DEDICATES AN ISSUE TO HIM AUGUST, 8, 1960, IN WHICH FIDEL IS CALLED THE HEART OF THE CUBAN REVOLUTION, RAÚL CASTRO THE FIST, AND CHE GUEVARRA THE BRAIN.

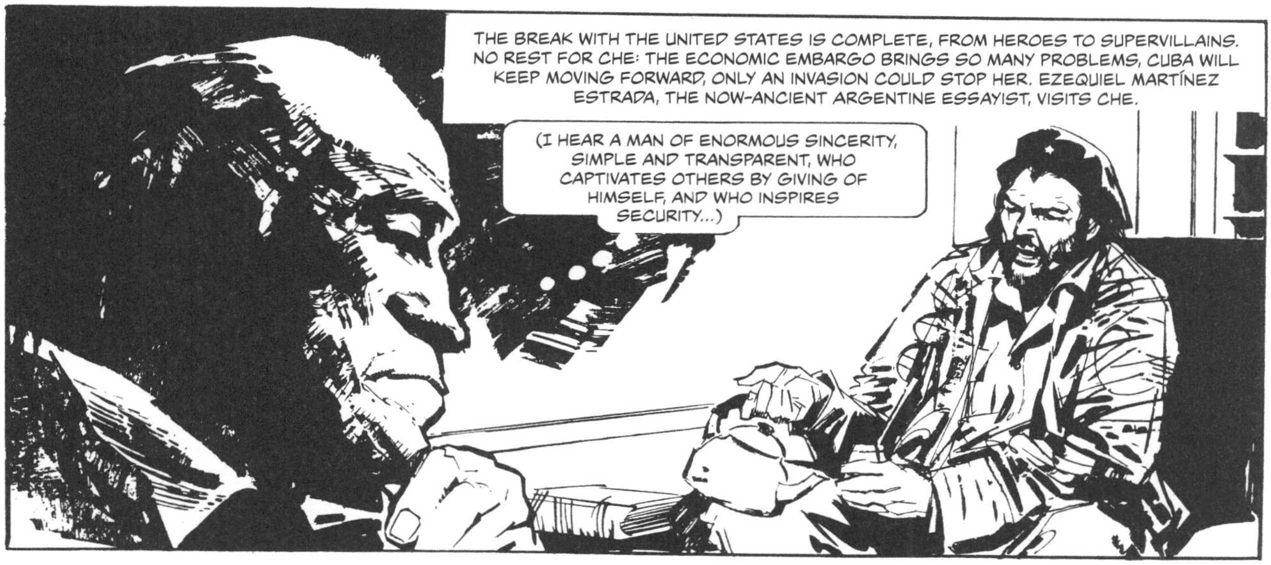
THE BREAK WITH THE UNITED STATES IS COMPLETE, FROM HEROES TO SUPERVILLAINS. NO REST FOR CHE: THE ECONOMIC EMBARGO BRINGS SO MANY PROBLEMS, CUBA WILL KEEP MOVING FORWARD, ONLY AN INVASION COULD STOP HER. EZEQUIEL MARTÍNEZ ESTRADA, THE NOW-ANCIENT ARGENTINE ESSAYIST, VISITS CHE.
(I HEAR A MAN OF ENORMOUS SINCERITY, SIMPLE AND TRANSPARENT, WHO CAPTIVATES OTHERS BY GIVING OF HIMSELF, AND WHO INSPIRES SECURITY...)

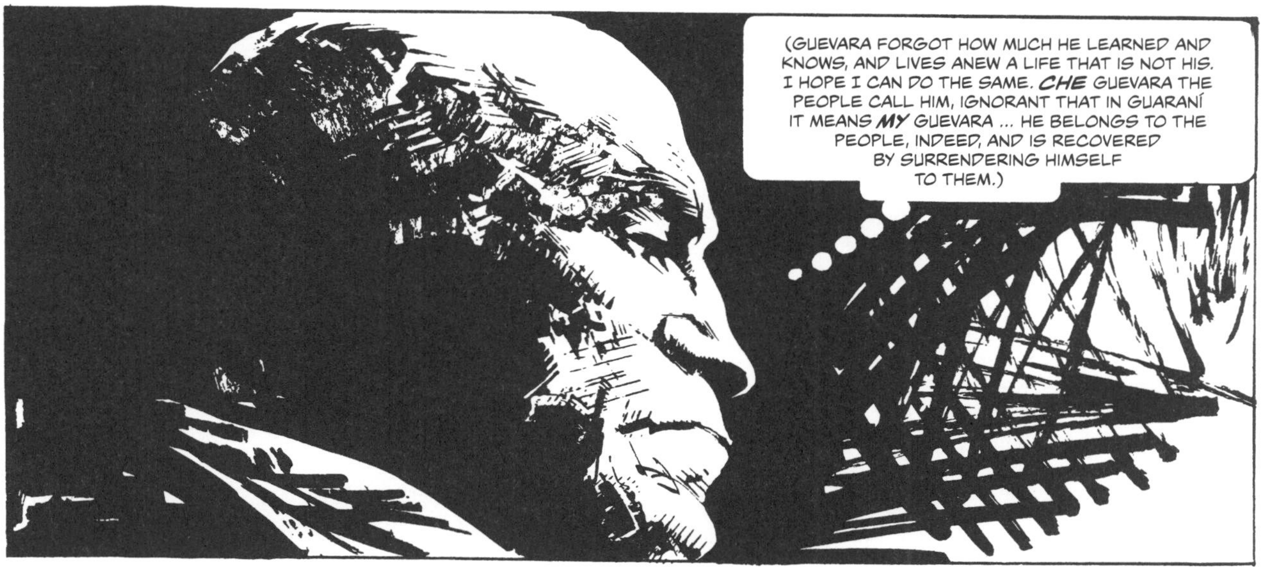
(GUEVARA FORGOT HOW MUCH HE LEARNED AND KNOWS, AND LIVES ANEW A LIFE THAT IS NOT HIS. I HOPE I CAN DO THE SAME. **CHE** GUEVARA THE PEOPLE CALL HIM, IGNORANT THAT IN GUARANÍ IT MEANS **MY** GUEVARA ... HE BELONGS TO THE PEOPLE, INDEED, AND IS RECOVERED BY SURRENDERING HIMSELF TO THEM.)

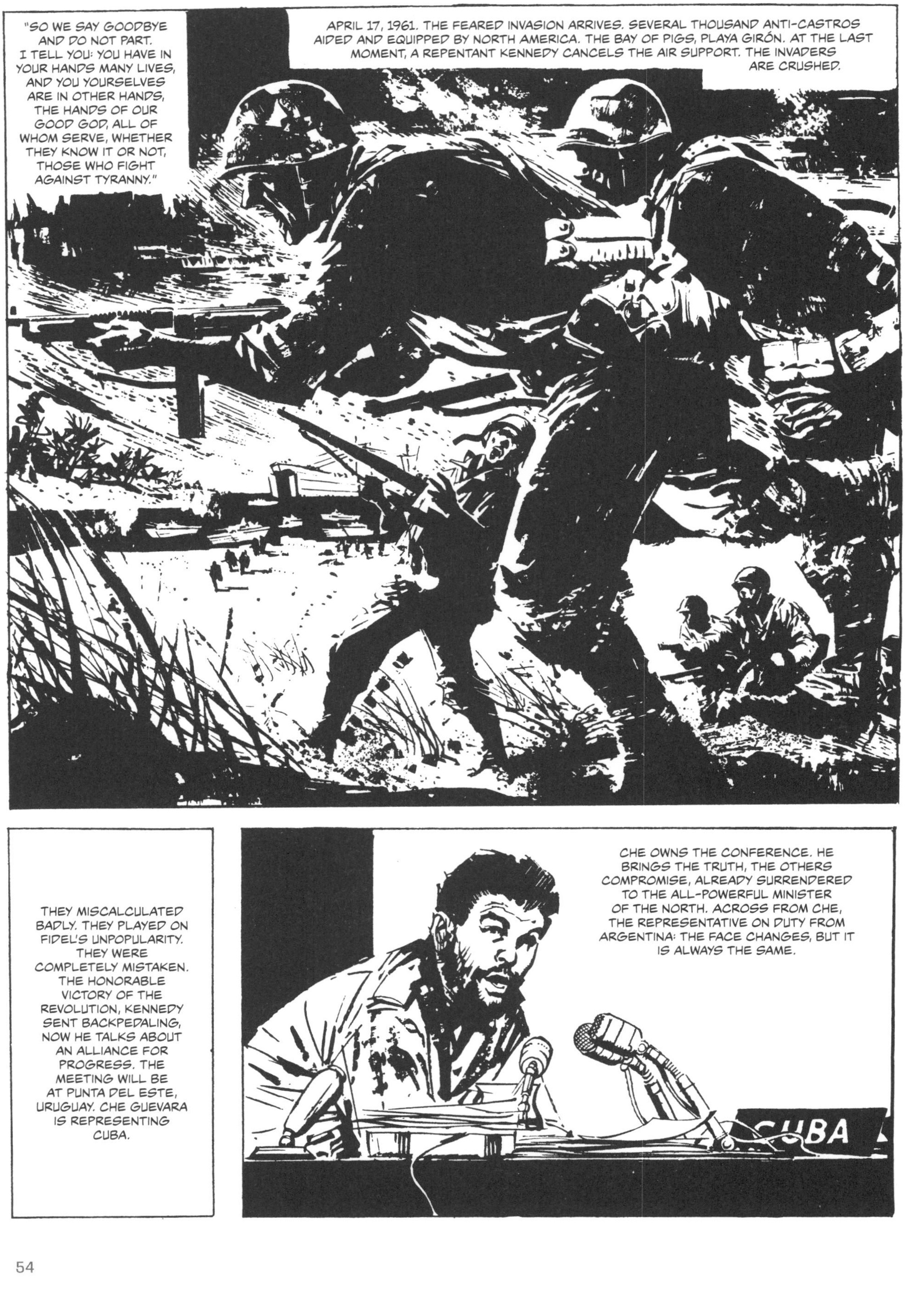
"SO WE SAY GOODBYE AND DO NOT PART. I TELL YOU: YOU HAVE IN YOUR HANDS MANY LIVES, AND YOU YOURSELVES ARE IN OTHER HANDS, THE HANDS OF OUR GOOD GOD, ALL OF WHOM SERVE, WHETHER THEY KNOW IT OR NOT, THOSE WHO FIGHT AGAINST TYRANNY."
APRIL 17, 1961. THE FEARED INVASION ARRIVES. SEVERAL THOUSAND ANTI-CASTROS AIDED AND EQUIPPED BY NORTH AMERICA. THE BAY OF PIGS, PLAYA GIRÓN. AT THE LAST MOMENT, A REPENTANT KENNEDY CANCELS THE AIR SUPPORT. THE INVADERS ARE CRUSHED.
THEY MISCALCULATED BADLY. THEY PLAYED ON FIDEL'S UNPOPULARITY. THEY WERE COMPLETELY MISTAKEN. THE HONORABLE VICTORY OF THE REVOLUTION, KENNEDY SENT BACKPEDALING, NOW HE TALKS ABOUT AN ALLIANCE FOR PROGRESS. THE MEETING WILL BE AT PUNTA DEL ESTE, URUGUAY. CHE GUEVARA IS REPRESENTING CUBA.
CHE OWNS THE CONFERENCE. HE BRINGS THE TRUTH, THE OTHERS COMPROMISE, ALREADY SURRENDERED TO THE ALL-POWERFUL MINISTER OF THE NORTH. ACROSS FROM CHE, THE REPRESENTATIVE ON DUTY FROM ARGENTINA: THE FACE CHANGES, BUT IT IS ALWAYS THE SAME.
CUBA

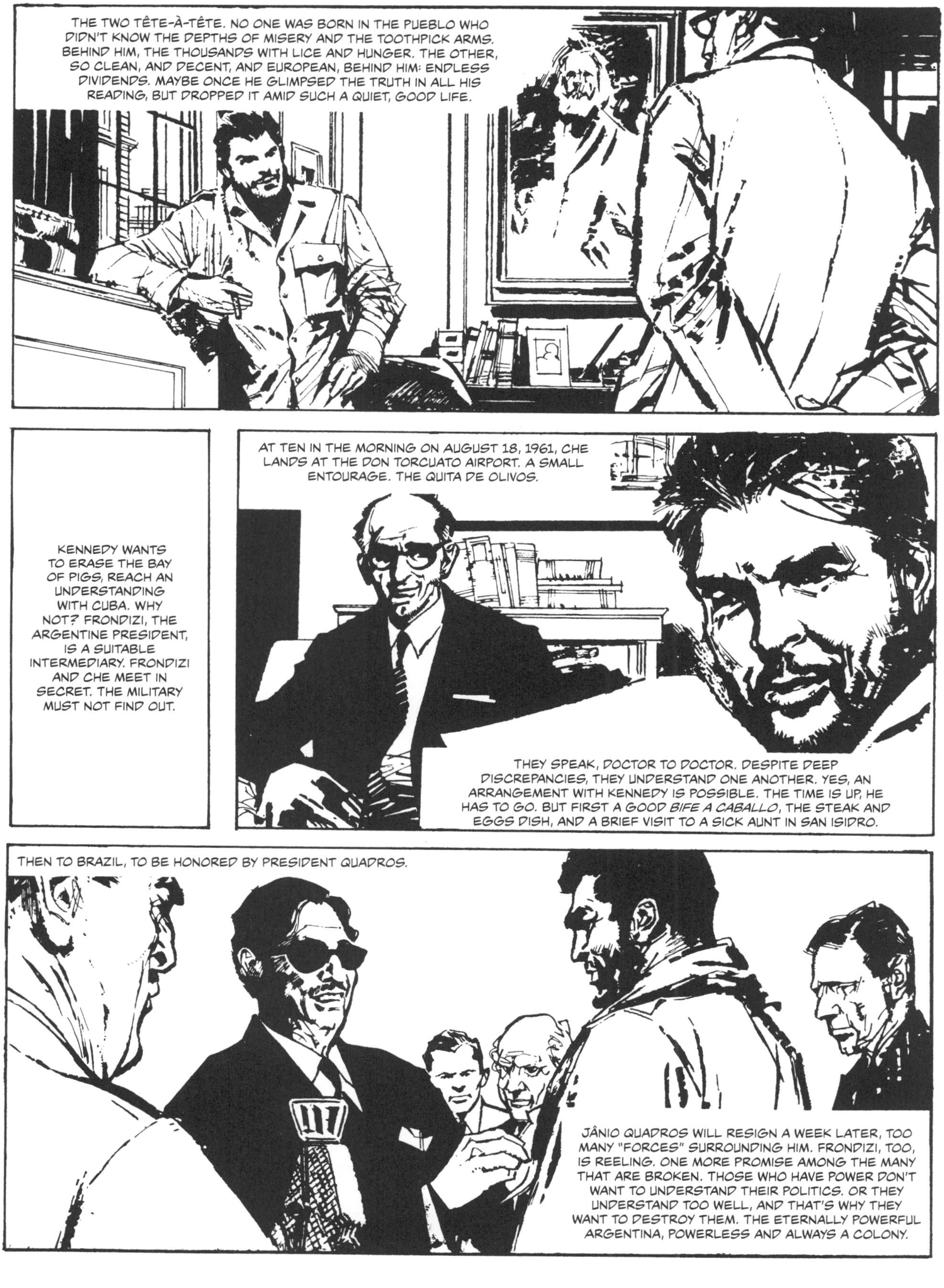

THE TWO TÊTE-À-TÊTE. NO ONE WAS BORN IN THE PUEBLO WHO DIDN'T KNOW THE DEPTHS OF MISERY AND THE TOOTHPICK ARMS. BEHIND HIM, THE THOUSANDS WITH LICE AND HUNGER. THE OTHER, SO CLEAN, AND DECENT, AND EUROPEAN, BEHIND HIM: ENDLESS DIVIDENDS. MAYBE ONCE HE GLIMPSED THE TRUTH IN ALL HIS READING, BUT DROPPED IT AMID SUCH A QUIET, GOOD LIFE.
KENNEDY WANTS TO ERASE THE BAY OF PIGS, REACH AN UNDERSTANDING WITH CUBA. WHY NOT? FRONDIZI, THE ARGENTINE PRESIDENT, IS A SUITABLE INTERMEDIARY. FRONDIZI AND CHE MEET IN SECRET. THE MILITARY MUST NOT FIND OUT.
AT TEN IN THE MORNING ON AUGUST 18, 1961, CHE LANDS AT THE DON TORCUATO AIRPORT. A SMALL ENTOURAGE. THE QUITA DE OLIVOS.
THEY SPEAK, DOCTOR TO DOCTOR. DESPITE DEEP DISCREPANCIES, THEY UNDERSTAND ONE ANOTHER. YES, AN ARRANGEMENT WITH KENNEDY IS POSSIBLE. THE TIME IS UP, HE HAS TO GO. BUT FIRST A GOOD *BIFE A CABALLO*, THE STEAK AND EGGS DISH, AND A BRIEF VISIT TO A SICK AUNT IN SAN ISIDRO.
THEN TO BRAZIL, TO BE HONORED BY PRESIDENT QUADROS.
JÂNIO QUADROS WILL RESIGN A WEEK LATER, TOO MANY "FORCES" SURROUNDING HIM. FRONDIZI, TOO, IS REELING. ONE MORE PROMISE AMONG THE MANY THAT ARE BROKEN. THOSE WHO HAVE POWER DON'T WANT TO UNDERSTAND THEIR POLITICS. OR THEY UNDERSTAND TOO WELL, AND THAT'S WHY THEY WANT TO DESTROY THEM. THE ETERNALLY POWERFUL ARGENTINA, POWERLESS AND ALWAYS A COLONY.

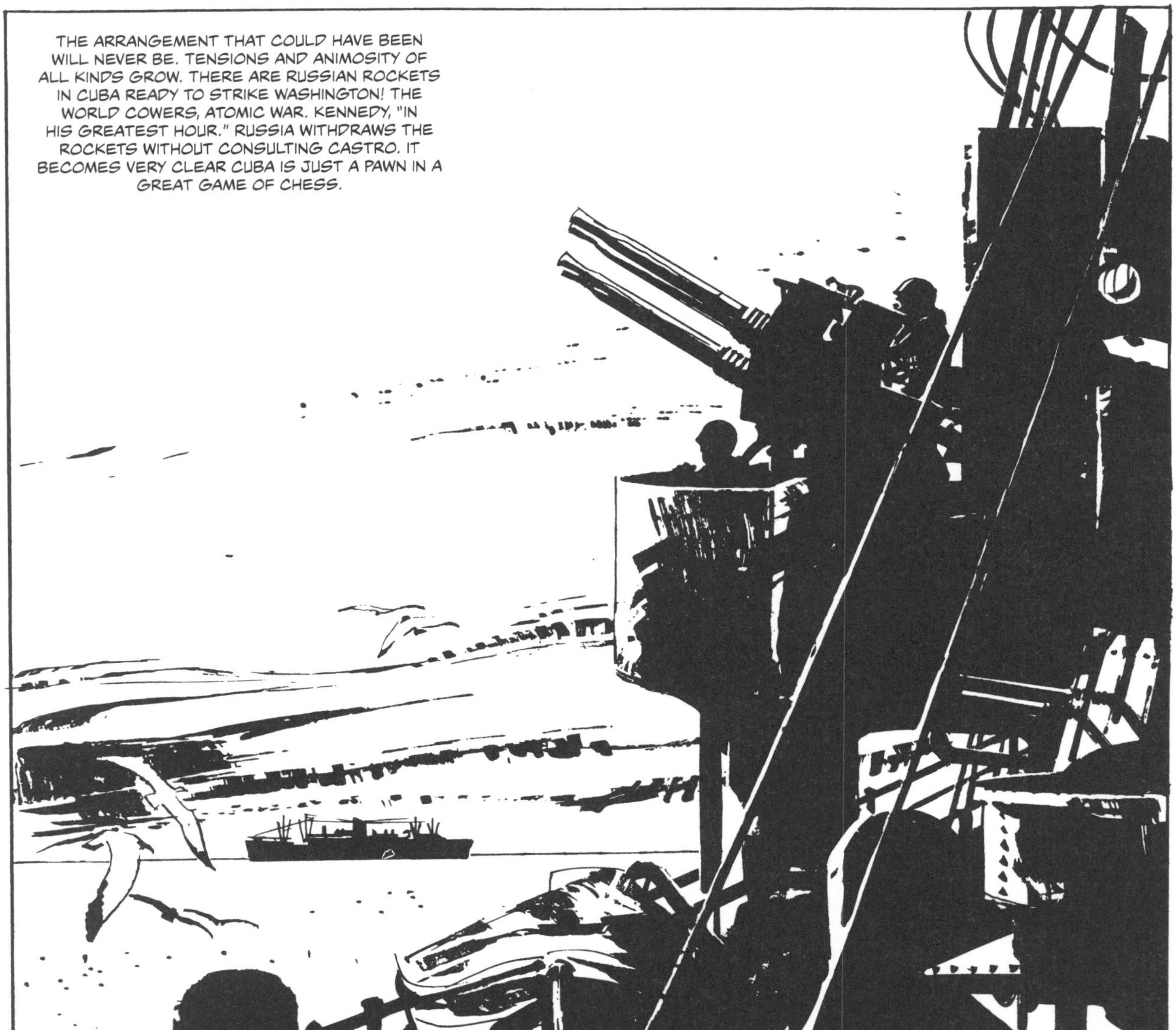
THE ARRANGEMENT THAT COULD HAVE BEEN WILL NEVER BE. TENSIONS AND ANIMOSITY OF ALL KINDS GROW. THERE ARE RUSSIAN ROCKETS IN CUBA READY TO STRIKE WASHINGTON! THE WORLD COWERS, ATOMIC WAR. KENNEDY, "IN HIS GREATEST HOUR." RUSSIA WITHDRAWS THE ROCKETS WITHOUT CONSULTING CASTRO. IT BECOMES VERY CLEAR CUBA IS JUST A PAWN IN A GREAT GAME OF CHESS.

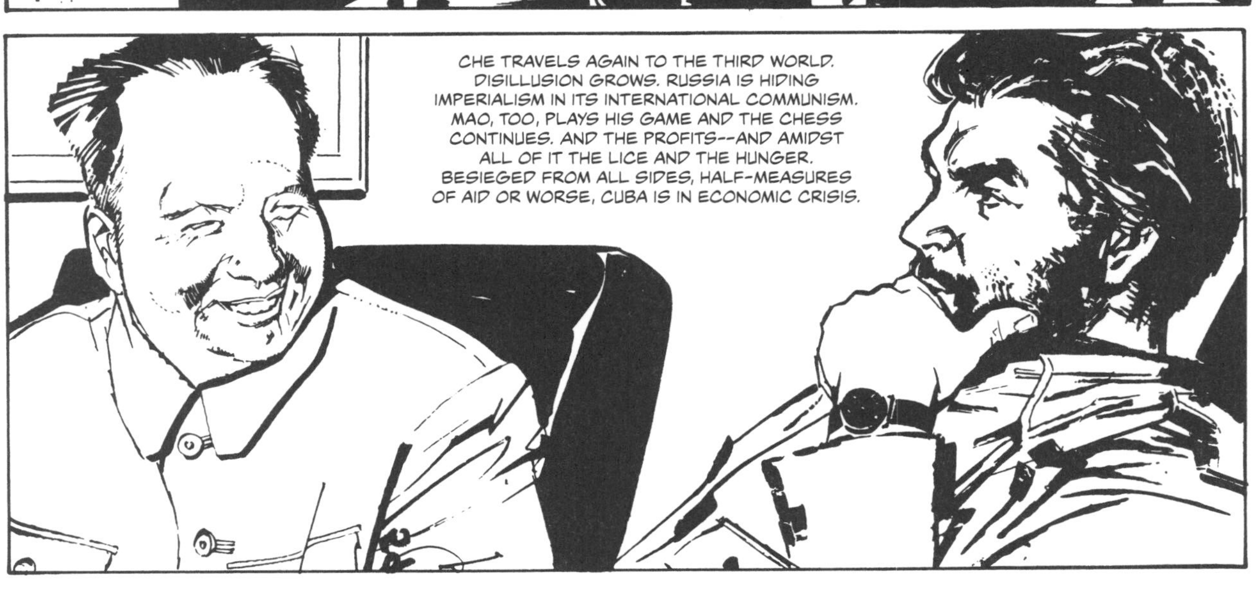
CHE TRAVELS AGAIN TO THE THIRD WORLD. DISILLUSION GROWS. RUSSIA IS HIDING IMPERIALISM IN ITS INTERNATIONAL COMMUNISM. MAO, TOO, PLAYS HIS GAME AND THE CHESS CONTINUES. AND THE PROFITS--AND AMIDST ALL OF IT THE LICE AND THE HUNGER. BESIEGED FROM ALL SIDES, HALF-MEASURES OF AID OR WORSE, CUBA IS IN ECONOMIC CRISIS.

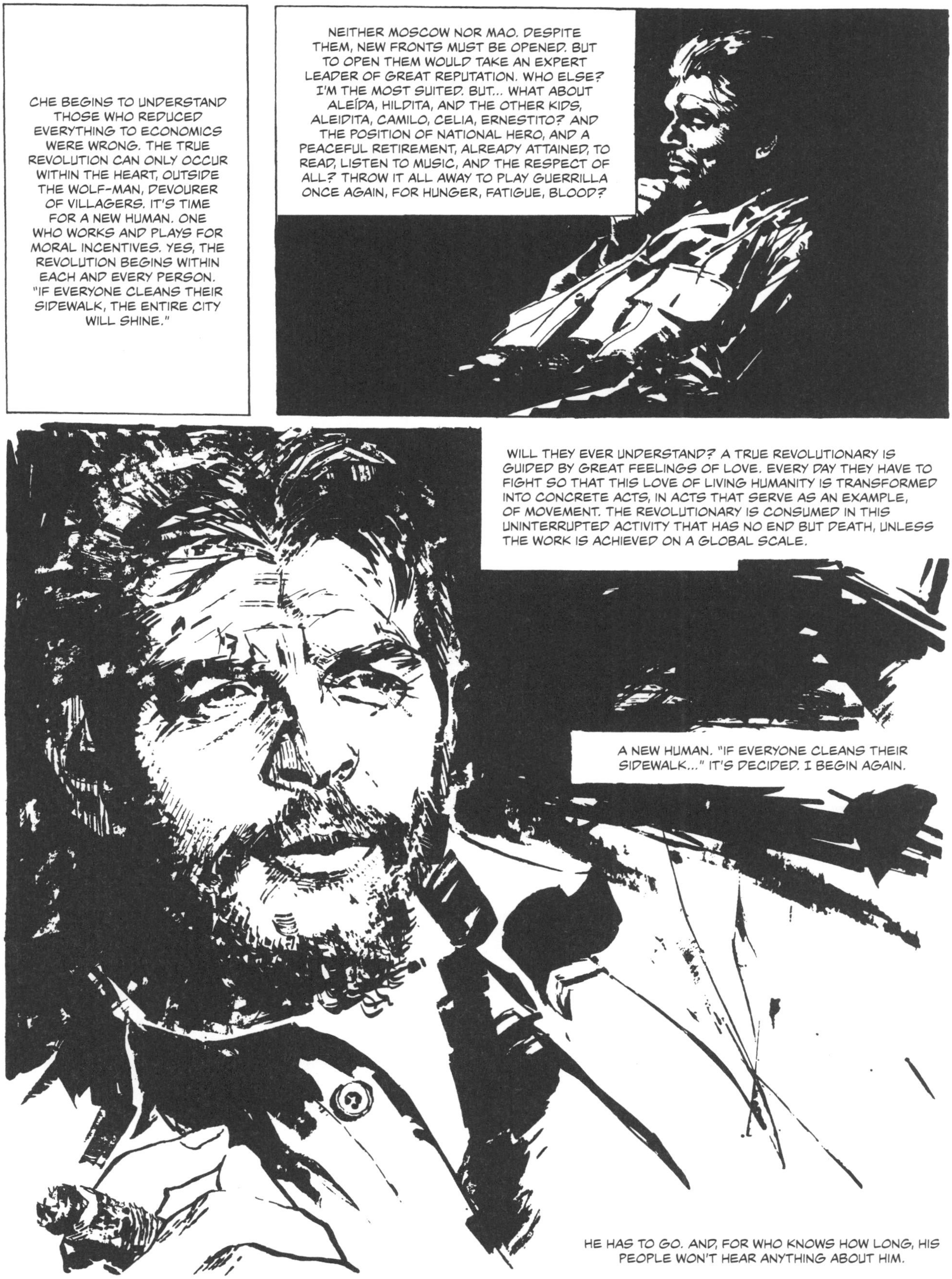
CHE BEGINS TO UNDERSTAND THOSE WHO REDUCED EVERYTHING TO ECONOMICS WERE WRONG. THE TRUE REVOLUTION CAN ONLY OCCUR WITHIN THE HEART, OUTSIDE THE WOLF-MAN, DEVOURER OF VILLAGERS. IT'S TIME FOR A NEW HUMAN. ONE WHO WORKS AND PLAYS FOR MORAL INCENTIVES. YES, THE REVOLUTION BEGINS WITHIN EACH AND EVERY PERSON. "IF EVERYONE CLEANS THEIR SIDEWALK, THE ENTIRE CITY WILL SHINE."
NEITHER MOSCOW NOR MAO. DESPITE THEM, NEW FRONTS MUST BE OPENED. BUT TO OPEN THEM WOULD TAKE AN EXPERT LEADER OF GREAT REPUTATION. WHO ELSE? I'M THE MOST SUITED. BUT... WHAT ABOUT ALEÍDA, HILDITA, AND THE OTHER KIDS, ALEIDITA, CAMILO, CELIA, ERNESTITO? AND THE POSITION OF NATIONAL HERO, AND A PEACEFUL RETIREMENT, ALREADY ATTAINED, TO READ, LISTEN TO MUSIC, AND THE RESPECT OF ALL? THROW IT ALL AWAY TO PLAY GUERRILLA ONCE AGAIN, FOR HUNGER, FATIGUE, BLOOD?
WILL THEY EVER UNDERSTAND? A TRUE REVOLUTIONARY IS GUIDED BY GREAT FEELINGS OF LOVE. EVERY DAY THEY HAVE TO FIGHT SO THAT THIS LOVE OF LIVING HUMANITY IS TRANSFORMED INTO CONCRETE ACTS, IN ACTS THAT SERVE AS AN EXAMPLE, OF MOVEMENT. THE REVOLUTIONARY IS CONSUMED IN THIS UNINTERRUPTED ACTIVITY THAT HAS NO END BUT DEATH, UNLESS THE WORK IS ACHIEVED ON A GLOBAL SCALE.
A NEW HUMAN. "IF EVERYONE CLEANS THEIR SIDEWALK..." IT'S DECIDED. I BEGIN AGAIN.
HE HAS TO GO. AND, FOR WHO KNOWS HOW LONG, HIS PEOPLE WON'T HEAR ANYTHING ABOUT HIM.

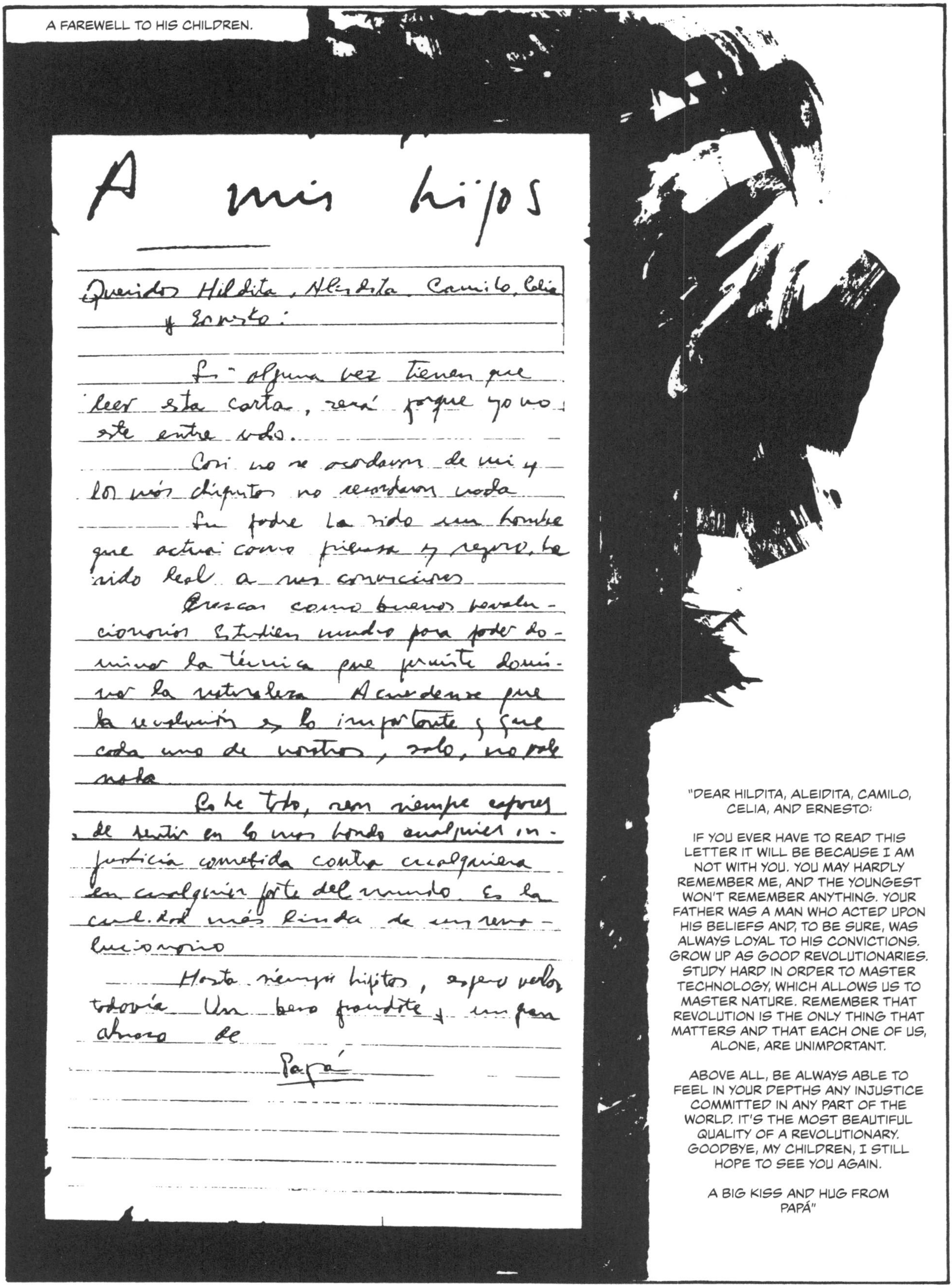
A FAREWELL TO HIS CHILDREN.
A mis hijos
Queridos Hildita, Aleidita, Camilo, Celia y Ernesto:
Si alguna vez tienen que leer esta carta, será porque yo no esté entre Uds.
Casi no se acordarán de mí y los más chiquitos no recordarán nada.
Su padre ha sido un hombre que actúa como piensa y, seguro, ha sido leal a sus convicciones.
Crezcan como buenos revolucionarios. Estudien mucho para poder dominar la técnica que permite dominar la naturaleza. Acuérdense que la revolución es lo importante y que cada uno de nosotros, solo, no vale nada.
Sobre todo, sean siempre capaces de sentir en lo más hondo cualquier injusticia cometida contra cualquiera en cualquier parte del mundo. Es la cualidad más linda de un revolucionario.
Hasta siempre hijitos, espero verlos todavía. Un beso grandote y un gran abrazo de
Papá
"DEAR HILDITA, ALEIDITA, CAMILO, CELIA, AND ERNESTO:
IF YOU EVER HAVE TO READ THIS LETTER IT WILL BE BECAUSE I AM NOT WITH YOU. YOU MAY HARDLY REMEMBER ME, AND THE YOUNGEST WON'T REMEMBER ANYTHING. YOUR FATHER WAS A MAN WHO ACTED UPON HIS BELIEFS AND, TO BE SURE, WAS ALWAYS LOYAL TO HIS CONVICTIONS. GROW UP AS GOOD REVOLUTIONARIES. STUDY HARD IN ORDER TO MASTER TECHNOLOGY, WHICH ALLOWS US TO MASTER NATURE. REMEMBER THAT REVOLUTION IS THE ONLY THING THAT MATTERS AND THAT EACH ONE OF US, ALONE, ARE UNIMPORTANT.
ABOVE ALL, BE ALWAYS ABLE TO FEEL IN YOUR DEPTHS ANY INJUSTICE COMMITTED IN ANY PART OF THE WORLD. IT'S THE MOST BEAUTIFUL QUALITY OF A REVOLUTIONARY. GOODBYE, MY CHILDREN, I STILL HOPE TO SEE YOU AGAIN.
A BIG KISS AND HUG FROM PAPÁ"

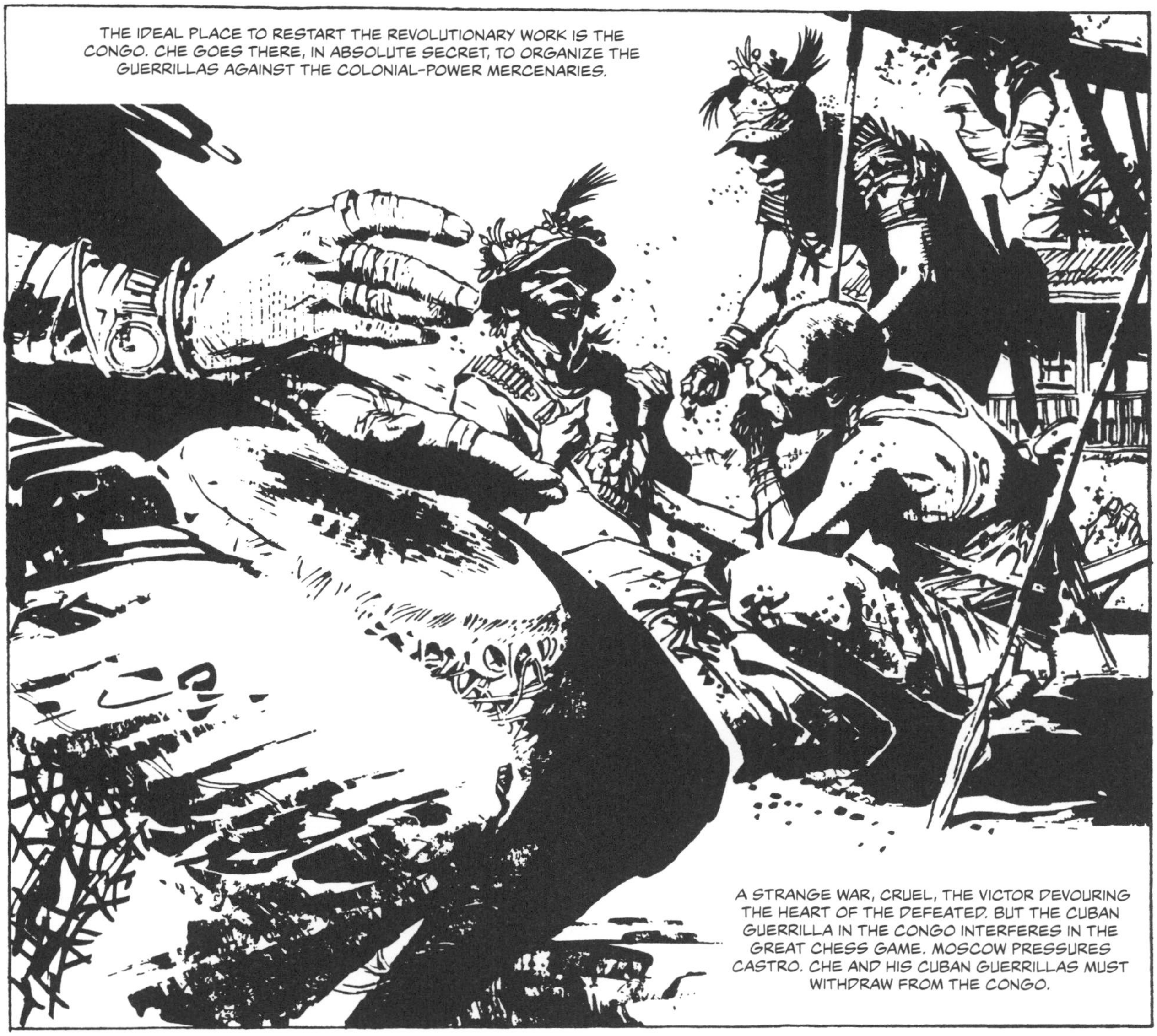
THE IDEAL PLACE TO RESTART THE REVOLUTIONARY WORK IS THE CONGO. CHE GOES THERE, IN ABSOLUTE SECRET, TO ORGANIZE THE GUERRILLAS AGAINST THE COLONIAL-POWER MERCENARIES.
A STRANGE WAR, CRUEL, THE VICTOR DEVOURING THE HEART OF THE DEFEATED. BUT THE CUBAN GUERRILLA IN THE CONGO INTERFERES IN THE GREAT CHESS GAME. MOSCOW PRESSURES CASTRO. CHE AND HIS CUBAN GUERRILLAS MUST WITHDRAW FROM THE CONGO.

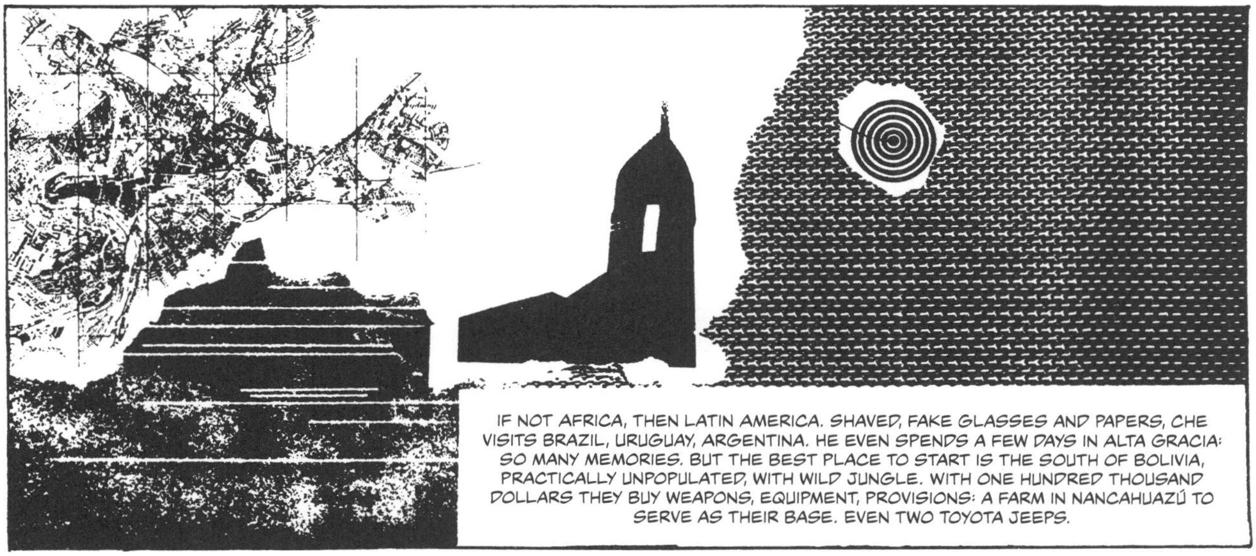
IF NOT AFRICA, THEN LATIN AMERICA. SHAVED, FAKE GLASSES AND PAPERS, CHE VISITS BRAZIL, URUGUAY, ARGENTINA. HE EVEN SPENDS A FEW DAYS IN ALTA GRACIA: SO MANY MEMORIES. BUT THE BEST PLACE TO START IS THE SOUTH OF BOLIVIA, PRACTICALLY UNPOPULATED, WITH WILD JUNGLE. WITH ONE HUNDRED THOUSAND DOLLARS THEY BUY WEAPONS, EQUIPMENT, PROVISIONS: A FARM IN NANCAHUAZÚ TO SERVE AS THEIR BASE. EVEN TWO TOYOTA JEEPS.

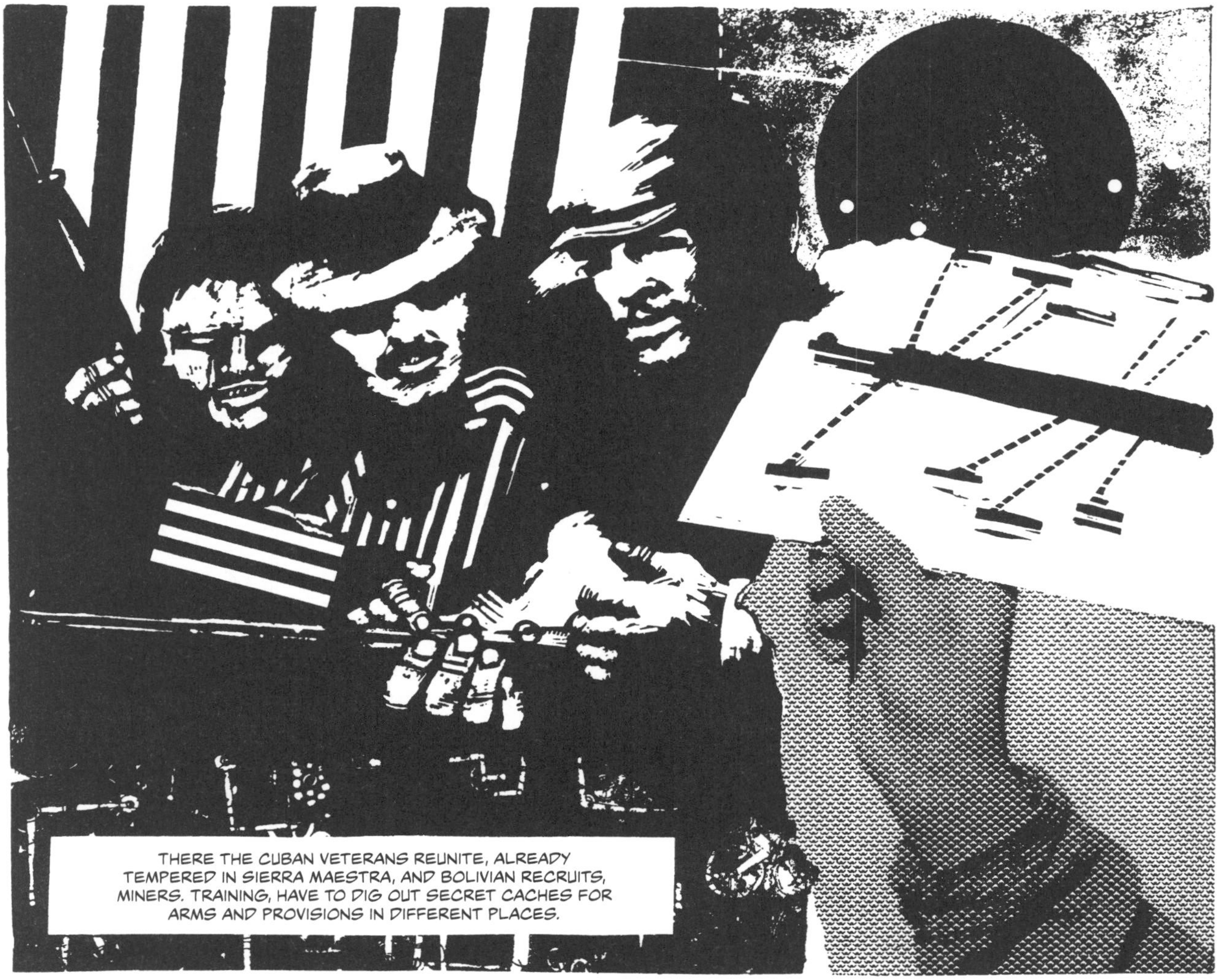
THERE THE CUBAN VETERANS REUNITE, ALREADY TEMPERED IN SIERRA MAESTRA, AND BOLIVIAN RECRUITS, MINERS. TRAINING, HAVE TO DIG OUT SECRET CACHES FOR ARMS AND PROVISIONS IN DIFFERENT PLACES.

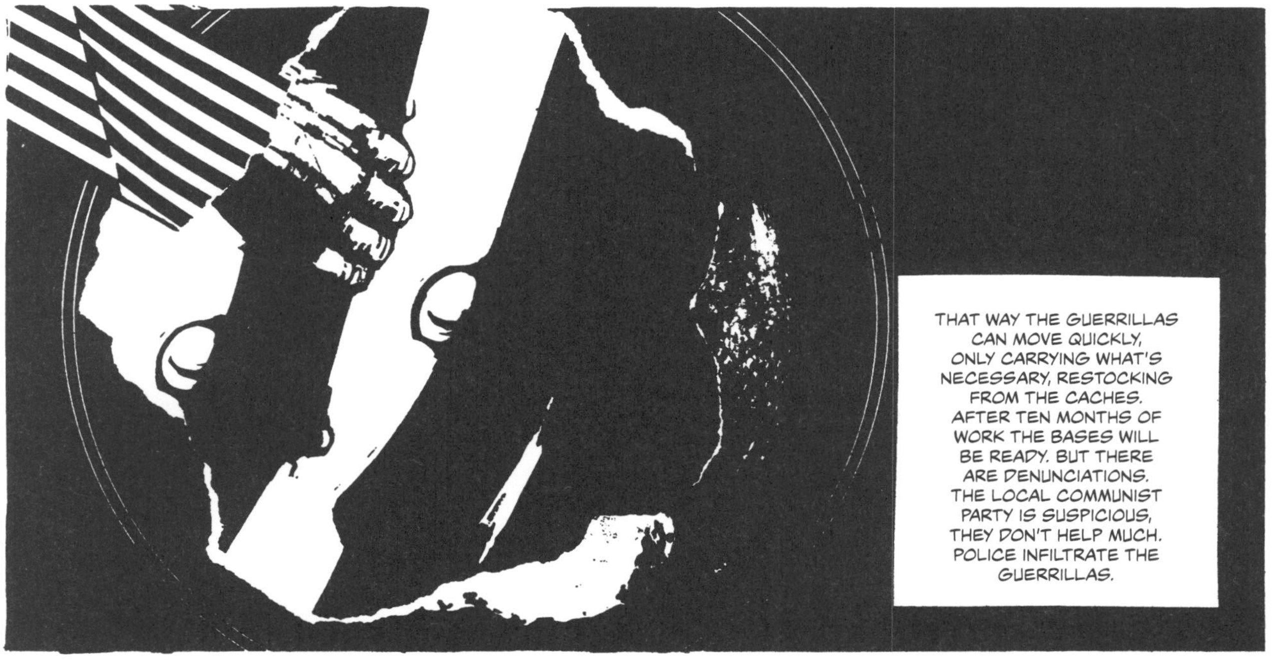
THAT WAY THE GUERRILLAS CAN MOVE QUICKLY, ONLY CARRYING WHAT'S NECESSARY, RESTOCKING FROM THE CACHES. AFTER TEN MONTHS OF WORK THE BASES WILL BE READY. BUT THERE ARE DENUNCIATIONS. THE LOCAL COMMUNIST PARTY IS SUSPICIOUS, THEY DON'T HELP MUCH. POLICE INFILTRATE THE GUERRILLAS.

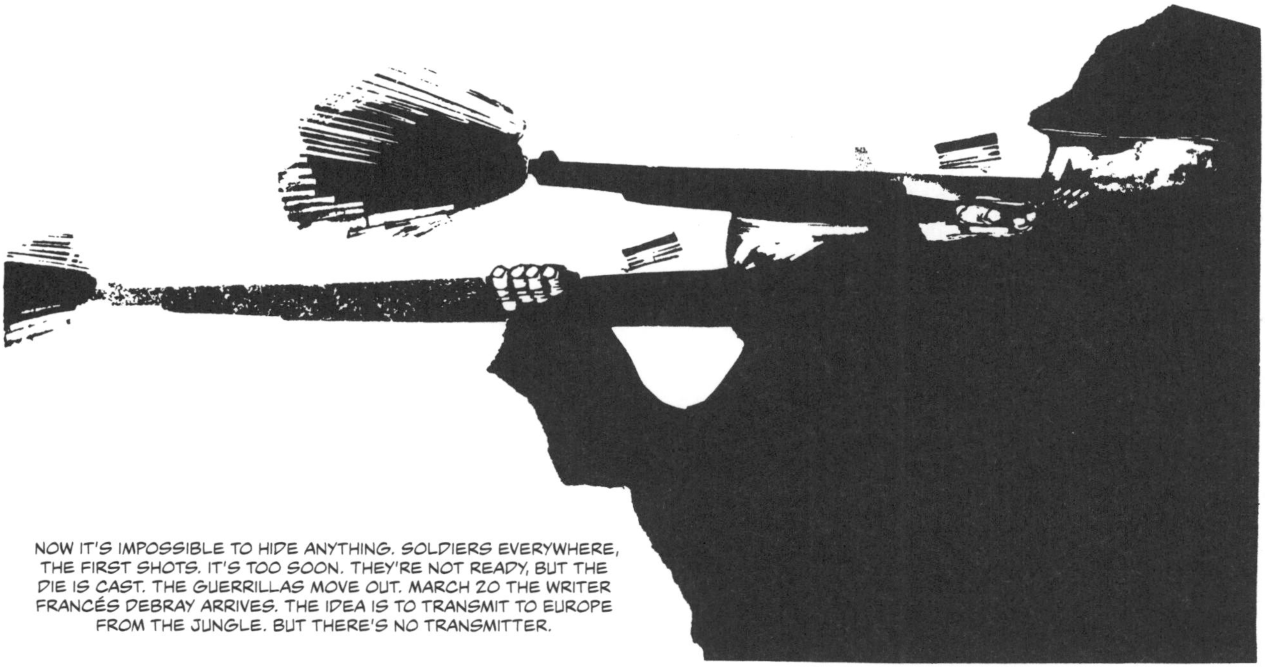
NOW IT'S IMPOSSIBLE TO HIDE ANYTHING. SOLDIERS EVERYWHERE, THE FIRST SHOTS. IT'S TOO SOON. THEY'RE NOT READY, BUT THE DIE IS CAST. THE GUERRILLAS MOVE OUT. MARCH 20 THE WRITER FRANCÉS DEBRAY ARRIVES. THE IDEA IS TO TRANSMIT TO EUROPE FROM THE JUNGLE. BUT THERE'S NO TRANSMITTER.

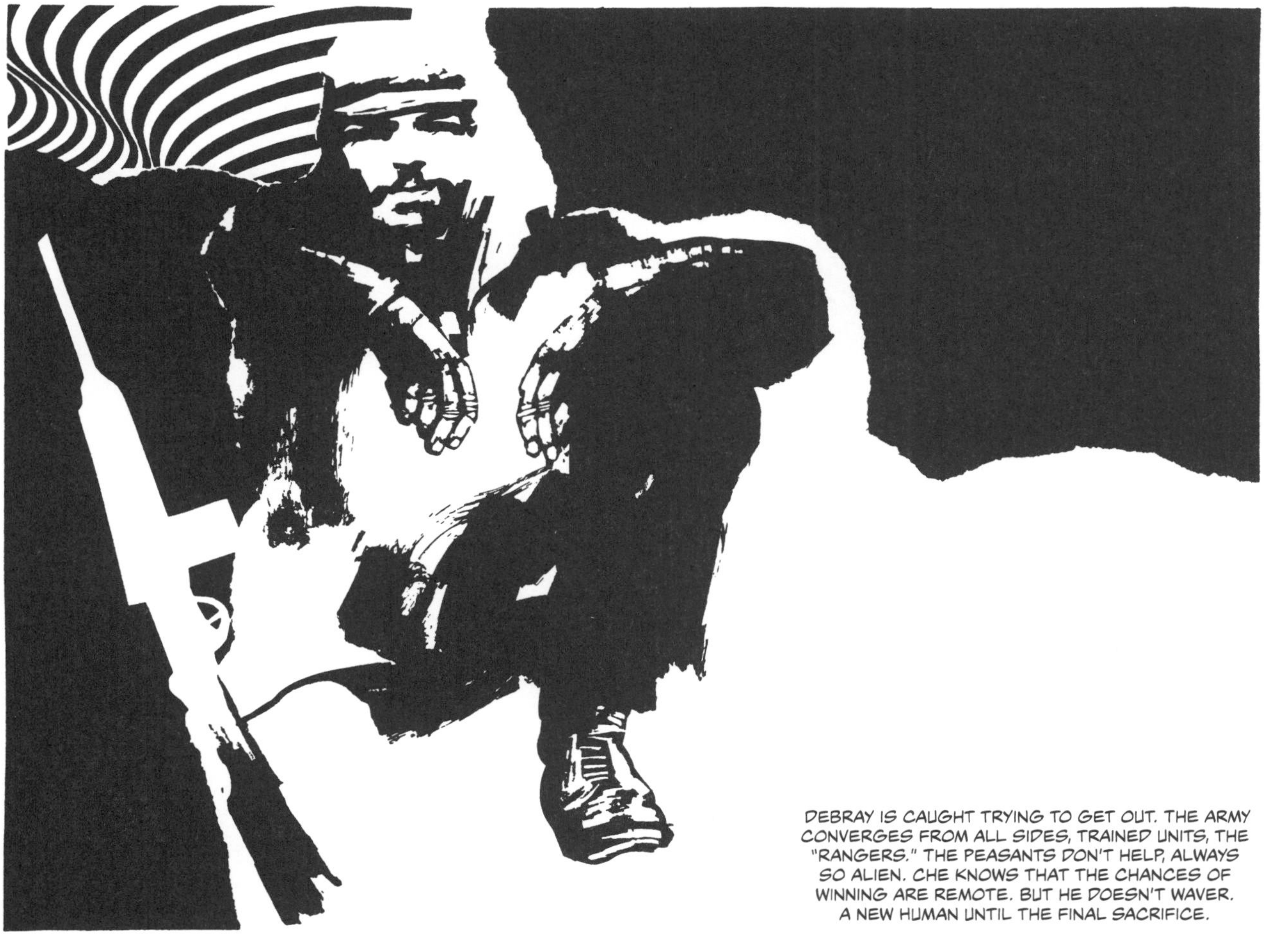
DEBRAY IS CAUGHT TRYING TO GET OUT. THE ARMY CONVERGES FROM ALL SIDES, TRAINED UNITS, THE "RANGERS." THE PEASANTS DON'T HELP, ALWAYS SO ALIEN. CHE KNOWS THAT THE CHANCES OF WINNING ARE REMOTE. BUT HE DOESN'T WAVER. A NEW HUMAN UNTIL THE FINAL SACRIFICE.

THE SEVENTH OF OCTOBER

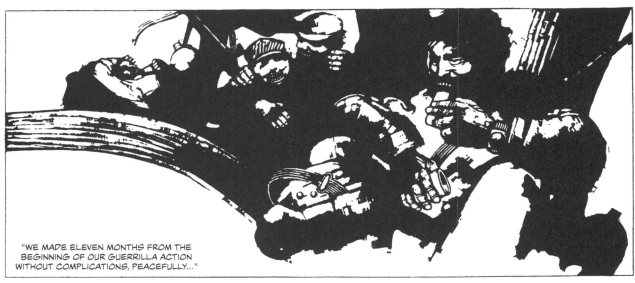

"WE MADE ELEVEN MONTHS FROM THE BEGINNING OF OUR GUERRILLA ACTION WITHOUT COMPLICATIONS, PEACEFULLY..."

SHHH, QUIET, GRANNY. WE'RE NOT GOING TO HURT YOU.

... AN OLD WOMAN HERDING GOATS CAME INTO THE CANYON WHERE OUR ENCAMPMENT WAS AND HAD TO BE DETAINED."

I... I DON'T KNOW ANYTHING... NO, I HAVEN'T SEEN ANY SOLDIERS, I DON'T KNOW ANYTHING...

"SHE DIDN'T WANT TO TALK, BARELY TOLD US ABOUT THE ROADS. WE'RE APPROXIMATELY ONE LEAGUE FROM HIGUERAS AND TWO FROM JAGÜEY..."

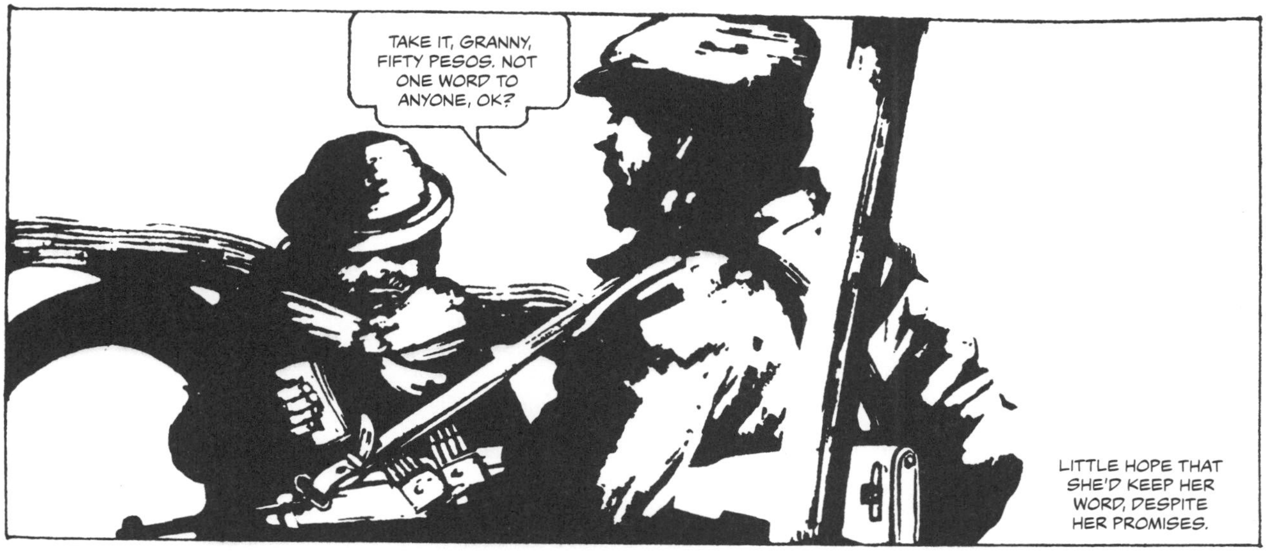
TAKE IT, GRANNY, FIFTY PESOS. NOT ONE WORD TO ANYONE, OK?
LITTLE HOPE THAT SHE'D KEEP HER WORD, DESPITE HER PROMISES.

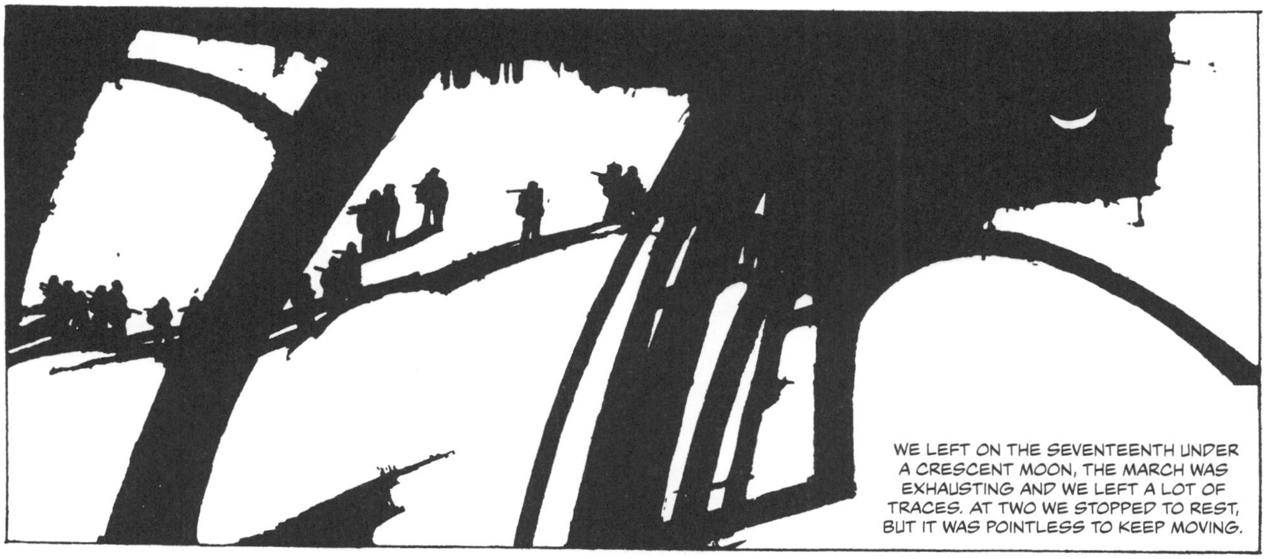
WE LEFT ON THE SEVENTEENTH UNDER A CRESCENT MOON, THE MARCH WAS EXHAUSTING AND WE LEFT A LOT OF TRACES. AT TWO WE STOPPED TO REST, BUT IT WAS POINTLESS TO KEEP MOVING.

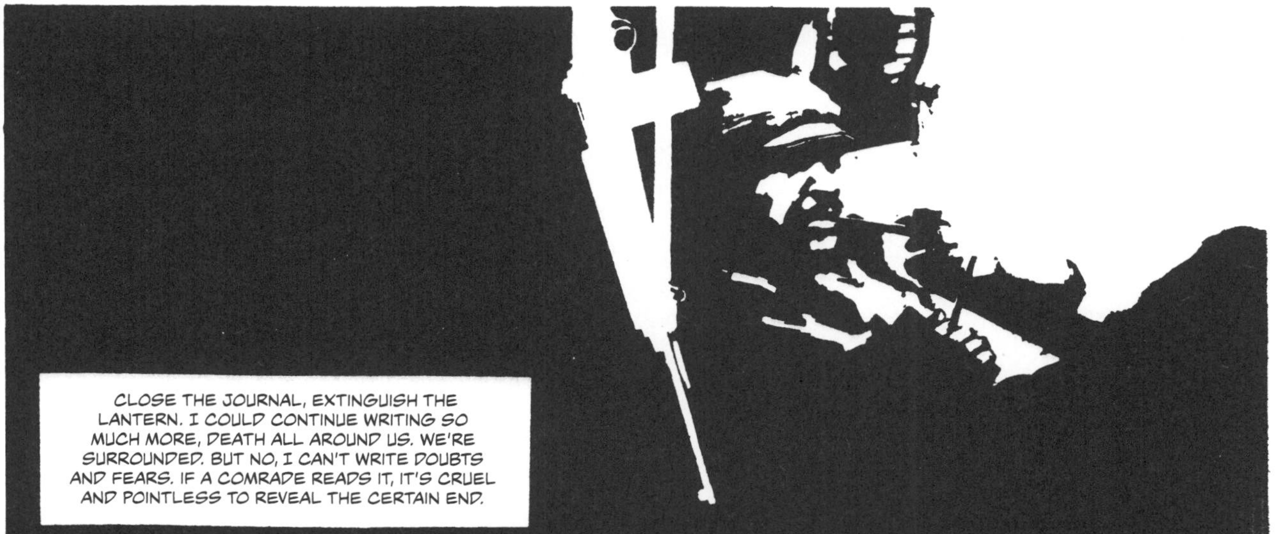
CLOSE THE JOURNAL, EXTINGUISH THE LANTERN. I COULD CONTINUE WRITING SO MUCH MORE, DEATH ALL AROUND US. WE'RE SURROUNDED. BUT NO, I CAN'T WRITE DOUBTS AND FEARS. IF A COMRADE READS IT, IT'S CRUEL AND POINTLESS TO REVEAL THE CERTAIN END.

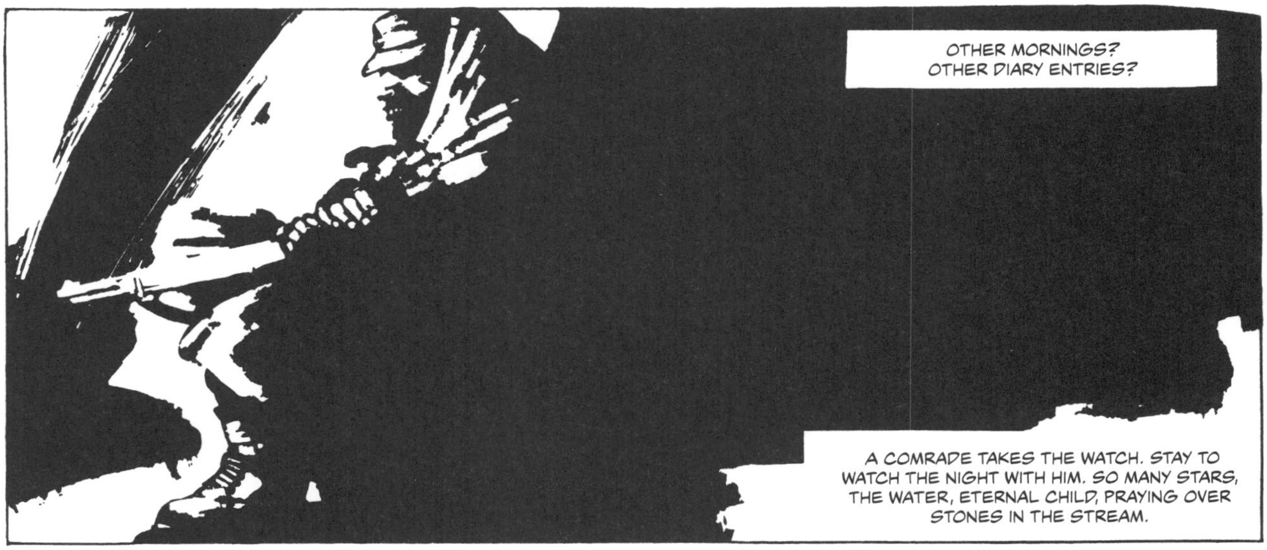
OTHER MORNINGS?
OTHER DIARY ENTRIES?
A COMRADE TAKES THE WATCH. STAY TO WATCH THE NIGHT WITH HIM. SO MANY STARS, THE WATER, ETERNAL CHILD, PRAYING OVER STONES IN THE STREAM.

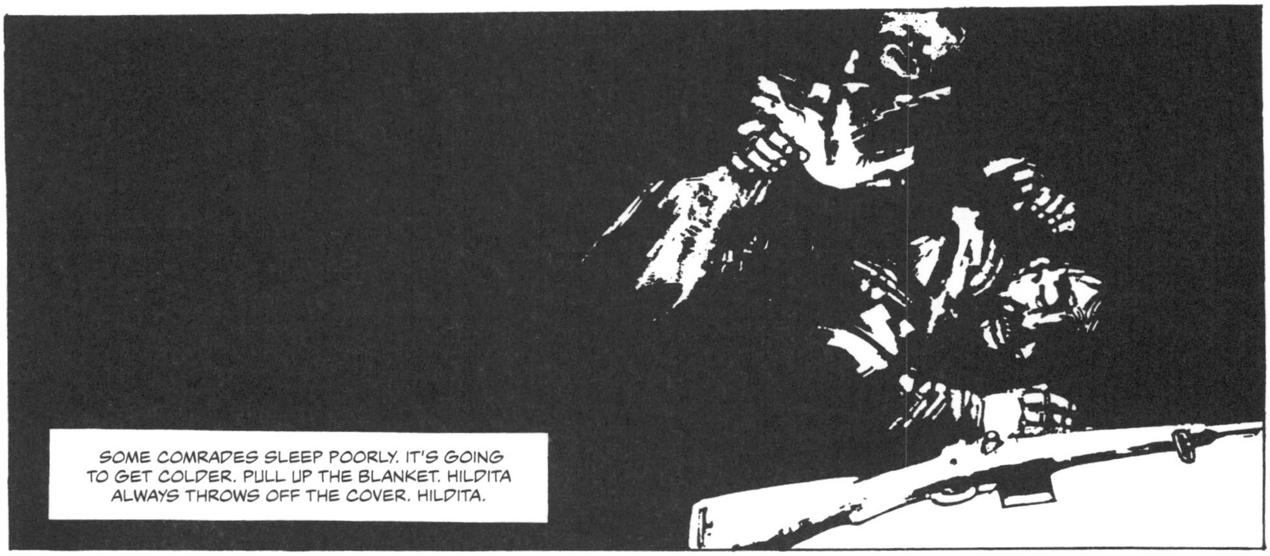
SOME COMRADES SLEEP POORLY. IT'S GOING TO GET COLDER. PULL UP THE BLANKET. HILDITA ALWAYS THROWS OFF THE COVER. HILDITA.

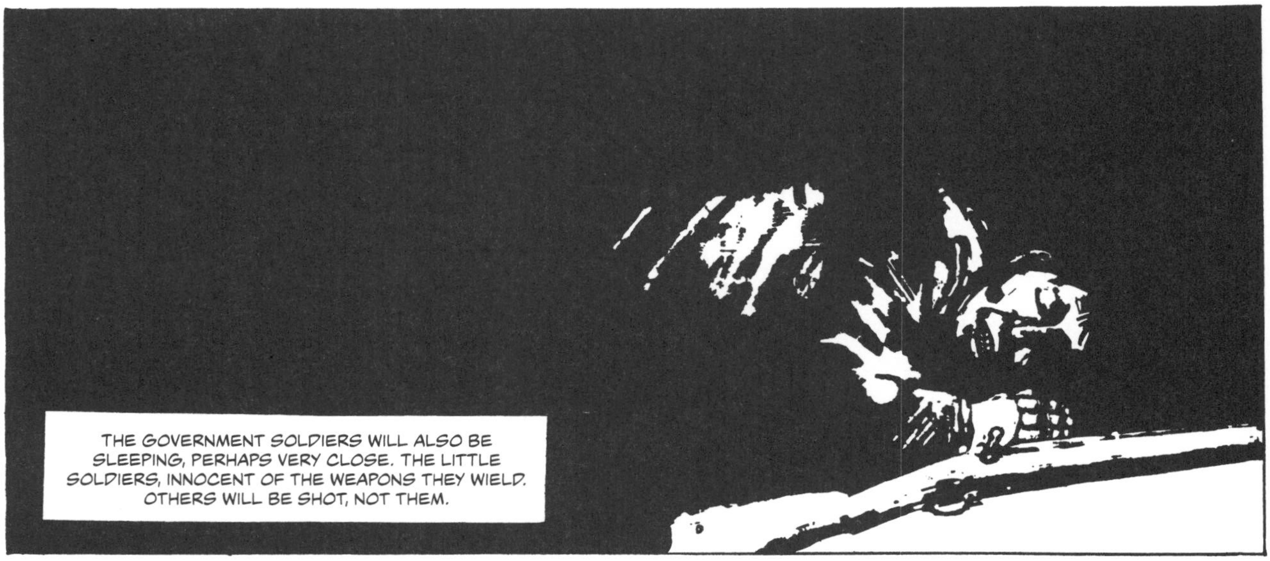
THE GOVERNMENT SOLDIERS WILL ALSO BE SLEEPING, PERHAPS VERY CLOSE. THE LITTLE SOLDIERS, INNOCENT OF THE WEAPONS THEY WIELD. OTHERS WILL BE SHOT, NOT THEM.

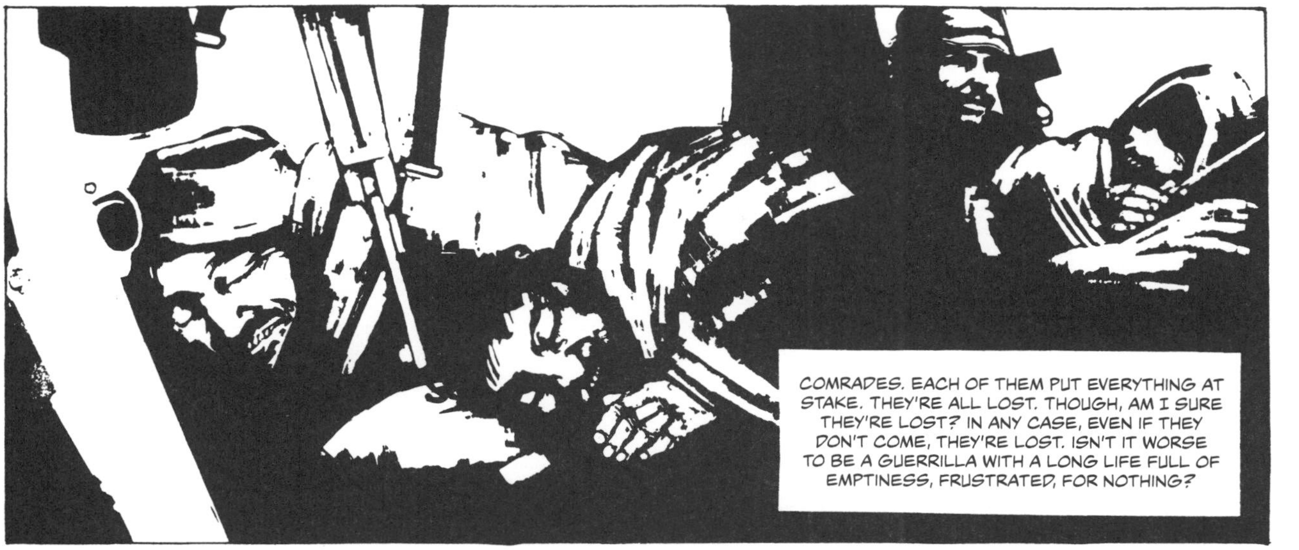
COMRADES. EACH OF THEM PUT EVERYTHING AT STAKE. THEY'RE ALL LOST. THOUGH, AM I SURE THEY'RE LOST? IN ANY CASE, EVEN IF THEY DON'T COME, THEY'RE LOST. ISN'T IT WORSE TO BE A GUERRILLA WITH A LONG LIFE FULL OF EMPTINESS, FRUSTRATED, FOR NOTHING?

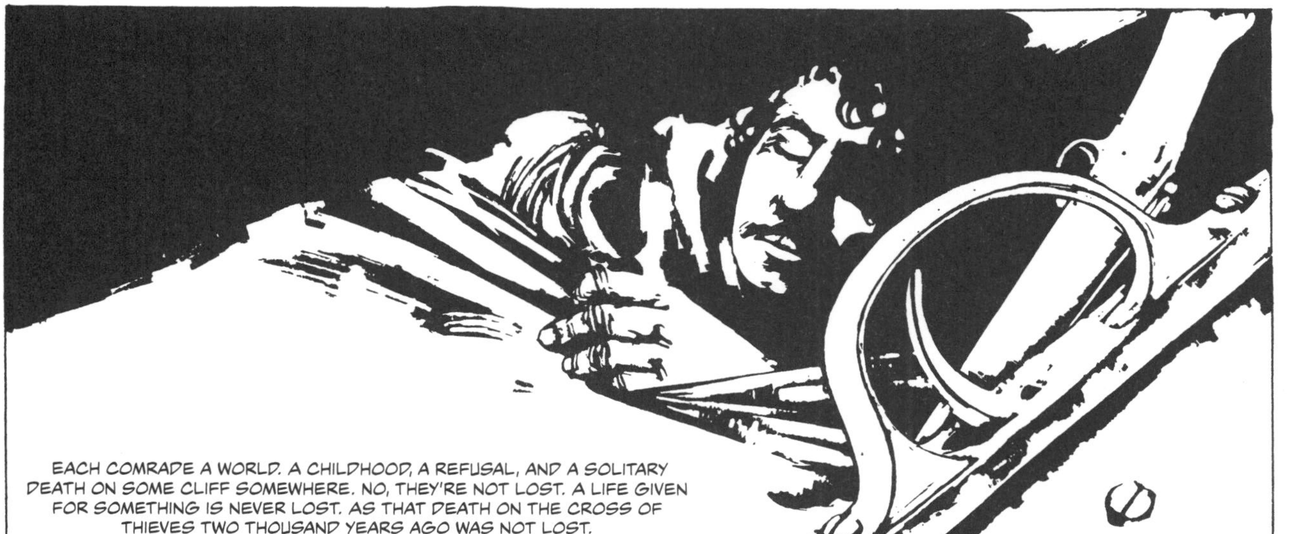
EACH COMRADE A WORLD. A CHILDHOOD, A REFUSAL, AND A SOLITARY DEATH ON SOME CLIFF SOMEWHERE. NO, THEY'RE NOT LOST. A LIFE GIVEN FOR SOMETHING IS NEVER LOST. AS THAT DEATH ON THE CROSS OF THIEVES TWO THOUSAND YEARS AGO WAS NOT LOST.

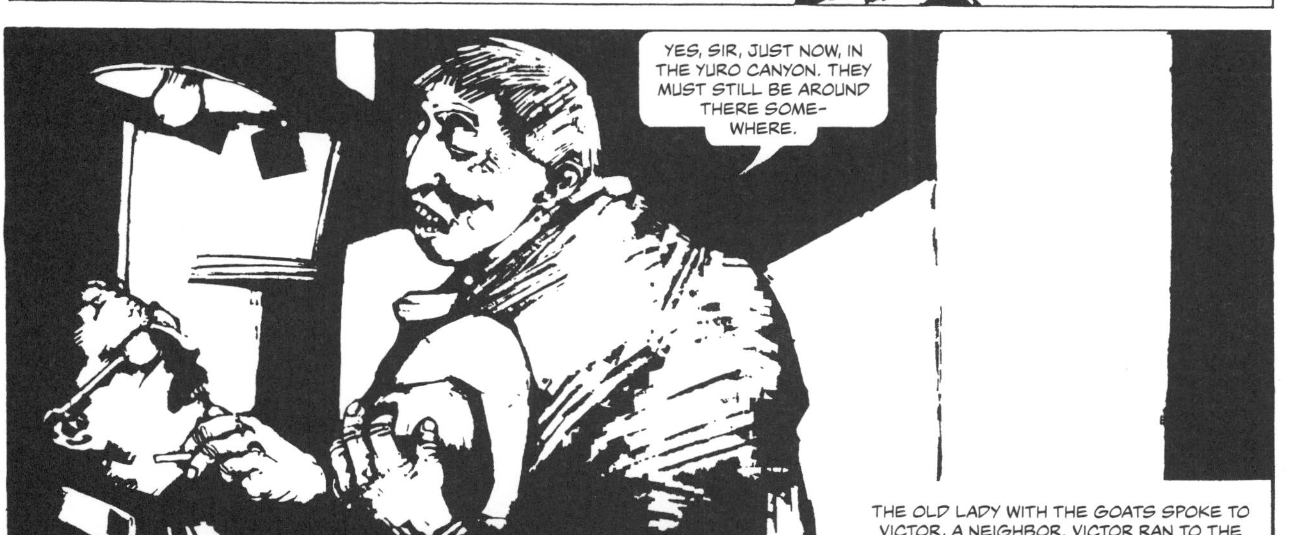
YES, SIR, JUST NOW, IN THE YURO CANYON. THEY MUST STILL BE AROUND THERE SOME-WHERE.
THE OLD LADY WITH THE GOATS SPOKE TO VICTOR, A NEIGHBOR. VICTOR RAN TO THE MILITARY BASE, THE ARMY HAS MONEY.

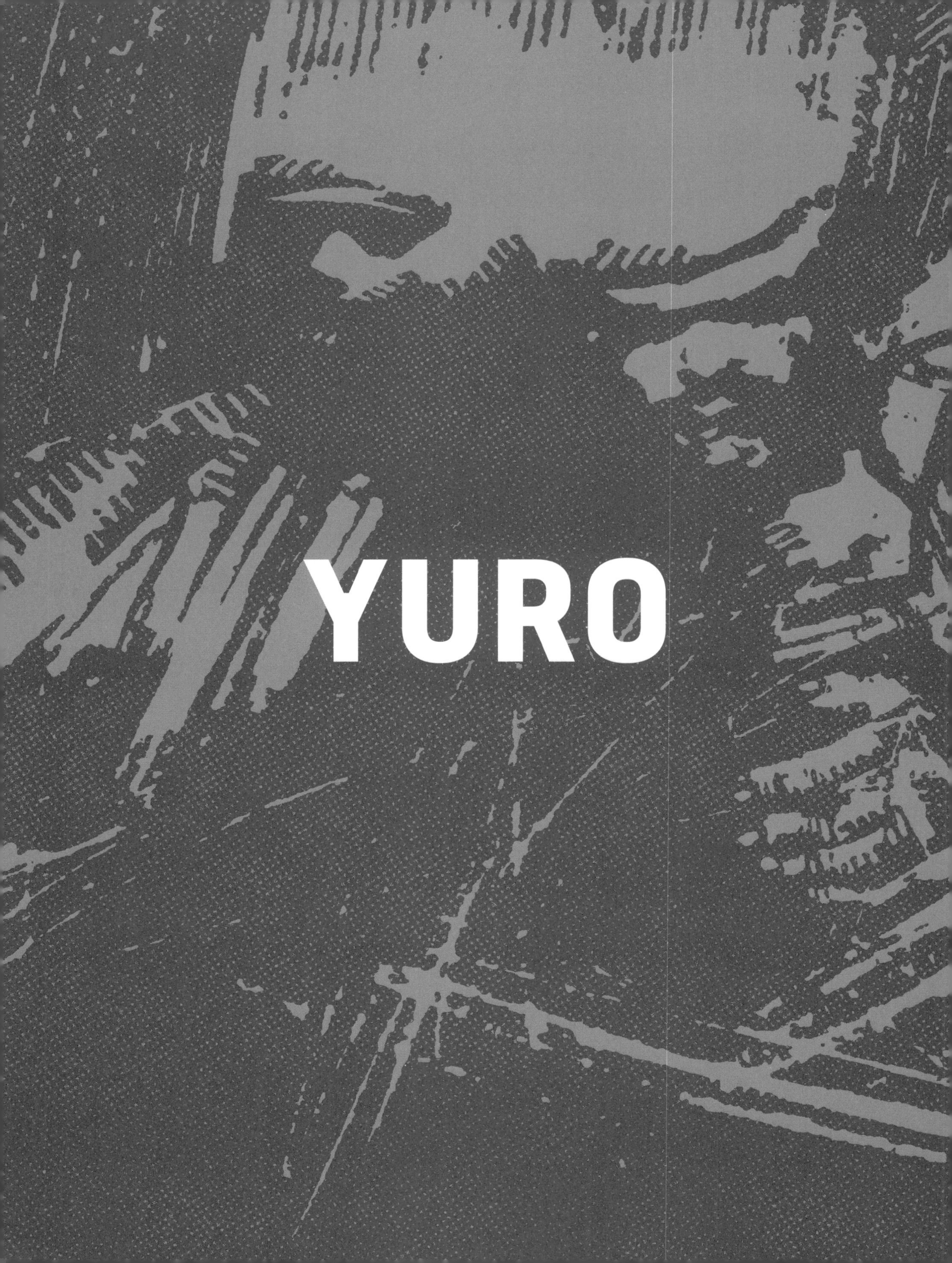

YURO

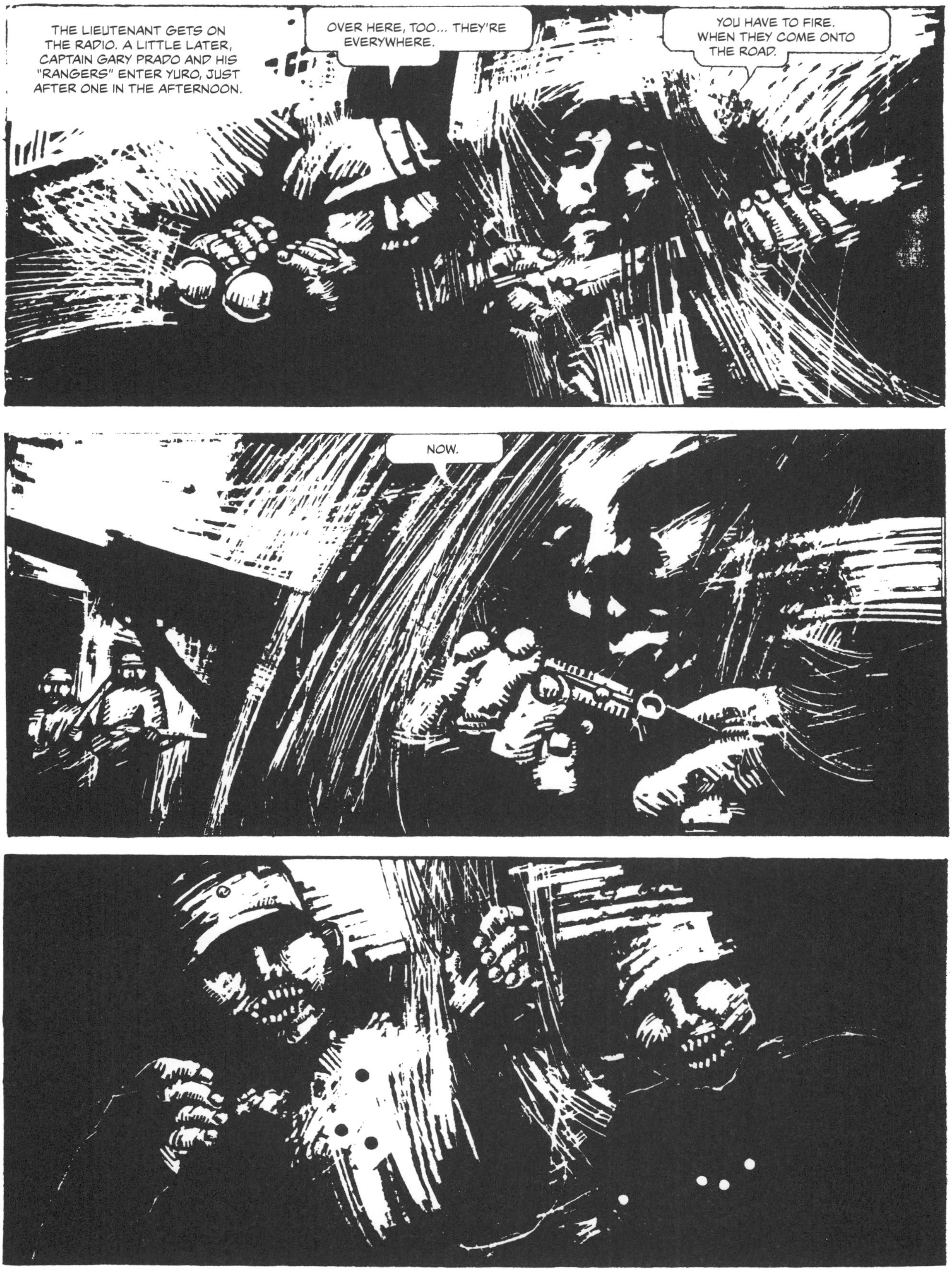
THE LIEUTENANT GETS ON THE RADIO. A LITTLE LATER, CAPTAIN GARY PRADO AND HIS "RANGERS" ENTER YURO, JUST AFTER ONE IN THE AFTERNOON.
OVER HERE, TOO... THEY'RE EVERYWHERE.
YOU HAVE TO FIRE. WHEN THEY COME ONTO THE ROAD.
NOW.

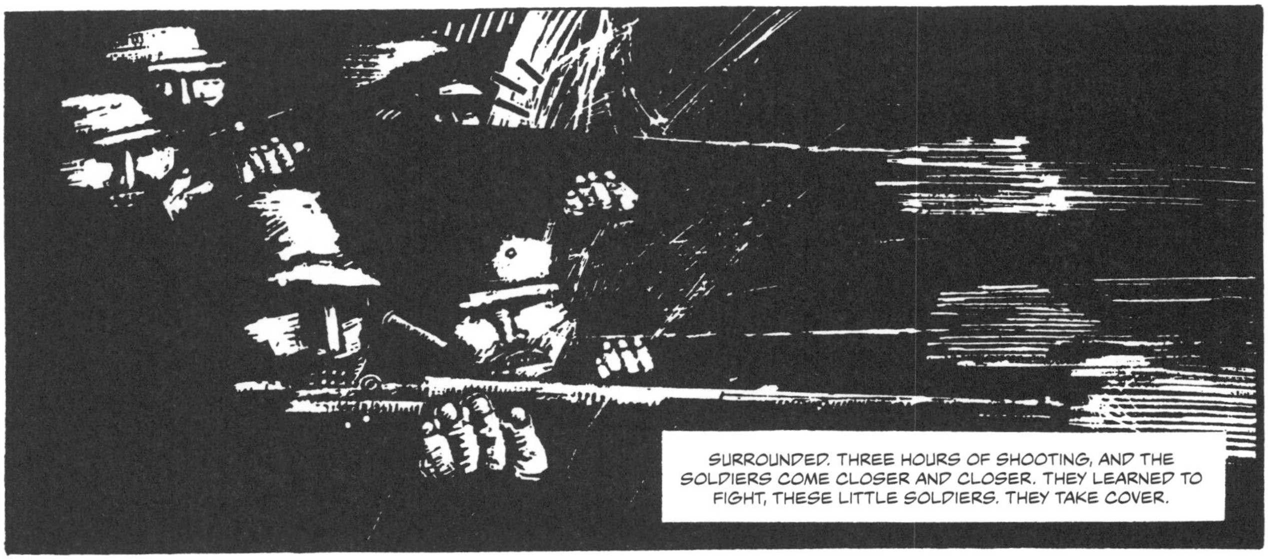
SURROUNDED. THREE HOURS OF SHOOTING, AND THE SOLDIERS COME CLOSER AND CLOSER. THEY LEARNED TO FIGHT, THESE LITTLE SOLDIERS. THEY TAKE COVER.

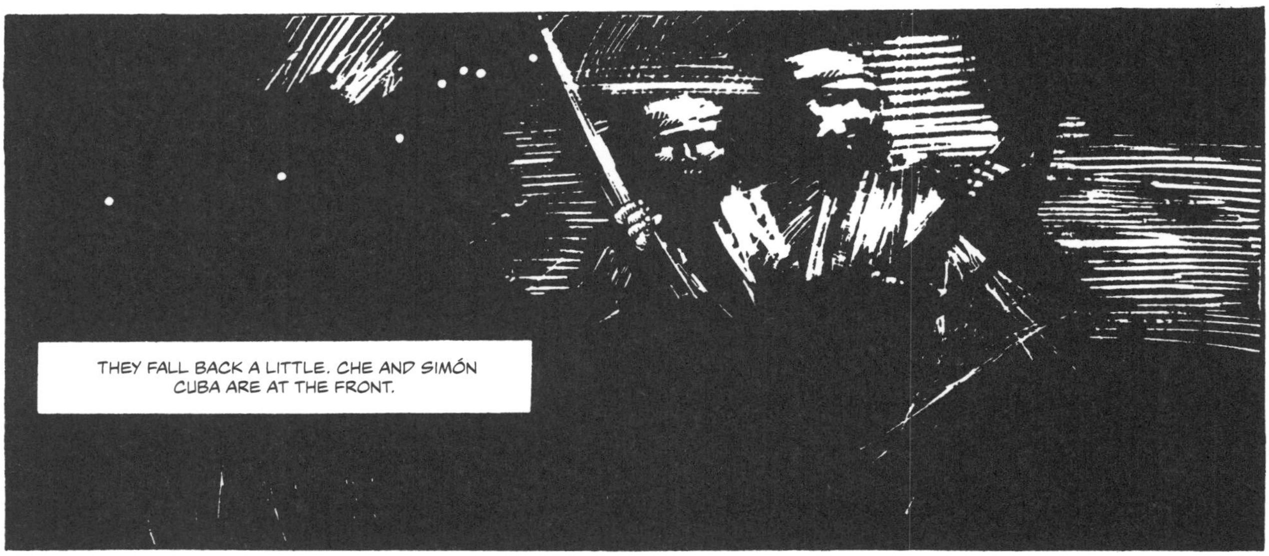
THEY FALL BACK A LITTLE. CHE AND SIMÓN CUBA ARE AT THE FRONT.

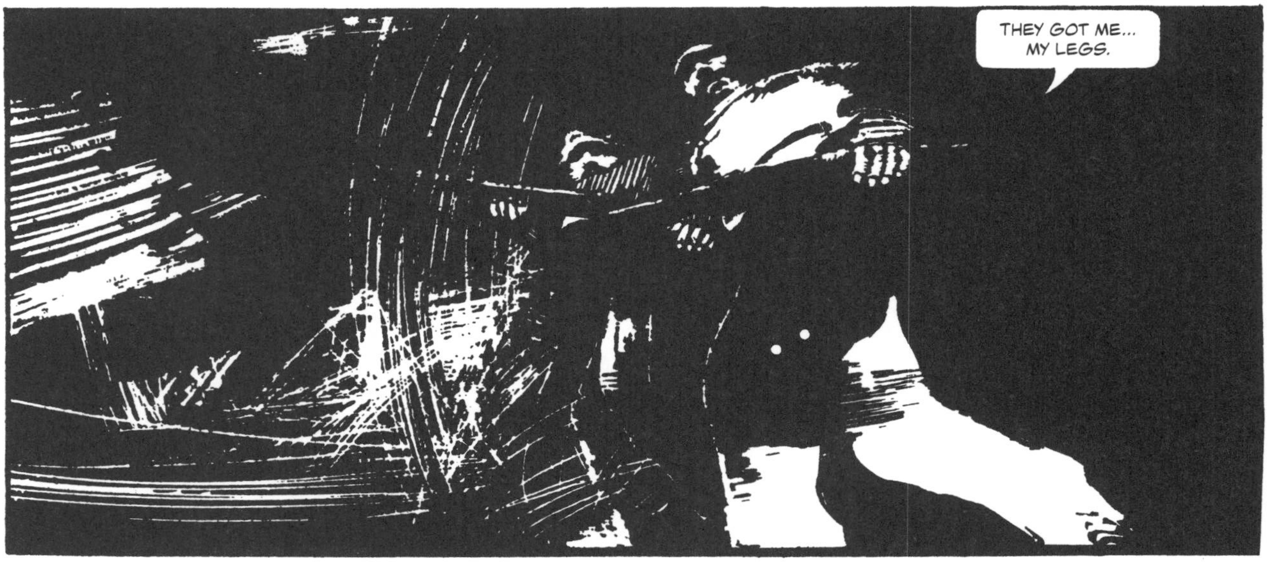
THEY GOT ME... MY LEGS.

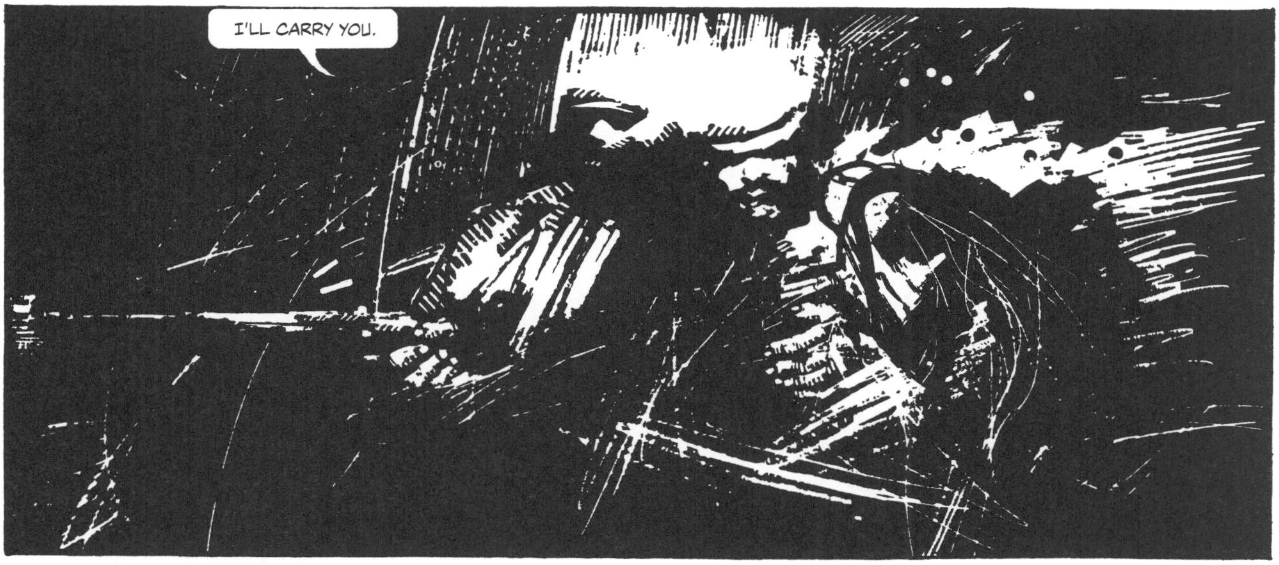
I'LL CARRY YOU.

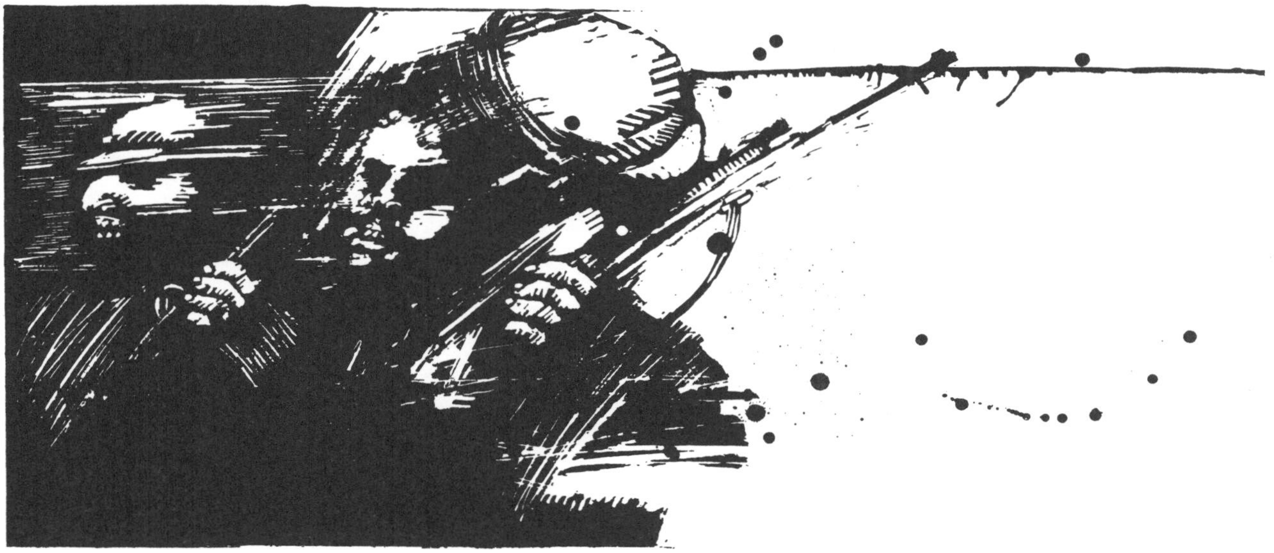

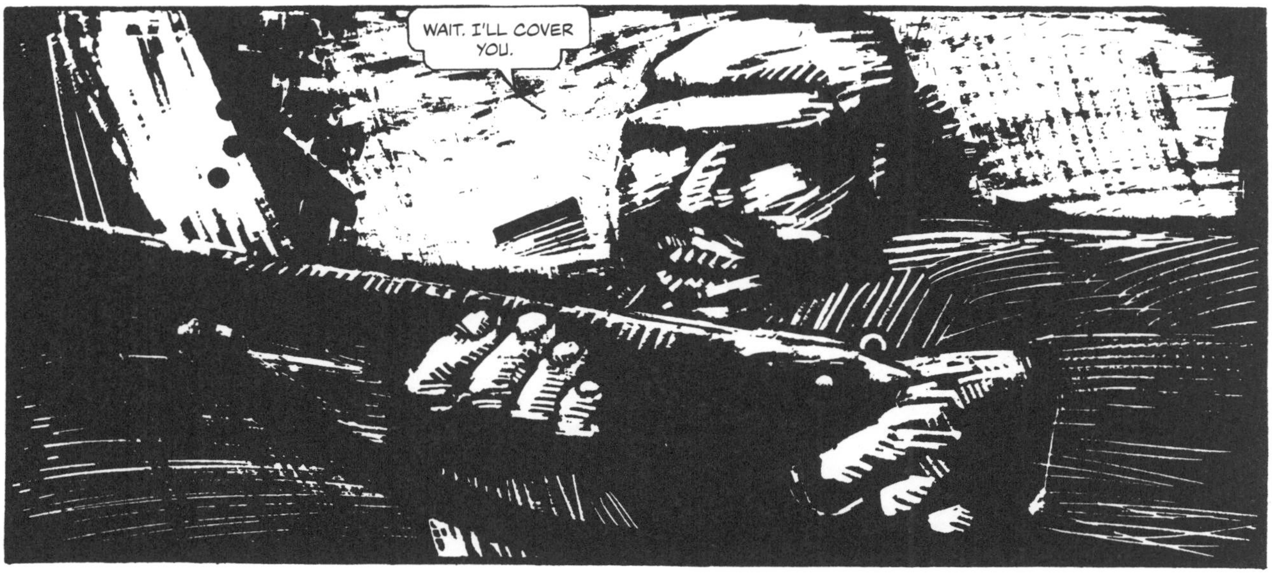
WAIT. I'LL COVER YOU.

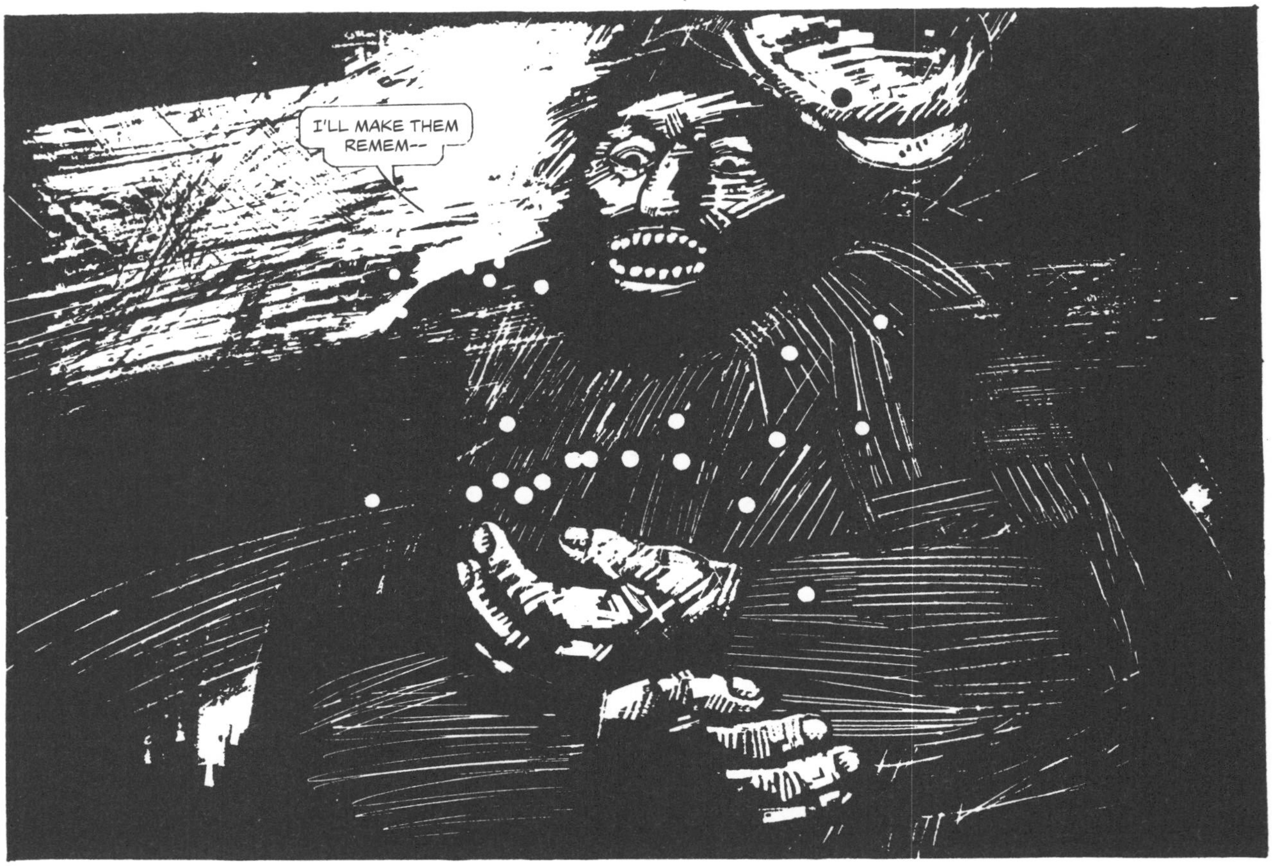
I'LL MAKE THEM REMEM--

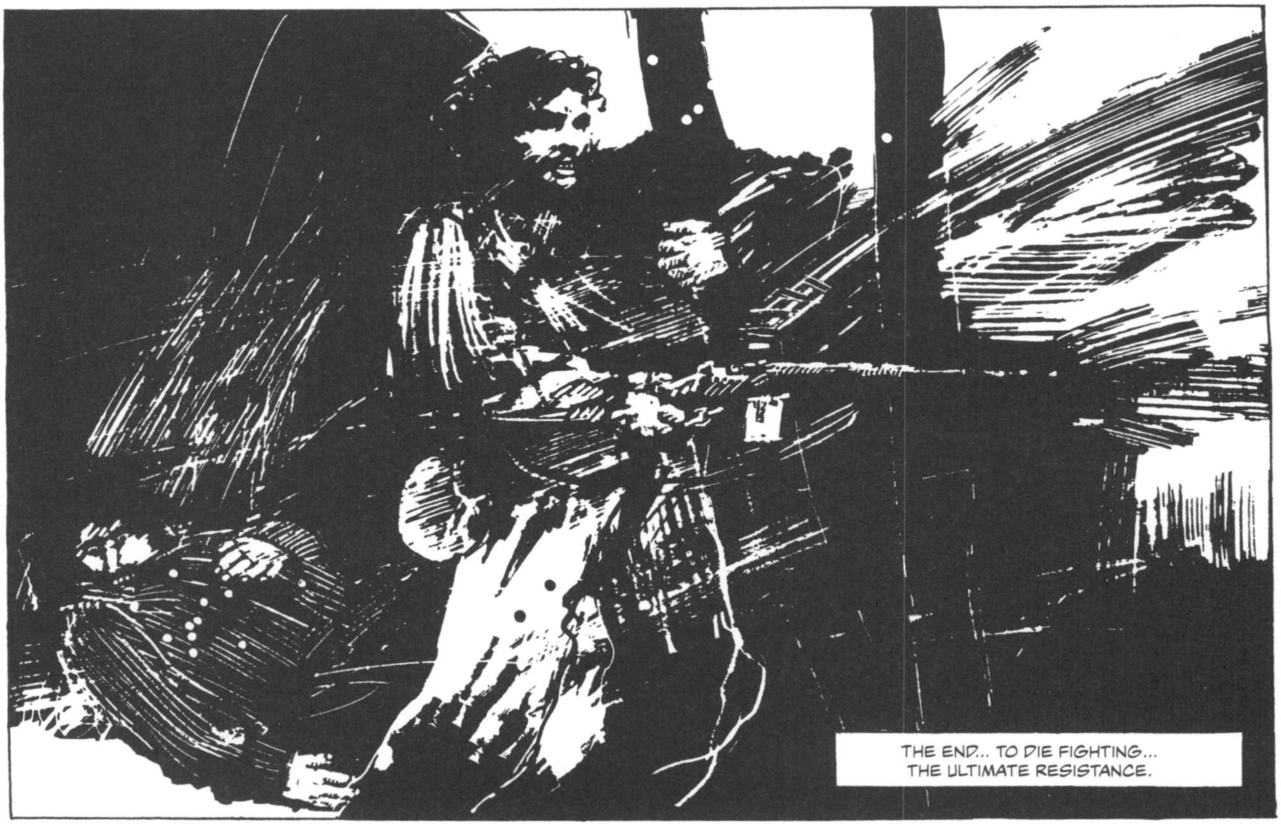
THE END... TO DIE FIGHTING... THE ULTIMATE RESISTANCE.

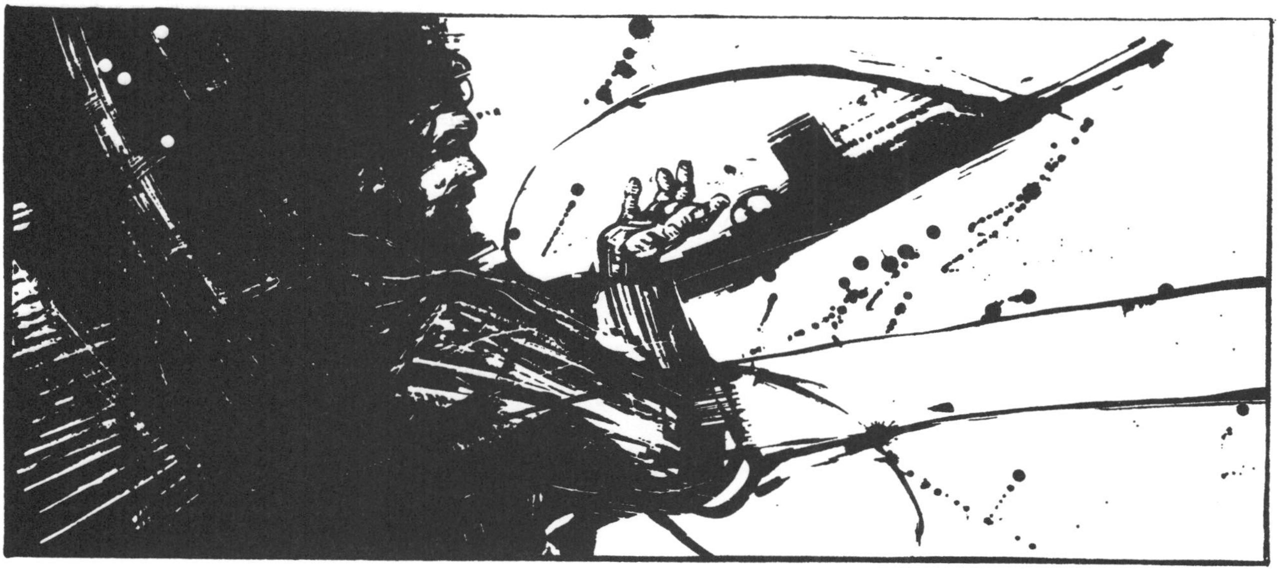
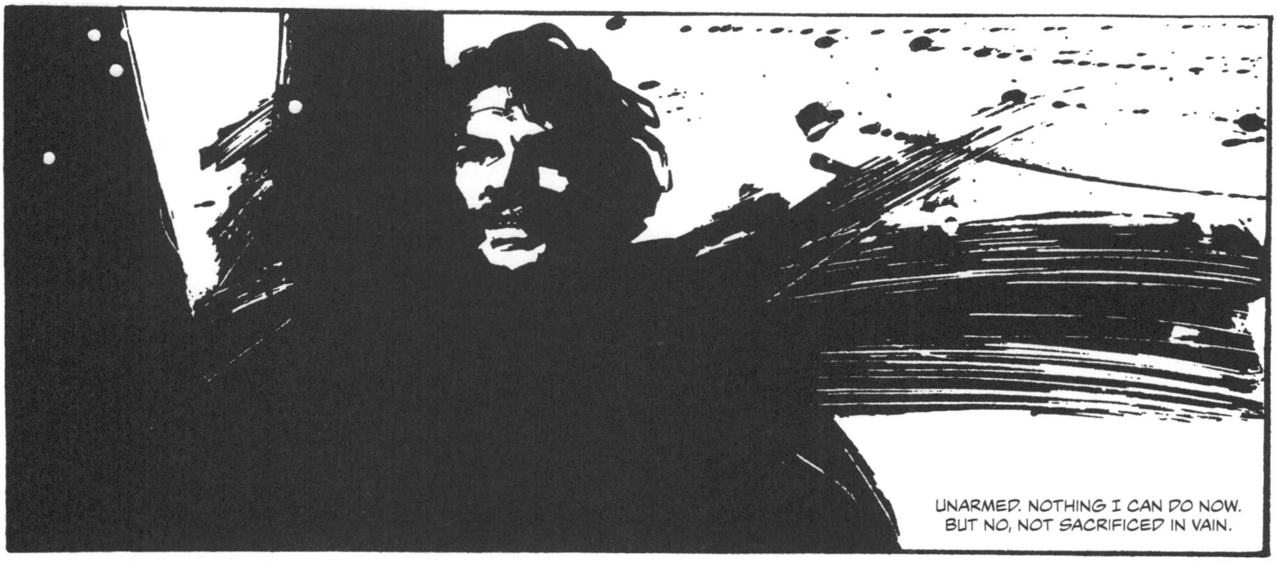
UNARMED. NOTHING I CAN DO NOW.
BUT NO, NOT SACRIFICED IN VAIN.
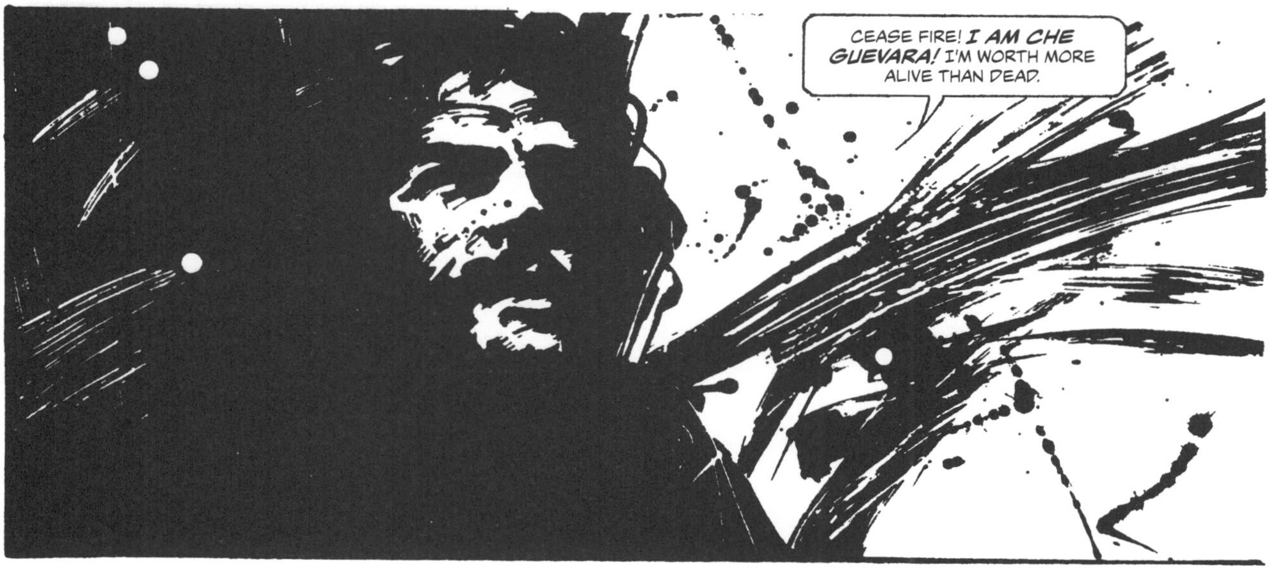
CEASE FIRE! **I AM CHE GUEVARA!** I'M WORTH MORE ALIVE THAN DEAD.

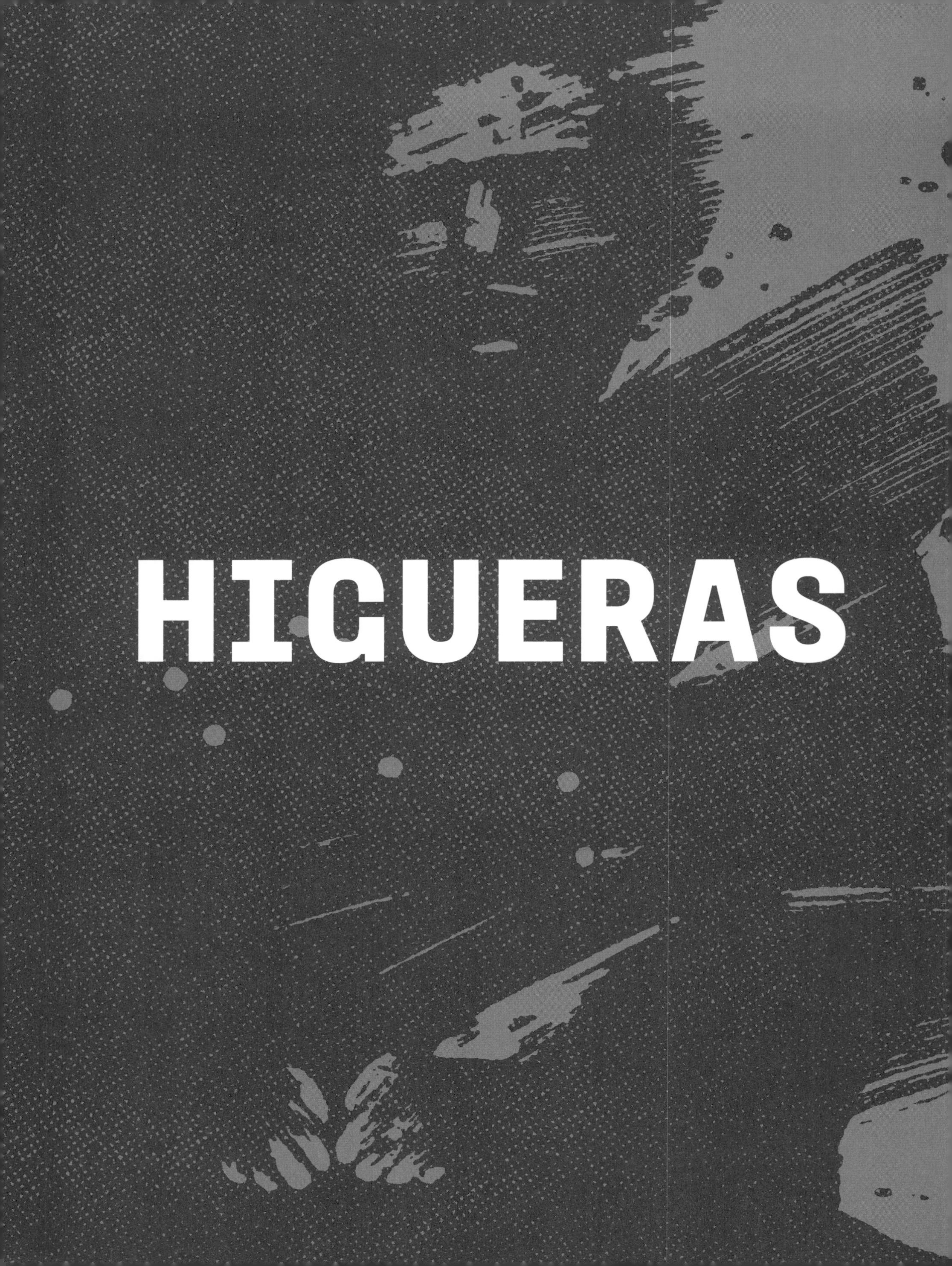

HIGUERAS

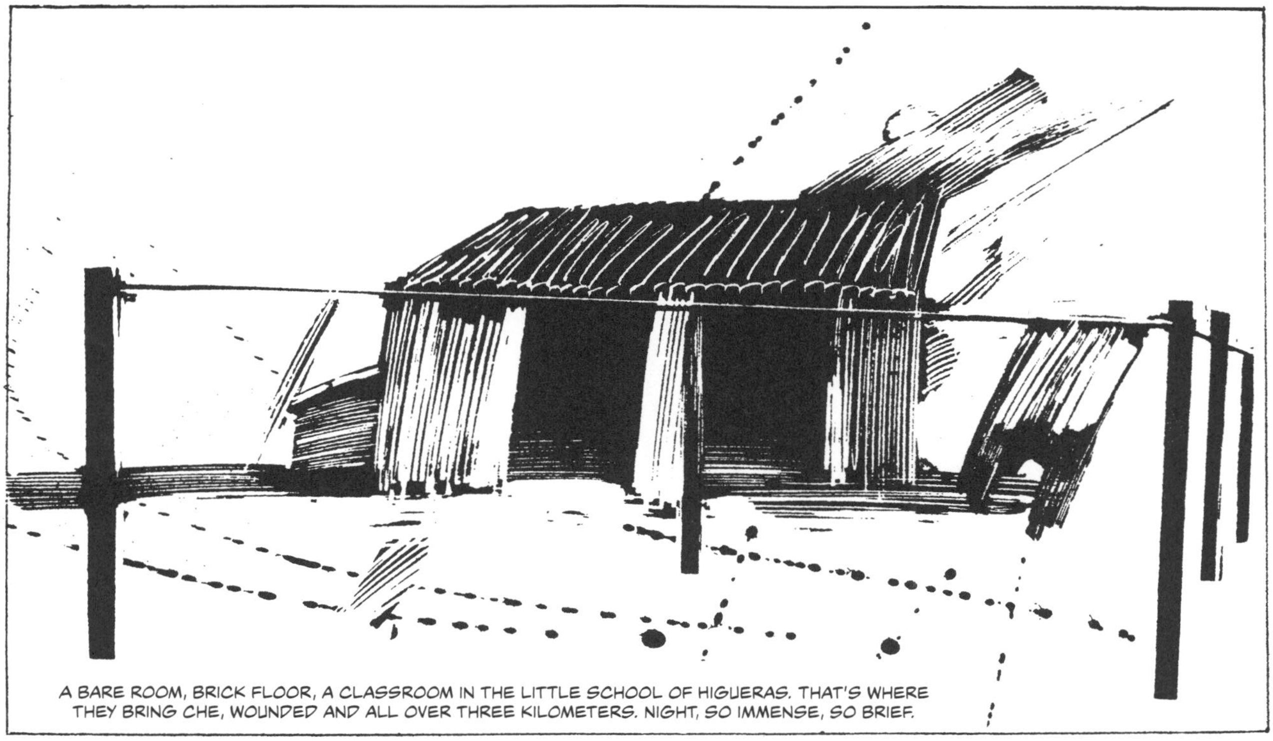
A BARE ROOM, BRICK FLOOR, A CLASSROOM IN THE LITTLE SCHOOL OF HIGUERAS. THAT'S WHERE THEY BRING CHE, WOUNDED AND ALL OVER THREE KILOMETERS. NIGHT, SO IMMENSE, SO BRIEF.

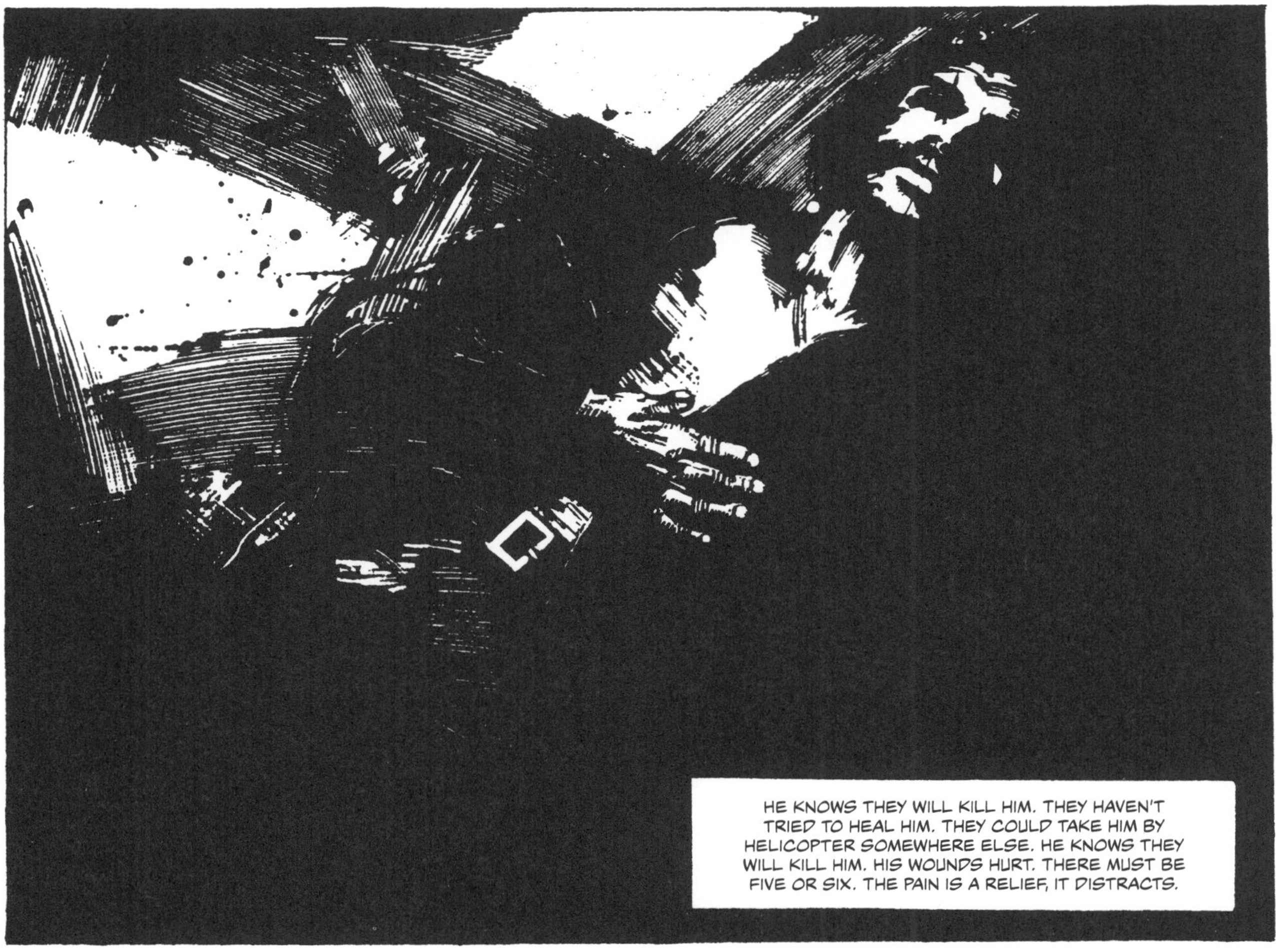
HE KNOWS THEY WILL KILL HIM. THEY HAVEN'T TRIED TO HEAL HIM. THEY COULD TAKE HIM BY HELICOPTER SOMEWHERE ELSE. HE KNOWS THEY WILL KILL HIM. HIS WOUNDS HURT. THERE MUST BE FIVE OR SIX. THE PAIN IS A RELIEF, IT DISTRACTS.

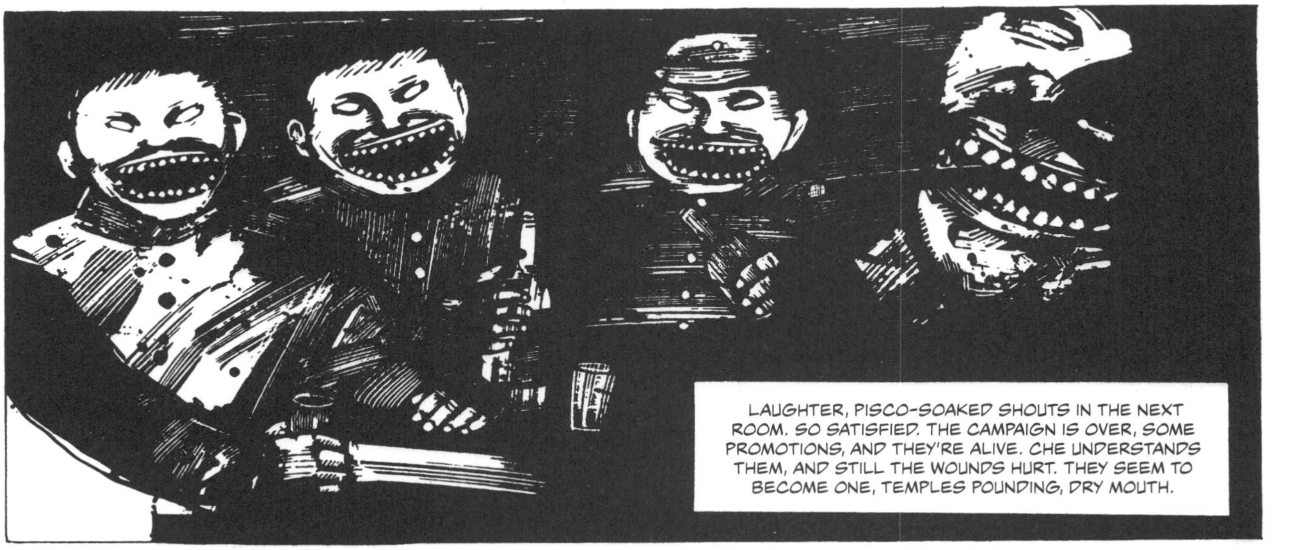
LAUGHTER, PISCO-SOAKED SHOUTS IN THE NEXT ROOM. SO SATISFIED. THE CAMPAIGN IS OVER, SOME PROMOTIONS, AND THEY'RE ALIVE. CHE UNDERSTANDS THEM, AND STILL THE WOUNDS HURT. THEY SEEM TO BECOME ONE, TEMPLES POUNDING, DRY MOUTH.

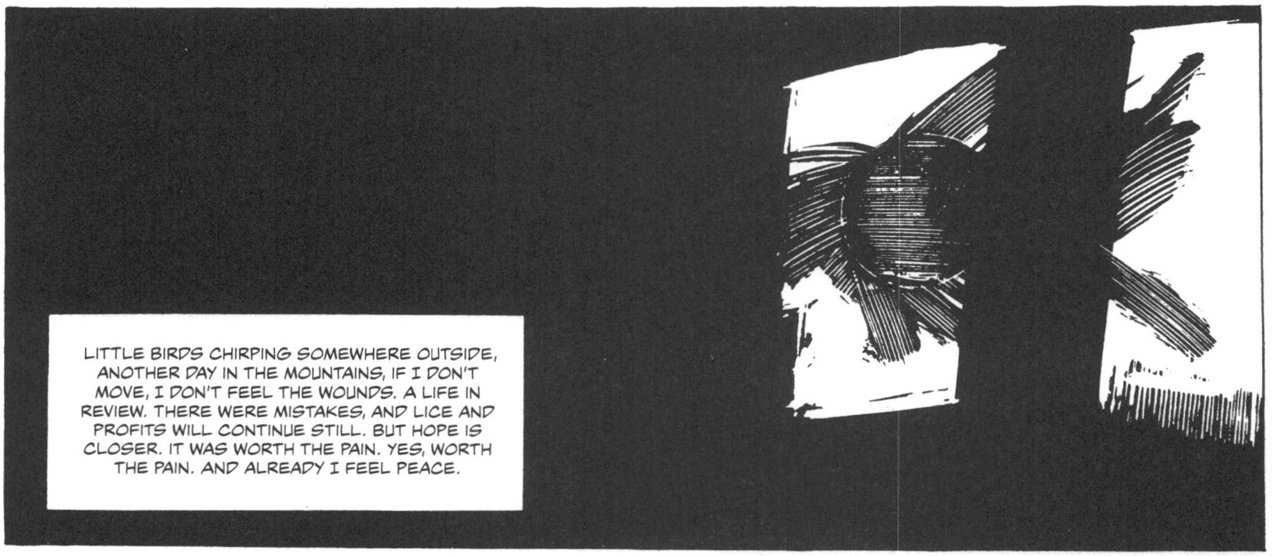
LITTLE BIRDS CHIRPING SOMEWHERE OUTSIDE, ANOTHER DAY IN THE MOUNTAINS, IF I DON'T MOVE, I DON'T FEEL THE WOUNDS. A LIFE IN REVIEW. THERE WERE MISTAKES, AND LICE AND PROFITS WILL CONTINUE STILL. BUT HOPE IS CLOSER. IT WAS WORTH THE PAIN. YES, WORTH THE PAIN. AND ALREADY I FEEL PEACE.

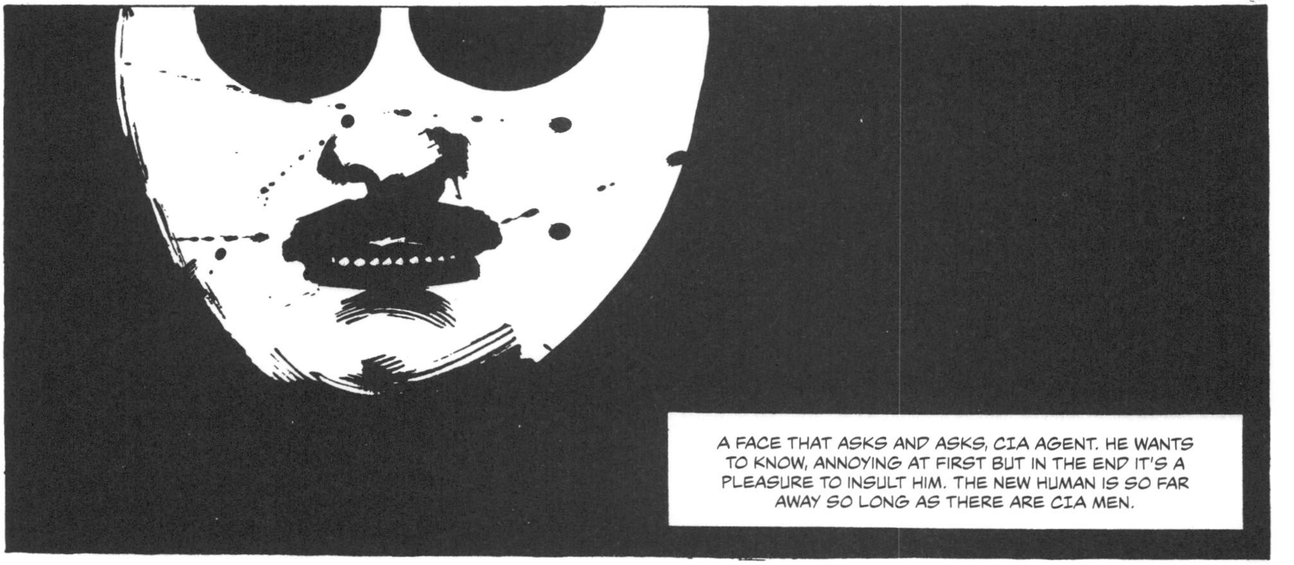
A FACE THAT ASKS AND ASKS, CIA AGENT. HE WANTS TO KNOW, ANNOYING AT FIRST BUT IN THE END IT'S A PLEASURE TO INSULT HIM. THE NEW HUMAN IS SO FAR AWAY SO LONG AS THERE ARE CIA MEN.

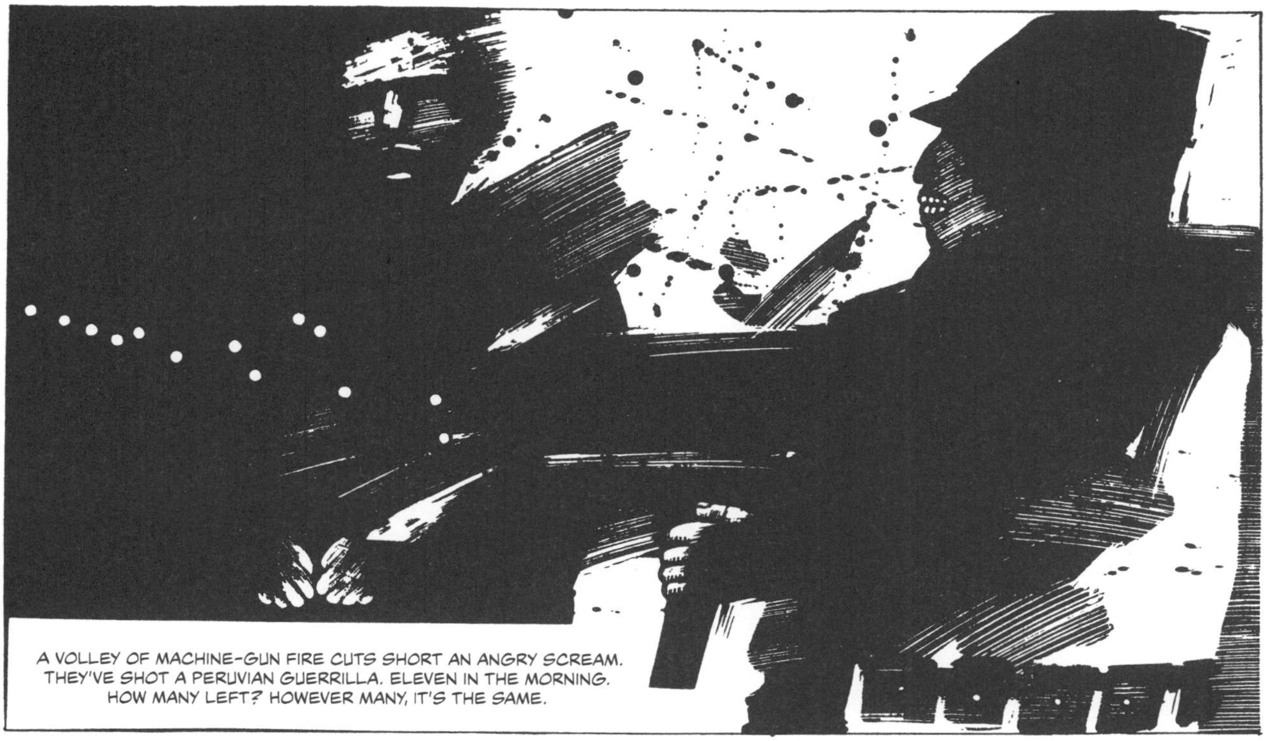
A VOLLEY OF MACHINE-GUN FIRE CUTS SHORT AN ANGRY SCREAM. THEY'VE SHOT A PERUVIAN GUERRILLA. ELEVEN IN THE MORNING. HOW MANY LEFT? HOWEVER MANY, IT'S THE SAME.

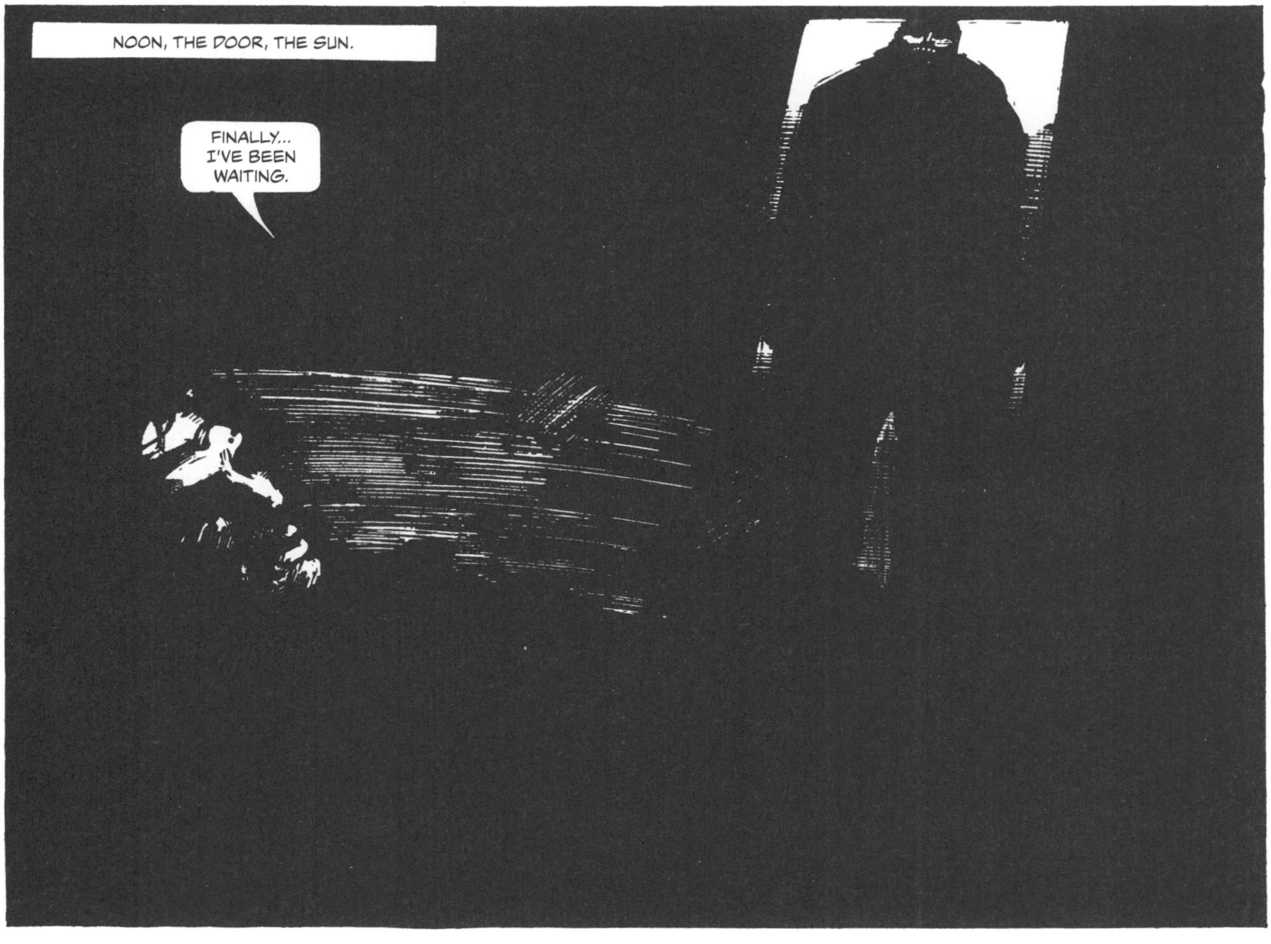
NOON, THE DOOR, THE SUN.
FINALLY... I'VE BEEN WAITING.

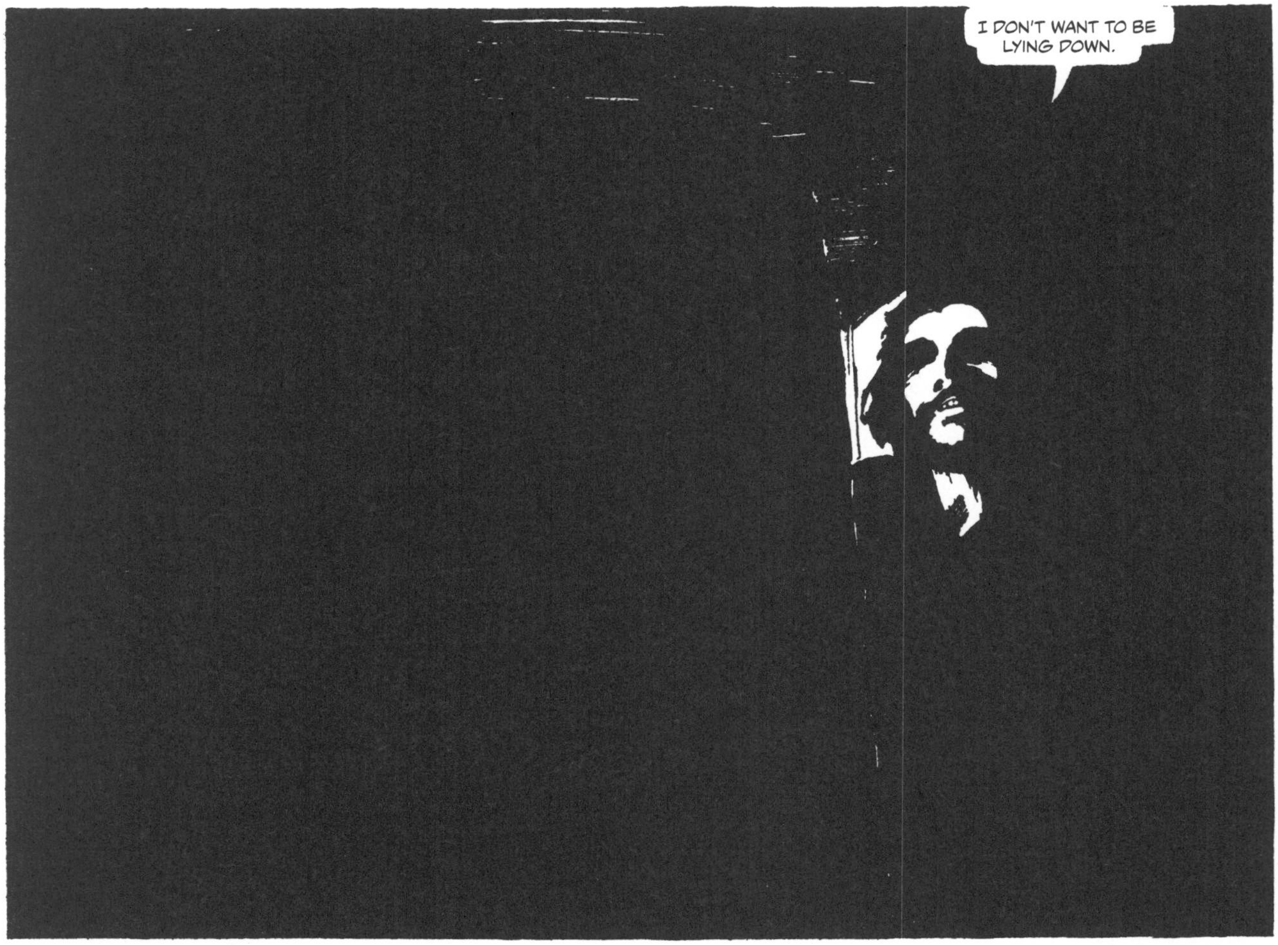
I DON'T WANT TO BE LYING DOWN.

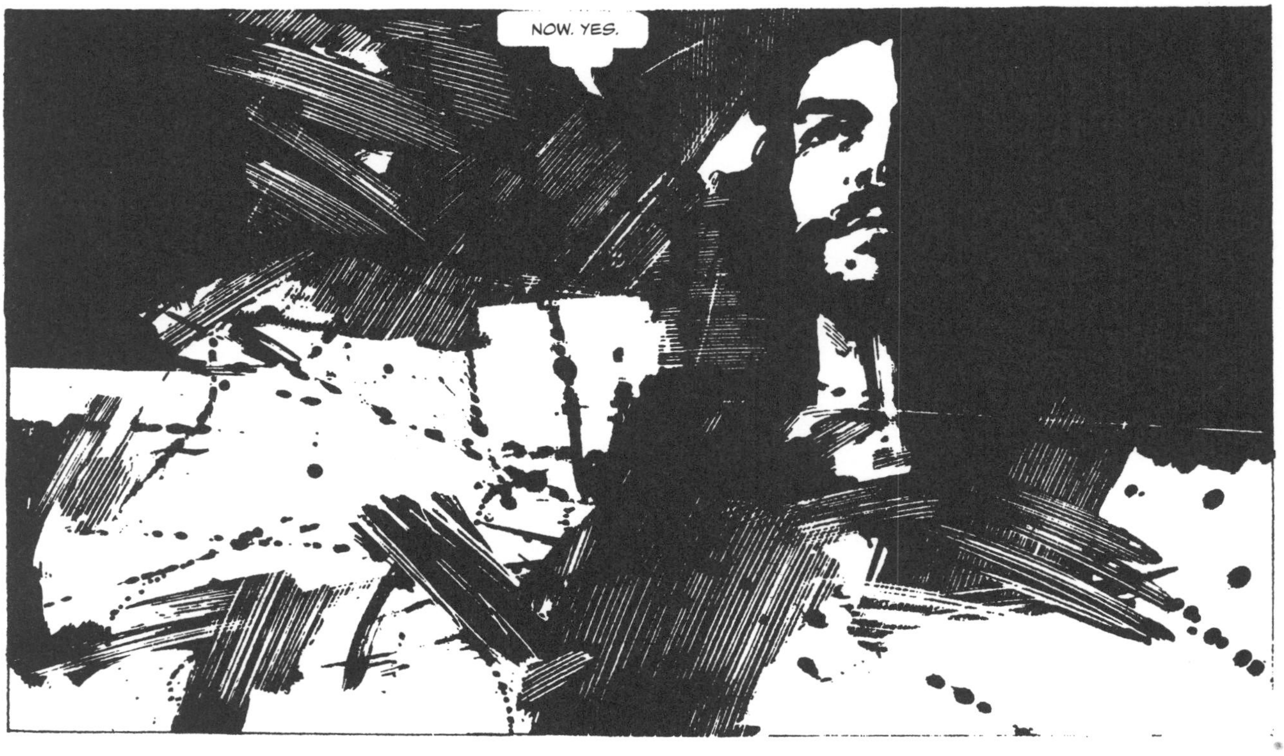
NOW. YES.

FIRE.

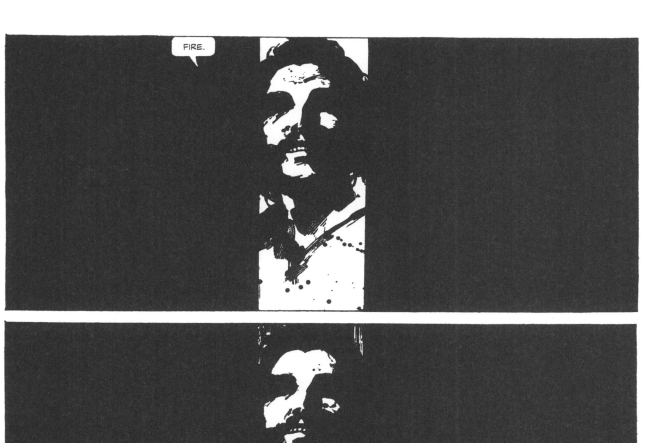

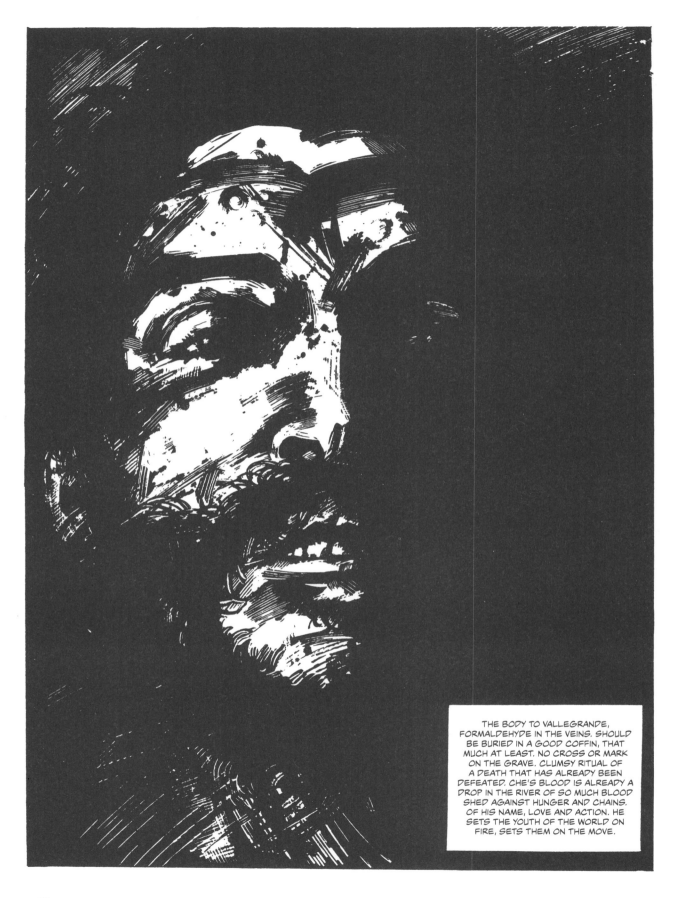

THE BODY TO VALLEGRANDE,
FORMALDEHYDE IN THE VEINS. SHOULD
BE BURIED IN A GOOD COFFIN, THAT
MUCH AT LEAST. NO CROSS OR MARK
ON THE GRAVE. CLUMSY RITUAL OF
A DEATH THAT HAS ALREADY BEEN
DEFEATED. CHE'S BLOOD IS ALREADY A
DROP IN THE RIVER OF SO MUCH BLOOD
SHED AGAINST HUNGER AND CHAINS.
OF HIS NAME, LOVE AND ACTION. HE
SETS THE YOUTH OF THE WORLD ON
FIRE, SETS THEM ON THE MOVE.

AFTERW

In 1969, Argentina was in turmoil: in 1966, members of the military had carried out a coup, calling it the Argentine Revolution and claiming to be engaged in a long-term project to restore the authority of the upper classes. General Juan Carlos Onganía, representing the conservative sectors of the Argentine Army, seized power as the *de facto* president. His administration strove to advance Argentina's development process by aligning the country with the United States in the Cold War context. Its anti-Peronist and anticommunist stances provoked domestic tensions that threatened the stability of the regime: widespread censorship, police brutality against labor activism, the impoverishment of the working classes, and a growing political radicalization, inspired by the Cuban Revolution, that saw the use of violence as a legitimate means to real change. By 1969, a mere three years after his rise to power, Onganía's presidency was falling apart.

January of that same year saw the publication of a work that, in the words of Héctor Germán Oesterheld, explored the "unexploited" possibilities of the adventure genre — that is, comics as a political and ideological weapon. The idea of making a comic about the life of Che Guevara had come out of a meeting between the editor Jorge Álvarez and comics artist Alberto Breccia a few months earlier, but the differing accounts suggest some tension and conflict over intellectual property and its meanings. According to Breccia, he had already completed some work — or was at least actively interested in the topic — at the time of his 1968 meeting with Álvarez at the First World Comics Biennial at the Di Tella Institute (an avant-garde artistic center in downtown Buenos Aires). It is most likely, however, that the idea originated with Álvarez, who was looking to publish a series of "illustrated lives" of major historical figures from North and South America. This innovative idea was a bid to capitalize on the Latin Americanist and revolutionary zeitgeist, dubiously tying together historical figures who could not have been farther apart in terms of time, space, and ideology. The inclusion of a John F. Kennedy biography alongside ones on Fidel Castro and Augusto César Sandino had all the subtlety of a bull in a china shop.

What was the reason for such incongruity? It was clearly a clumsy attempt to evade government censorship by introducing the name of the U.S. president as a kind of progressive representative of the North, and thus "disguise" the subversive rhetoric incorporated into the comics version of Che Guevara's life. One indication of this attempt at camouflage is that the edition was released not under the name of Jorge Álvarez's publishing house but under the nonexistent Ediko label, with no other credits given besides the names of the authors and the printers. Even the prologue was signed by E. V., the initialism for the semiologist and renowned intellectual Eliseo Verón, without further clarification. Everyone involved was all too aware that such a project was a risky affair at the time. The comic was scheduled for publication in October 1968 but ended up coming out in January 1969. Oesterheld remarked that even though the comic was released on a date when fewer students were around — January is the month when everybody goes on summer vacation in the southern hemisphere — the print run sold out quickly.

Oesterheld's comment offers two insights: first, the comic was aimed at a young, largely student audience; second, the fact that *Vida del Che* (Life of Che) sold out even when less of that demographic was seemingly available could suggest that the audience was expanding beyond the core at which the comic was initially targeted. Álvarez clearly knew what he was doing: a biographical comic on a major figure like Che in that context, just over a year after his death in Bolivia, with incredible art throughout, was bound to achieve its goal. Soon after, the publishing house was raided by government forces, and all publication materials were seized — including the

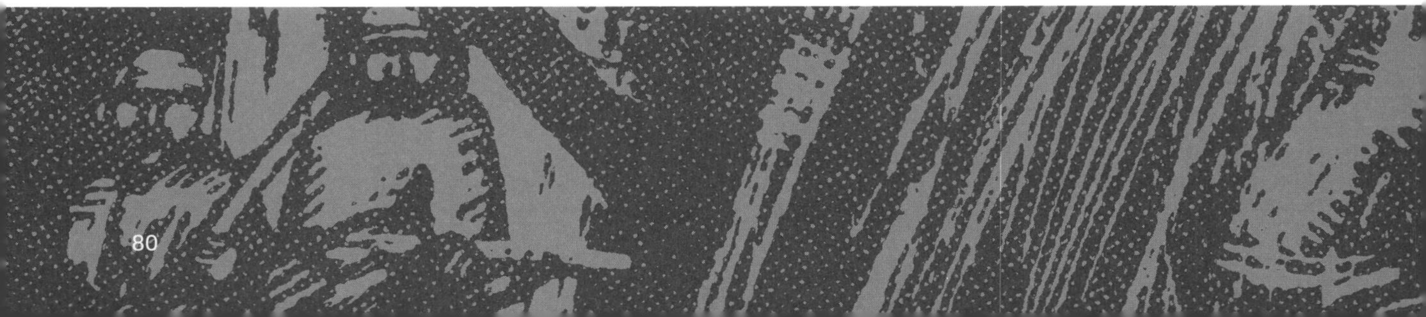

BY PABLO TURNES

original pages of *Life of Che* — and presumably destroyed, though their fate was never clear.

A REVOLUTIONARY PEDAGOGY

Although a certain romanticized version of the story tends to cast the government raid as a specific operation targeted against the comic, in fact the publisher and its entire catalog were in the authorities' crosshairs. When the Che comic was released, they finally decided to intervene. Some years later, Alberto Breccia offered his account of events to the Spanish magazine *Bang!*: "It was a bad deal financially speaking, but very nice to do it. *Life of Che* provoked a huge wave of opinion, especially within the Onganía administration; an editorial bashing me was even published in *La Nación* newspaper. That caused the United States embassy to buy it, and from there the Embassy alerted the [State Intelligence Secretariat (SIDE)], who came to my house and opened a file on me. The Embassy called me, called us to congratulate us and ask us to make [a comic about] Kennedy's life, which we never did, even though they paid for the publication.... And then the Army — even as the SINE [sic] was classifying me as a subversive element — asked me to do a 'History of the Argentine Army' to distribute among the soldiers. I asked for a very high price per page and then never did it.... [*Life of Che*] was only available for a very short time; it ended up being confiscated and burned, the originals too... Everything."

In an interview with comics writers Carlos Trillo and Guillermo Saccomanno shortly before his kidnapping and disappearance, Oesterheld agreed with Breccia when recalling both the actions of the SIDE and the editorial published in the conservative newspaper *La Nación*, which had probably served as a wake-up call to the authorities. According to Oesterheld, the editorial "talked about the danger of publicizing a revolutionary figure like Che." And he

detailed his contact with the intelligence services: "They called my house several times; they had to have been from the SIDE, looking for information. Knowing that they were going to get it anyway, I gave them what they wanted."

However, the comics writer disagreed with some crucial elements of the artist's version: "In that *Bang!* interview, Breccia says the American embassy wanted to buy it. The real story is this: the Embassy called me, not him. I must have told him about it and then, with that habit that cartoonists have of taking over..." These tensions gave the comic an interesting dynamic, since they not only led its creators to take a political-ideological stance but also created a community of voices that included two comics artists, a scriptwriter, an editor, and a semiologist. Breccia admitted to feeling a bit of a thrill at the possibility of needling the authorities. Oesterheld described his decision to acknowledge his authorial role as a deliberate one. When the editor suggested publishing the comic anonymously, Oesterheld was adamant: "Not only do I want to publish it under my name, I want my name on the cover." Oesterheld wanted to transform the pedagogical role traditionally associated with comics, directing it now not at children but at budding revolutionaries.

In that same Oesterheld interview from 1975, two years after the *Bang!* interview with Breccia, it seems clear that the stressed relationship between the pair had reached a breaking point: "Breccia has always behaved very well, except for that interview in *Bang!*, where he says I'm a good storyteller but a bad scriptwriter, where he makes me look like a cheap-ass scriptwriter... " In turn, Breccia admitted, "With Héctor [Oesterheld] there never was much camaraderie, there wasn't much affinity."

In general, it has been argued that the ideological commitment was on Oesterheld's side. For Breccia Senior, it was merely a job that added nothing to his work: "After *Mort Cinder*, I didn't intend to make any more comics.... I did *Life of Che* the same way I could have done nothing,

the same way I could have done advertising, that's it." But whereas for Breccia the project was (almost) always just work, often painful, driven only by the need for money and an agonizing economic — and creative — malaise, Oesterheld used it to explore his political commitment as an author/writer. In a way, writing a comic book was an "avant-garde" solution to a key debate in artistic and intellectual circles at the time: how to reach the masses, how to break through the strictures of one's field, how to transcend the quest for fame and recognition.

Breccia, in his account, did not finish explaining what had happened with the U.S. embassy's proposal. Oesterheld, however, in addition to clarifying that the Embassy had called him and not the artists, recalled that the Americans had invited him to travel to the United States for a year, visiting the places where Kennedy had lived, documenting and earning U.S. dollars. Oesterheld did not make his rejection of their offer explicit, but it was understood: he chose his commitment to the Latin American reality, radicalizing his political position by joining the Montoneros revolutionary group shortly after.

For their part, the Breccias were somewhat skeptical about the work. Though Enrique had briefly been a member of the Movimiento Nacionalista Tacuara (a far-right political organization) and was part of the Peronist Youth at the time, his account is that of a working man who finds the job to be like "any other." Even so, he was clearly aware of what a project like *Life of Che* meant in that context, remarking, "I can't speak for Héctor, but for my old man and me it was a job like any other, although there's no denying that Guevara galvanized everyone's attention in those days. From what I remember, J. Álvarez had a project to publish a collection of prominent political figures in comic form. After *Life of Che*, the life of John F. Kennedy was going to come out next."

It is not that his task lacked ideological weight but rather that he rejected any overt engagement with the political valence of the work. For a cartoonist, political commitment lies in how he faces his task, in the visual construction of a narrative's meaning. At this point, editor Álvarez's intervention was crucial: it was he who had the brilliant and provocative idea of joining these two stories (the more formal biography by Alberto and the account of the final period of Che's life in Bolivia by Enrique) into one, alternating them.

This visual contrast created a dialogue between the two different styles of drawing, which were, in turn, stitched together by Oesterheld's text. Oesterheld, for his part, pushed his literary capacities to the limit, in dialogue with Guevara's testimonial voice. The narrative switched back and forth between first and third person, to the point that it was difficult to discern where Guevara's voice ended and Oesterheld's began, and vice versa.

The lineage of woodcut adds to the visual impact. While the technique is not directly tied to a particular ideology or political position, woodcuts have traditionally been linked to avant-garde groups, such as the German expressionist group Die Brücke (The Bridge), and especially with early-twentieth-century leftist artists, socialists, and anarchists, such as the Belgian Frans Masereel, the German Otto Nückel, the North American Lynd Ward, the Italian American Giacomo Patri and, in Argentina, the group known as the Artistas del Pueblo [Artists of the People] (José Arato, Adolfo Bellocq, Guillermo Facio Hebequer, Agustín Riganelli, and Abraham Vigo).

In the Breccias's case, Alberto indisputably had some experience with woodcuts — which he would deploy more obviously in later works — since he had come into contact with some of the members of the Artistas del Pueblo, among others, through the covers and interior illustrations of many of the books published by the socialist publishing house Claridad, which he had read in his youth. Enrique, for his part, stated that "two or three years before drawing *Life of Che*, I carved and made woodcuts. My

drawing in *Life of Che* was a natural continuation of that activity, transferring the pure, clear black-and-white of the xylographic technique to paper."

AN URGENT COMIC

The original edition was considered lost except for the surviving copies: at least until the 1987 Spanish reissue, probably made from one of the 1969 copies. These losses and recoveries also affect the ways the work has been read. Take, for example, the famous opening page of the biographical section of *Life of Che* drawn by Alberto. The idea was to start with a copy of Guevara's original birth certificate. However, the copy did not arrive in time and the page had to be printed as a blank box. When the comic strip became known in Europe, particularly in France, it was read as an allegory of Che as a universal figure, since by not having a homeland he became a citizen of the world. The Breccias recounted this anecdote sardonically, mocking the "intellectualized" reading of the comic that was due to an accident of the production process.

Later editions incorporated the famous copy of the birth certificate that had been missing for so long. Does this allow us a better and more complete reading than all of those preceding it? Not really, because that box had been reduced to an anecdote that readers might or might not be aware of, or about which they could have reached conclusions other than those made by the French — or even none at all. This leads us to discuss — and (why not?) to dispute — the "official" account of Alberto's role in this work. Based on his own testimony and the drawings in the biographical section, Enrique's work has been viewed as experimental and avant-garde, relegating Alberto to the more classical and conservative part.

This interpretation was understandable back when the comic was first published, but with the advantage of hindsight it is possible to understand Alberto's contribution as residing within a genealogy that implied gradually breaking with the work of previous decades, in terms of style but above all in the search for and construction of a new way of viewing comics. This involves both the technical aspect — particularly the use of collage — and the political-ideological aspect, the use of a graphic biography.

We know that the project was on tight deadlines, with Oesterheld's script feverishly reworking Che's diaries and the Cuban newspaper *Granma* as a photojournalistic source. Meanwhile, the two comics artists divided up their work and had no contact during the drawing process. This dynamic can also be understood as political, as a sort of activism with all the urgency of a statement, racing to continue fanning the flame of revolution inspired by Che's legacy.

Alberto Breccia, on the other hand, though he kept his distance from the project's political implications, could not help feeling a certain sympathy with or interest in a man who embodied adventure in such a particular and present way. His task, in any case, was to produce this work while incorporating his experience drawing scholarly biographical stories and the use of collage as a technique of urgency. Alberto's true innovation, in this case, lay in reimagining the biographical genre in a way that fit with the character portrayed — that is, a revolutionary.

Another issue that the cartoonist had to solve was Oesterheld's script. The refined chaos of Alberto's collage was combined with Oesterheld's "textual guerrilla warfare," which fired bursts of literary fragments, fragments of meaning that were difficult to decode — at least at times — for non-Argentine readers.

ALL FIRES THE FIRE

Oesterheld wanted to apply that revolutionary pedagogy as an extension of Guevara's legacy, which indicates the commitment inherent to this task on the part of the

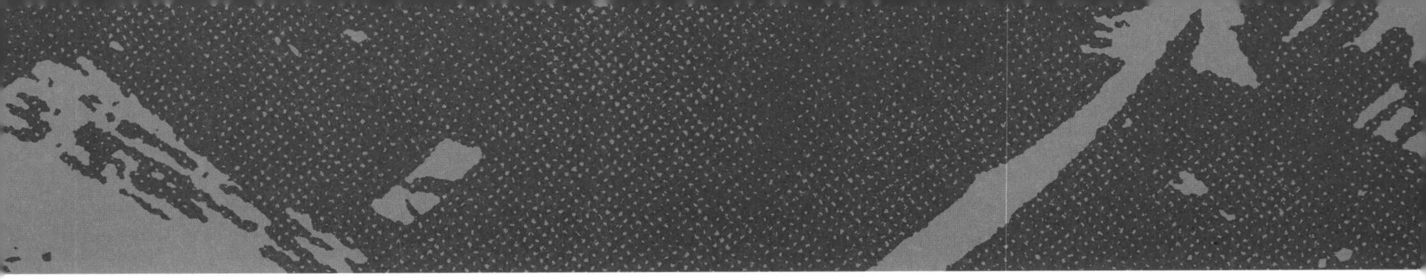

scriptwriter. Just as the Breccias created a zone of exchange in which the lines are blurred, the same happens with the text when it changes from the third person to the first person: "Close the journal, extinguish the lantern. I could continue writing so much more, death all around us. We're surrounded. But no, I can't write doubts and fears. If a comrade reads it, it's cruel and pointless to show the certain end." Somehow Oesterheld anticipates his own fate, consciously expressed in *The Eternaut II*, which continued to be published even after the scriptwriter was already missing and dead: the testament of someone consciously marching toward his revolutionary death.

The striking final three pages are presented as if they were a roll of photographic film advancing vertically, zooming in from the wider shot of Guevara's living space until only his face remains, surrounded by darkness, a white dot representing the final gunshot. Readers are confronted by a face that, despite being dead, gazes frankly back at the viewer: it is the ultimate conversion of Che into a myth, a man who dies to multiply himself, who "impels the youth of the world to their feet, sets them marching." It is shocking to picture the scene of that last page being consumed by fire, a scene to which only the imagination can give us access, since of this — if it ever happened — there are no images extant.

Héctor Germán Oesterheld was kidnapped by a task force on April 27, 1977, in the city of La Plata. By that time, his four daughters and two of his sons-in-law (all of them involved with Montoneros) had already been killed or disappeared. Oesterheld was seen in different clandestine detention centers between late 1977 and early 1978. According to survivor Eduardo Arias, "He was in terrible condition. We stayed together for a long time.... One of the most unforgettable memories I have of Héctor is from Christmas Eve in '77. The guards gave us permission to take off our hoods and smoke a cigarette. And they

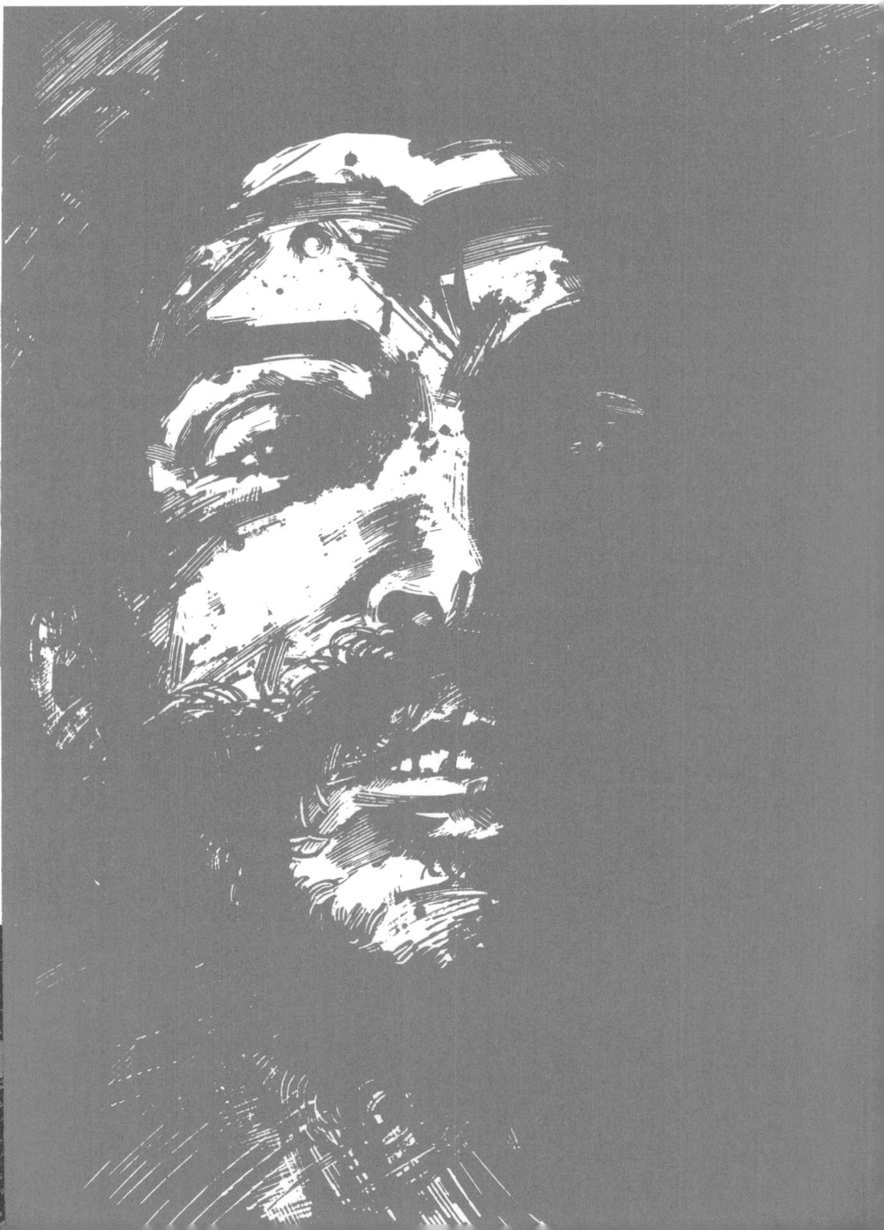

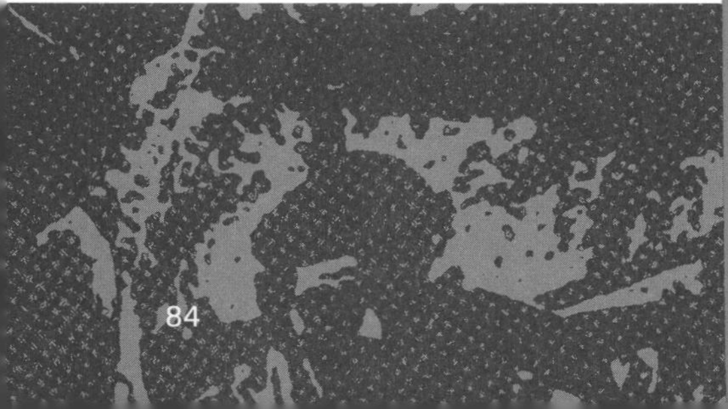

allowed us to talk to each other for five minutes. Then Héctor said that since he was the oldest of all the prisoners, he wanted to greet all the prisoners who were there one by one. I will never forget that last handshake. These events happened. He was in a very grim physical state." (Excerpt from an interview published in *Feriado Nacional* (National Holiday) magazine, October 1983). While his ultimate fate is unknown (as is the case with most disappeared people), it is suspected that he was executed in 1978, in a field outside the town of Mercedes, in the Province of Buenos Aires.

Alberto Breccia returned to comics in the early 1970s, working for the Italian comics market. There, he quickly became an *auteur* and a star, being awarded with the Yellow Kid award in 1973, during the Lucca Comics Convention. He produced challenging, experimental works that pushed the boundaries of the comics medium to another level. His works were published in Italy, Spain, and France in magazines such as *Linus*, *Charlie Mensuel*, and *Comics + Ilustración Internacional*; and to a lesser degree, in Argentina, in *Fierro* magazine. He kept working until his death in 1993, in Buenos Aires.

Enrique Breccia also continued working in comics, mainly for European markets (namely, Italy and France) and for the United States (DC and Marvel). He also pursued a career as a painter and illustrator, something he continues to practice. After living for a long time in Mar del Sur, a small coastal village in the province of Buenos Aires, he now resides in Rome. His relationship with his father was always contentious, as recently described in the book *Mi padre y yo: conversaciones con Enrique Breccia* (My father and me: Conversations with Enrique Breccia), a series of conversations between Enrique Breccia and the journalist Gonzalo Santos.

Jorge Álvarez quit the publishing business and founded Mandioca, a seminal record label in the second wave of Argentine rock 'n' roll. He experienced ongoing financial and legal problems because of the economic and cultural politics of the dictatorship. In 1977, after receiving threats, he went into exile and lived in Spain for thirty-four years. There, he became a key figure in the music industry, producing pop albums for bands such as Olé Olé and Mecano that defined an era for Spain's post-dictatorship culture. He returned to Buenos Aires in 2013 and died there in 2015. A forgotten figure during those decades, he has come to be recognized as one of the most influential figures in Argentine culture in the second half of the twentieth century. ★

Pablo Turnes (Mar del Plata, Argentina, 1979) is a Professor in History from the National University of Mar del Plata, M.A. in History of Argentine and Latin American Art from the Institute of High Social Studies - National University of San Martín and Doctor in Social Sciences from the University of Buenos Aires. He completed his doctorate as a fellow of the National Council for Scientific and Technical Research (CONICET). He was an organizing member of the International Comics Conference "Viñetas Serias" in its three editions (2010, 2012, and 2014), and provides comic critic workshops with Amadeo Gandolfo, with whom he also co-edits the web magazine *Kamandi* (www.revistak-amandi.com). His Master's thesis published in 2018 by Tren en Movimiento under the title *The Exile of Forms: Alack Sinner by José Muñoz and Carlos Sampayo*. His doctoral thesis was published in 2019 by Miño & Dávila under the title *The Exception Within the Rule: The Comics Work of Alberto Breccia* (1962–1993). He is currently living in Berlin as a postdoctoral fellow for the Alexander von Humboldt Foundation. His research focuses on the issue of contemporary Latin American comics and their relationship to memory, trauma, and recent Latin American history.

Afterword translated by Andrea Rosenberg.

OESTERH

Héctor Germán Oesterheld (HGO) courtesy of the Oesterheld estate.

Héctor Germán Oesterheld was born in Buenos Aires in 1919 and is considered one of South America's greatest comic writers. He wrote in and redefined a number of highly diverse genres, ranging from tales of adventure and war to science fiction, detective, and Western stories. The stories Oesterheld created were drawn by the best comic artists of his time, including Alberto Breccia, Hugo Pratt, and Francisco Solano López. Oesterheld's profoundly humanist work features mature themes, complex characters dealing with deep inner conflicts, and, particularly in his caption boxes, elegant prose. Still, this added complexity never interferes with the reading or enjoyment of the stories.

In the mid-1940s, while working as a geologist, Oesterheld wrote children's books and scientific articles for two publishers, Codex and Abril. It was with the latter

that he made his debut as a comic strip writer and his series were prolifically published in the 1950s, especially in the magazine *Misterix*. Two works from that period stand out. In 1952, he created, with Italian artist Paul Campani (later replaced by Solano López), *Bull Rockett*, whose main character is a test pilot and scientist. Then, in 1953, with another Italian artist, Hugo Pratt (who would go on to be world-renowned), he created the successful Western strip, *Sergeant Kirk*. Its protagonist is a prototypical Oesterheld character, a humanist who stands firm against violence. Kirk deserts the army, regretting that he took part in massacring Native Americans, and becomes a member of the Chattooga tribe.

In 1956, Oesterheld founded the Frontera (Frontier) publishing company with the help of his brother, Jorge. They wrote, sometimes under pseudonyms, most of the comic strips published in the magazines *Frontera* and *Hora Cero* (Zero Hour). Oesterheld created some of his most celebrated works during this period of success, such as *Ernie Pike* (1957) with Hugo Pratt, a series featuring a war reporter in which the soldiers are portrayed as humans first, rather than as fighters belonging to a particular side. They also collaborated on *Ticonderoga*, a comic strip situated in the U.S. during the colonial period.

The series *Rolo, el marciano adoptivo* (Rolo, the Adoptive Martian) also dates from 1957. This strip, drawn by Solano López, has certain similarities with Oesterheld's best-known work *El Eternauta* (The Eternaut), also drawn by Solano López. Both appeared at a time of great political agitation in Argentina and are science fiction series that start with extraterrestrials invading Earth — and groups of humans forming a resistance. As in other Oesterheld comics, although the adventure strip is named after the point-of-view character, it features a collective protagonist. The characters in both series are ordinary people who end up becoming heroes. Another connection is that the adventure bursts in on everyday life rather than a faraway

ELD

BY JOSÉ ENRIQUE NAVARRO

time or place; the action takes place in what could be any Buenos Aires street or neighborhood. Also set in Buenos Aires, *Sherlock Time* (1958), is a comic featuring a time-traveling detective. This story, a cross between a detective novel and science fiction, marked the first time Oesterheld worked with Uruguayan artist Alberto Breccia, who was able to create a disquieting atmosphere through the generous use of shadows.

The 1960s were a difficult period for the printed media industry due to the economic situation in Argentina as well as to the arrival of television. Overwhelmed by debt, Oesterheld was forced to close his own publishing company. He returned to the magazine *Misterix*, where, in 1962, once again with Breccia, he published *Mort Cinder*, considered by critics to be their masterpiece. The protagonist is another time traveler, an immortal who dies only to be reborn and witness the smaller stories within history. Breccia's *Mort Cinder* drawings mark yet another milestone in his aesthetic experimentation.

Oesterheld had to combine his work at *Misterix* with a great deal of writing for other small publishing houses. In addition, the political upheaval in Argentina (with a military dictatorship from 1966 to 1973) led to Oesterheld's growing political commitment, which is clearly reflected in his work. For example, in 1969, he released a biography of Che Guevara, *Vida del Che* (Life of Che), drawn by Alberto Breccia and his son, Enrique Breccia. The work was subsequently seized and the originals destroyed. *Vida y obra de Eva Perón. Una historia gráfica* (The Life and Work of Eva Perón: A Graphic History, 1970), which Oesterheld had outlined and Peronist journalist Luis Alberto Murray completed, suffered a similar fate. With art by Alberto Breccia and published without any indications as to the publisher, printer, or distributor, the work was confiscated and the printing plates destroyed.

The end of the decade saw Oesterheld's first return to the Eternaut character; a new version of the story first published in 1957 reappeared in the magazine *Gente*, in 1969, this time drawn by Alberto Breccia. This version, which was much bolder in terms of graphics and political content, was never finished due to the protests of the magazine's readership, which had a conservative bent.

The combination of Oesterheld's increasing political commitment and his family's financial woes had a profound effect on his production in the 1970s. From his work with Columba, the only firm publishing adventure comics at the time, the series *Kabul de Bengala* (Kabul of Bengala) stands out. Record, a new company, reprinted some of his previous works and published new ones, including *Nekrodamus* and the *El Eternauta* sequel, which came out in 1976. By this time, Oesterheld had joined the press committee for the Montoneros, an armed leftist organization, and was living in hiding. Other comic strips that he wrote during this last period, all highly political, were published either by media shut down by the Isabel Perón government or by underground organizations. Such was the case of the unfinished *Guerra de los Antartes* (The War of the Antartes), the installments of *450 años de guerra contra el imperialismo* (450 Years of War Against Imperialism), and *Camote*.

With the return of the military to power in Argentina in 1976, many of Oesterheld's works, including *The Eternaut*, were banned. Oesterheld was arrested in 1977 by a group of soldiers, and it is suspected that he was killed some time in 1978. He and his four daughters are among the more than 30,000 people who disappeared during the last Argentine military dictatorship. ★

José Enrique Navarro is an Associate Professor of Hispanic Studies at Wichita State University.

BRECCIA

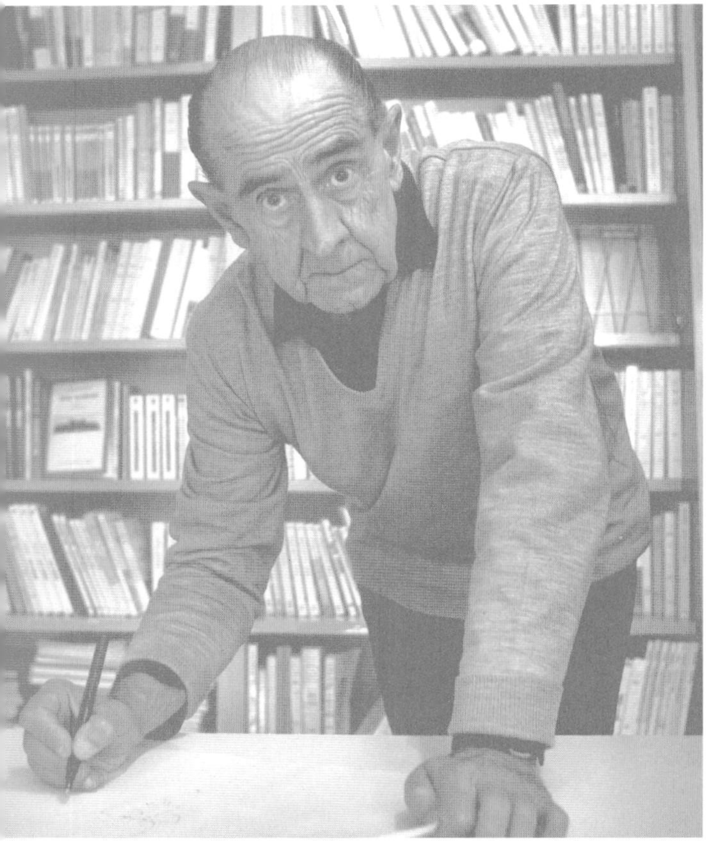

Breccia in Paris in 1987. Photo courtesy of the Breccia estate..

Alberto Breccia was born in Montevideo, Uruguay, in 1919. When he was three, he moved to Buenos Aires, Argentina. At a young age, he worked in a slaughterhouse. But he was soon part of Argentina's "golden age" of comics, which began in the '40s, and for which he drew dozens of pages per week — mostly in the action, adventure, humor, or film adaptation genres. In addition, he did commercial artwork for advertising and children's books. In 1946, he began to draw his first recognizable character, Vito Nervio, (written by Leonardo Wadel). There were glimmers of it beforehand, but with this character, Breccia's personal style came to the surface. In 1958, he collaborated for the first time with scriptwriter Héctor Germán Oesterheld (HGO), on *Sherlock Time*, and his graphic art cohered and darkened. He delivered lots of Westerns and war comics to Europe, but the turning point in his career arrived in 1962, when he collaborated with HGO on *Mort Cinder*, a masterpiece of narrative, drawing, and graphic experimentation, published serially in the Argentine magazine *Misterix* until 1964.

In debt, with three children and a sick wife, Breccia abandoned comics for several years and dedicated himself to teaching at the Panamerican School of Art and IDA-Institute of Art Directors. During that time, he only completed the three-page comic "Richard Long" (which Oesterheld also wrote), continuing his graphic experiments by means of collage. One of the first times Breccia was recognized as an *auteur* came shortly afterward in an essay by Argentine intellectual Oscar Masotta, co-director of the World Comics Biennial. (The Biennial was held in 1968 at the Di Tella Institute, the heart of Buenos Aires's pop art scene at that time.)

The year 1968 also marked Breccia's return to comics, once again via stories written by Oesterheld. Together, they completed the surprisingly contemporary *Vida del Che* (it also had sequences drawn by his son, Enrique Breccia) and a retelling of Oesterheld's seminal *The Eternaut*, published weekly in — oddly — a gossip magazine. Times were not the same as when Oesterheld wrote the original version (in 1957, drawn by Francisco Solano López). As dictatorships became more frequent and bloody all over the world, events led HGO to change a central detail in the script: in this new version, the great world powers hand Latin America over to the invaders...

and Breccia's graphic innovations became even more psychedelic. Readers considered it "inexplicable" and "confusing," so Oesterheld himself shortened the script to quickly complete its publication. The following year, they collaborated on *The Life and Work of Eva Perón: A Graphic History.* Both this and *Che* were controversial because of political figures they depicted and — due to persecution by successive Argentine dictatorships — their original pages and hard copies of the graphic novels disappeared. They were confiscated or lost.

The beginning of the '70s meant recognition in Europe for Breccia: much of his work was republished in books and magazines, and he was invited to and given awards at comics festivals and conventions. From that moment on, he stopped making commissioned comics to become "a professional who dedicates the required time" to comics and started to "feel the joy of drawing in another way," according to *Breccia, El Viejo: Conversations with Juan Sasturain.*

He worked with writers such as Carlos Trillo, Guillermo Saccomanno, Juan Sasturain, and Norberto Buscaglia on original scripts; he also adapted tales by Edgar Allan Poe, H. P. Lovecraft, W. W. Jacobs, the Brothers Grimm, Lord Dunsany, and the Latin Americans Horacio Quiroga, Jorge Luis Borges, Gabriel García Márquez, Juan Rulfo, Juan Carlos Onetti, Alejo Carpentier, and João Guimarães Rosa.

With his expertise, Breccia was able to take advantage of the short story comics form and innovate, narrate, and experiment without repeating himself. Breccia also drew long-running series like *Nadie* [Nobody] (1997), *El Viajero de Gris* [The Traveler in Gray] (1978), *Buscavidas* [The Life-Seeker] (1981), *Drácula, Dacul, Vlad?, Bah...* (1984), and *El Dorado: el delirio de Lope de Aguirre* [El Dorado: Lope de Aguirre's Delirium] (1992). The four-volume series *Perramus*, which Sasturain wrote, was recognized in 1989 by Amnesty International. *Report on the Blind*, an excerpt adapted from Ernesto Sábato's classic novel *On Heroes and Tombs* was published during Breccia's final year. He had resumed teaching dozens of students who valued new and personal aesthetics. Cancer metastasized and carried Breccia away on November 10, 1993, just when, in Argentina, Cartoonist Day is commemorated. ★

Ezequiel Garcìa is an Argentine artist born in 1975. After studying under Alberto Breccia, Garcìa co-edited several comics anthologies and has had short works appear in comics magazines in Europe and South America. In 2000, he was given the comics award at the Salão del Humor de Piraci-caba in Brazil. Garcìa's first graphic novel, *Turning 30,* was released in Argentina in 2007. More recently, Garcìa has served as a comics teacher, art gallery curator, and co-organizer of the Festival Increìble de Historietas, Fanzines y Afines. Fantagraphics published his graphic novel *Growing Up in Public* in the U.S. in 2016. Further updates can be found at www.ezequielgarcia.com.ar.

BRECCIA

Enrique Breccia (b. 1945, Buenos Aires), an acclaimed Argentine painter, illustrator, and cartoonist, is probably best known to American audiences for his *Swamp Thing* run for DC's Vertigo imprint. In addition to DC, he has worked for Marvel, Fleetway, Delcourt, Bonelli Editore, and many other global comics publishers; he has also illustrated literary works by Lovecraft, Melville, and others.

Already an accomplished fine and commercial artist, his comics career began in earnest in 1968. Although he had previously assisted his father, Alberto Breccia, on series like *Mort Cinder*, he contributed artwork to the bestselling graphic biography *Life of Che*, depicting Che's diary entries from the time he enters Bolivia until his death. Other notable projects include his 1970s series of war history comics for *Linus* magazine, art for the Alvar Mayor character (written by Carlos Trillo) in the 1980s, the recent *The Sentinels* series with Xavier Dorison, and the graphic novel *Golgotha*, scripted by Bollée and Alcante, for the publisher Delcourt/Soleil. Breccia currently lives in Italy.★

Enrique Breccia, photo courtesy of the Breccia Estate.

Erica Mena is a Puerto Rican poet, translator, and book artist, who holds an MFA in poetry from Brown University and an MFA in literary translation from the University of Iowa. Their book *Featherbone* (Ricochet Editions, 2015) won a 2016 Hoffer First Horizons Award, and their English translation of the Argentine graphic novel *The Eternaut* won a 2016 Eisner Award. Their artist books are collected widely. Most recently they created the artist books *Puerto Rico en mi corazón*, a collection of letterpress printed broadsides by Puerto Rican poets in response to Hurricane Maria, printed in Spanish and English, and *Gringo Death Coloring Book* by Raquel Salas Rivera with collaborator Mariana Ramos Ortiz. They have taught Book Arts, Translation, and Poetry at Brown University, Mills College, Harvard University, and elsewhere. They currently live in Fiskars, Finland. Mena is online at acyborgkitty.com.★

MENA

TRANSLATION OF CHE'S BIRTH CERTIFICATE, PAGE 7

LEFT MARGIN

24 *Exhibit A.*

b. Cert. Fil. 12-7-1946
auth 4A

Guevara
Ernesto

MAIN TEXT

Exhibit A

Record number *Three-hundred-fifty-four.*

In department of the *City of Rosario* Department of *itself* [illegible], Province of Santa Fe, on the *fifteenth* day of *June* of the year nineteen *twenty eight* at *ten-oh-seven* in the morning *Ernesto* [illegible] charged to the Civil Status Registry, is presented [illegible] *Rafael Guevara, residing on* [illegible] *Rios Street four hundred* [illegible] at *twenty-five* years of age of status *married* of nationality *Argentine* of profession *land-owner* neighbor of *this city* declares [illegible] that in *his residence* the *fourteenth of the current* month of *June* at *three-oh-five* in the morning was born a boy of race *white* and that this boy is *legitimately his and* of *his wife Snra Celia de la Serna y Llosa, of twenty-two years of age, Argentine.* Who is grandson in the paternal line of *Don Roberto Guevara and of Doña Ana Lynch.* And in the maternal line of *Don Juan Martín de la Serna* [illegible] *Llosa.*

SECOND PAGE OF CERTIFICATE

And in the maternal line of *Don Juan Martín de la Serna. And of Doña Edelmira Llosa.* And that the aforementioned child has been given the name *Ernesto.*

He further declared.

All of which presentation witnessed as witness by Don *Raul Lyn* of *twenty-two* years of age, of status *single* of nationality *Argentine* of profession [Illegible] and residing at *this city* and D[cut off] *José Beltran* of *thirty years* [cut off] age, of status *single* of nationality *Brazilian* of profession *chauffeur* residing at *Street* [illegible] *two thousand and seventy.*

After reading this record, it is ratified in its contents by signing with me [cut off] [cut off] *and the declarant.*

[Signatures]

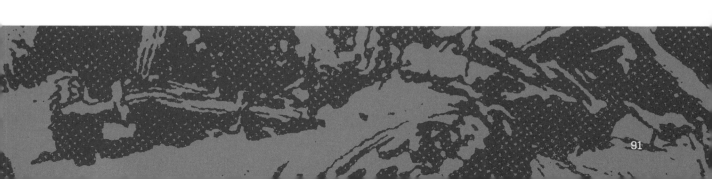

91

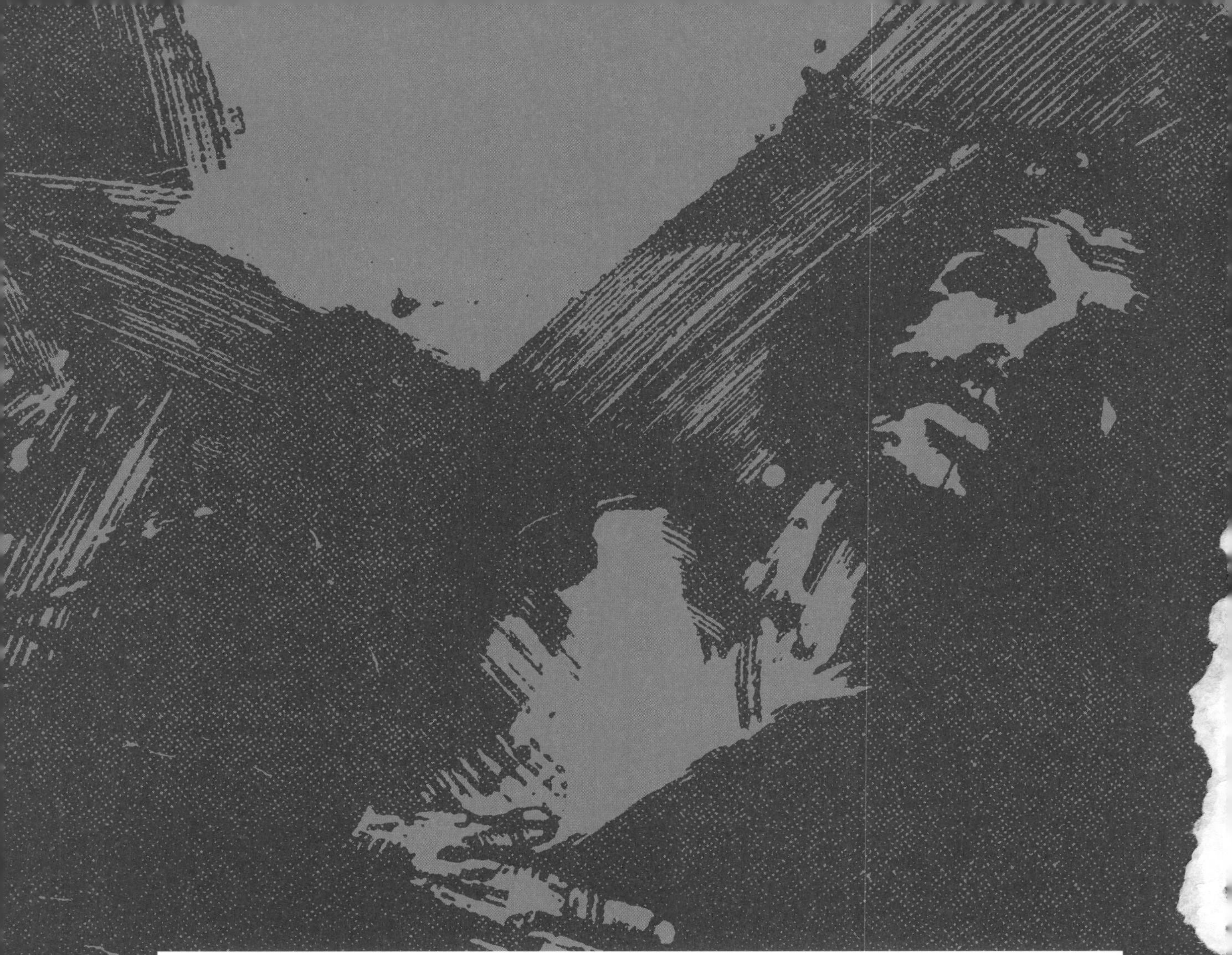

NEXT TIME

After they completed the bestselling *Life of Che*, Héctor Germán Oesterheld, Alberto Breccia, and Enrique Breccia began to work on a companion graphic biography about controversial First Lady, actress, and activist for the rights of the poorest: *Vida y obra de Eva Perón. Una historia gráfica* (The Life and Work of Eva Perón: A Graphic History, 1970). However, the governmental backlash to *Life of Che* meant that, while the Breccias' art was unchanged, editorial had Oesterheld's script rewritten to be more "politically neutral." The book appeared in 1970, poorly colored and printed. In 2001, editor Javier Doeyo discovered and updated Oesterheld's script, and *The Life and Work of Eva Perón: A Graphic History* was restored. Fantagraphics is proud to present this work in English for the first time.★

OTHER BOOKS IN THE ALBERTO BRECCIA LIBRARY

Mort Cinder drawn by Alberto Breccia;
written by Héctor Germán Oesterheld; translated by Erica Mena (2018)

Perramus: The City and Oblivion drawn by Alberto Breccia;
written by Juan Sasturain; translated by Erica Mena (2020)

The Eternaut 1969 drawn by Alberto Breccia;
written by Héctor Germán Oesterheld; translated by Erica Mena (2020)

Alberto Breccia's Dracula drawn by Alberto Breccia (2021)